# SEARCH MY HEART, O GOD

# SEARCH MY HEART, O GOD

## 365 APPOINTMENTS WITH GOD

# KAY ARTHUR

WATERBROOK
PRESS

SEARCH MY HEART, O GOD
PUBLISHED BY WATERBROOK PRESS
5446 North Academy Boulevard, Suite 200
Colorado Springs, Colorado 80918
*A division of Random House, Inc.*

Scriptures in this book, unless otherwise noted, are from the *New American Standard Bible* (NASB), copyright © 1960, 1962, 1963, 1968, 1971, 1973, 1975, 1977, 1995 by The Lockman Foundation. Scripture quotations marked (NIV) are taken from the *Holy Bible, New International Version®*. NIV®. Copyright © 1973, 1978, 1984 by International Bible Society. Used by permission of Zondervan Publishing House. All rights reserved. Scripture quotations marked (NKJV) are taken from the *New King James Version.* Copyright © 1982 by Thomas Nelson, Inc. Scripture quotations marked (KJV) are taken from the King James Version. All used by permission, all rights reserved. Italicized words in Scripture quotations reflect the author's emphasis.

Some of the material in this book originally aired on Kay Arthur's *Precepts from God's Word* radio broadcast.

ISBN 1-57856-274-0

Printed in the United States of America
1999—First Edition

10 9 8 7 6 5 4 3 2 1

# CONTENTS

# A WORD FROM KAY

The heart is the innermost part of our being. No matter how hard we might try, we cannot disguise the true state of our heart; it will be revealed in our thoughts, our conversations, our actions, our relationships. Of course, we may fool others for a while, but we can never deceive God, "for man looks at the outward appearance, but the Lord looks at the heart" (1 Samuel 16:7).

Have you ever taken time, beloved, in the busyness of life to allow God to take you by the hand and, in the gentleness of His love, search your heart, to see if there is any hurtful way in you? How often have you looked deeply, allowing God to shine the spotlight of His holiness into every corner and hidden recess of your innermost self? What dangerous temptations, pet sins, or wrong beliefs have you been quietly entertaining? What passion drives you through each day? What secret guilts or worries are creeping over your heart, stifling your God-given joy and stealing away your peace?

While living with hidden sin, guilt, or pain will lead only to sorrow, a heart cleansed by and filled with the Holy Spirit will lead to joy and peace. As you allow God to reveal the true state of your heart, I encourage you to pray along with King David, "Create in me a clean heart, O God, and renew a steadfast spirit within me.… Restore to me the joy of Your salvation and sustain me with a willing spirit" (Psalm 51:10,12).

There's so much that goes on inside us that no one sees or knows or even realizes, isn't there? Private thoughts, fears, temptations, wrestlings, conflicts, hurts, doubts. Things we want to hide, to keep to ourselves for fear of condemnation…rejection…embarrassment…or even something as simple as the possibility of disappointing another person should they discover what we deal with in our inner man.

We can hide it all except from One, the One who is omnipresent, omniscient. The One whose name is El Roi, the God who sees. And that's all right, because He's also a God who loves, who cares, who desires our highest good. A God who promises to be our ever-present help in the time of need. Thus our prayer, our heart's cry, "Search my heart, O God," is not only safe, it's wise and pleasing to our creator for it's the pure in heart who will see God.

This, beloved, is the purpose of this book: taking a moment each day to allow God to search your heart and cleanse you with the washing of His Word, that you might ascend His hill of holiness with clean hands and a pure heart.

# SEARCH
# MY HEART

You may have heard it before under many and varied circumstances—maybe as a warning: "The heart is deceitful above all things, and desperately wicked: who can know it?" (Jeremiah 17:9, KJV). It's a true statement and a biblical one, but the Word of God also tells us our hearts don't have to stay that way.

God is in the business of heart transplants, taking hearts of stone and replacing them with hearts of flesh. It happens at salvation. When God awesomely performs this divine transplant, He then writes His laws upon our hearts and puts His Spirit within us. He becomes our God, and we become His people. Life begins—life eternal—and with it the process of making us more and more like our Lord and Savior, Jesus Christ. "Moreover, I will give you a new heart and put a new spirit within you; and I will remove the heart of stone from your flesh and give you a heart of flesh" (Ezekiel 36:26).

So on this first day of a new year, examine your heart, beloved. Are you sure that you have a new heart, that you are a child of God, born truly from above—a new creature in Christ Jesus?

*O God, You know all things. There's nothing hidden from Your sight. If I am Your child, let Your Spirit bear witness with my spirit. And if not, bring me into Your family. Give me a heart for You, a new beginning that leads to life eternal and grants me the privilege of calling You Abba, Father, forever and ever.*

Have you become a slave to someone or something?

Don't faint, precious child of God. Soon in the midst of the darkest of days, maybe even sooner than you think, your day of jubilee is coming!

Leviticus 25 describes the year of jubilee, a joyous time in which those who'd been sold into slavery could return to their families and others regained land they had lost through financial troubles.

All this, my friend, provides a picture of what is promised when you receive the Lord Jesus Christ as your Redeemer! Through Him we are set free from the bondage of sin and become heirs of the kingdom "which He promised to those who love Him" (James 2:5).

"Therefore you are no longer a slave, but a son; and if a son, then an heir through God" (Galatians 4:7).

God's Word is full of such wonderful symbols of His love, care, and protection of us. Determine to know your God and His Word. Take time to study God's Word and to realize afresh that He is God and He offers hope that can hold you through any dark night of your soul.

*I thank You, Lord, that I have been bought with a price, paid by Jesus. I am no longer a slave to sin. I have the Holy Spirit, and "where the Spirit of the Lord is, there is liberty" (2 Corinthians 3:17).*

Are there times when you doubt God's love for you?

When things aren't going as you had hoped, when your life is reeling out of control, do you wonder how a loving God could allow you to suffer such pain?

What a comfort it is to remember that God paid the dearest of prices to redeem you from your life of sin. You were dead in your trespasses and sins; you were condemned to death row for all eternity—and justly so. Yet the Father gave His Son to die in your place, enduring the most brutal of deaths. He did this when you were still walking your own way, not even realizing the price He was paying. And had you known it, you probably wouldn't even have cared. That's how lost you—and I—were!

Romans 5:6-10 says that God loved you when you were His enemy. When you were a sinner, ungodly and without hope, He loved you, pursued you, and wooed you. And He did not let go until you gave in and succumbed to His desire to be your Father, your God, your Lord, your Master, your Redeemer. Isn't that awesome?

*O Father, thank You for demonstrating Your love for me in that, while I was yet a willful, wandering sinner, Christ died for me. Help me to focus on Your proven love when life isn't quite what I had hoped for. May I remember Your sacrifice and realize that because You are working on my behalf, as Romans 8:28-29 says, even this will result in my good and Your glory.*

Are you feeling anxious, my friend?

It's hard sometimes, isn't it…

…to have peace when your circumstances are difficult?

…to have joy when your heart is filled with anxiety?

Circumstances, as well as our frustration with and anxiety about life, can rob us of our joy. The apostle Paul was well aware of this as he wrote from prison:

"I have learned to be content in whatever circumstances I am. I know how to get along with humble means, and I also know how to live in prosperity; in any and every circumstance I have learned the secret of being filled and going hungry, both of having abundance and suffering need. I can do [bear] all things through Him who strengthens me" (Philippians 4:11-13).

If you'll let Jesus infuse you with His strength, you'll find contentment to carry you through each day. When your heart is overwhelmed by anxiety, ask yourself what Jesus would do. Then, beloved, do it in His strength.

*Lord, in an act of my will, I roll the anxiety in my heart onto Your shoulders. Help me to remember that my circumstances are well within Your sovereign control and that You have offered me Your strength to endure every challenge that comes my way. In faith's confidence I appropriate Your strength right now.*

When the report says "storms ahead," do you trust God or evacuate the area? It's difficult, isn't it, to trust God when the "forecast" is contrary to what we want—or feel we need?

Maybe you're in financial straits, you're agonizing over a broken relationship, or you've lost your job. Whatever your situation, it seems the forecast is bleak at best!

So what will you do?

When the apostle Peter urged the hurting, suffering, persecuted Christians scattered throughout Asia Minor to "stand firm" in the grace of God (1 Peter 5:12), some of them thought it strange that suffering would come their way. So he wrote, "Therefore humble yourselves under the mighty hand of God, that He may exalt you at the proper time, casting all your anxiety on Him, because He cares for you" (1 Peter 5:6-7).

Have you asked God to hear your cry? He has promised never to desert you (Hebrews 13:5).

You can boldly say, "The Lord is my helper; I will not fear what man does to me!"

*Lord, I give You today's anxieties and worries, realizing that I am helpless without Your strength and grace. I thank You that the Holy Spirit will help me to stand firm, if I will only choose to appropriate His love, joy, peace, patience, kindness, goodness, faithfulness, gentleness, and self-control.*

Have you been crying out to God for relief from a difficult situation—and it hasn't come? Does it feel as if an elephant is standing on your chest? Have tears been your food day in and day out? Oh, beloved, there is hope and help no matter how dark things may seem. Run to God and cry out these words found in chapter 3 of Lamentations:

"Waters flowed over my head; I said, 'I am cut off!' I called on Your name, O LORD, out of the lowest pit. You have heard my voice, 'Do not hide Your ear from my prayer for relief, from my cry for help.' You drew near when I called on You; You said, 'Do not fear!' O Lord, You have pleaded my soul's cause; You have redeemed my life" (verses 54-58).

My friend, God *will* sustain you. He has promised—and He never breaks His word. When the burden weighs heavily on your heart, deliberately choose to give it to God, "casting all your anxiety on Him, because He cares for you" (1 Peter 5:7).

Remember, He's the burden bearer, not you. Sheep are not burden-bearing animals! ✗

*Dear Lord, thank You for this reminder that You offer the strength I need to endure the trials of today. I choose this moment to give You my burdens, and I claim Your promise to hear my cry for help. You lead. I will follow.*

Beloved, I know how distressing, how disappointing it is when God doesn't seem to be answering our prayers, but I urge you to persevere.

Perhaps you're agonizing over a son or daughter…or a husband or wife. Whatever the situation, beloved, don't give up. God has not forgotten you.

In Luke 11 Jesus tells a parable that urges us to persist in prayer. We're to keep on asking, keep on seeking, keep on knocking until the door is opened. And while the answer may or may not be what we hoped for, you and I can rest assured it will be in line with God's perfect and holy will.

I know it's difficult to continue in prayer when heaven seems to be silent, but a major key to answered prayer, according to Jesus, is persistence. Isn't this where we often fail? We give up before we receive an answer.

I know the process is hard. But the answer to your prayers rests in the hands of our sovereign God, "who is able to do far more abundantly beyond all that we ask" (Ephesians 3:20).

*O Father, with the writer of Psalm 55, I ask that You would give ear to my prayer. Do not hide Yourself from my supplication. I claim the promise that when I cast my burden upon You, Lord, You will sustain me. In an act of faith, therefore, I will keep on praying, asking, seeking until You open the door. I trust in You for You are my God.*

Have you experienced a time when God seemed so distant, so far away that you felt as if the joy of His presence was lost to you? A shroud covered your soul. You felt devoid of the emotions that once inflamed your heart with passion for your Lord and your God.

At times like these I am so thankful for the years I have spent in the Word of God. When our relationship with God seems devoid of joy and excitement, we have to walk in the gut-level knowledge of all that we have studied. We have to believe God is there, that He has not moved, and that for some reason He has chosen to be silent for awhile.

God's silence is not like our human silence. It does not mean that He is not working or that He has abandoned us. God does not change, and His promises are not made null and void, for even "if we are faithless, He remains faithful, for He cannot deny Himself" (2 Timothy 2:13).

Wrap yourself in the blanket of faith, steep yourself in His Word, and cling to Him. God will never abandon the work of His hands. "He who began a good work in you will perfect it until the day of Christ Jesus" (Philippians 1:6).

*"O God, You are my God; I shall seek You earnestly; my soul thirsts for You, my flesh yearns for You, in a dry and weary land where there is no water.... For You have been my help, and in the shadow of Your wings I sing for joy. My soul clings to You; Your right hand upholds me" (Psalm 63:1,7).*

Have you ever wondered why some Christians seem to have a greater passion for the things of God than others? Do they somehow have an extra blessing? Does God play favorites?

No, for the Bible says each believer is complete in Christ. So what makes the difference? Consider Matthew 13:12: "For whoever has, to him more shall be given, and he will have an abundance; but whoever does not have, even what he has shall be taken away from him."

Each believer has been given a new heart that reflects God's own passion. But when we ignore the Holy Spirit's beckoning, it gradually becomes quieter and quieter, until it seems as if all passion has disappeared from our spiritual lives.

It's a matter of choice, my friend. Only *you* can put a limit on how God uses your life. Matthew 13:9 says, "He who has ears, let him hear." How well are you listening? Are you content with the status quo? Why not take a minute right now to examine your heart. It may be the best investment of time you'll ever make!

*O Lord, forgive me for forgetting You, for not realizing how much I need You, for not actively listening to Your Holy Spirit. Renew my passion for You. Keep me mindful of my need of You and of Your power.*

Each of us was created with a longing for unconditional love, and sometimes that yearning creates an ache within our hearts. Do you feel that ache today? Perhaps you've blown it. You've made a mess of your life, or you've cruelly wounded someone close to you. Deep inside you wonder if anyone could love someone like you.

God does.

He loves you so much that He sent His only Son, Jesus Christ, to die on a cross nearly two thousand years ago. Jesus died for you because God knew you would fail to measure up. "By this the love of God was manifested in us, that God has sent His only begotten Son into the world so that we might live through Him" (1 John 4:9).

God loves you just the way you are, yet He loves you too much to leave you that way: "He made Him who knew no sin to be sin on our behalf, so that we might become the righteousness of God in Him" (2 Corinthians 5:21). "Therefore if anyone is in Christ, he is a new creature; the old things passed away; behold, new things have come" (verse 17).

*Lord, I embrace the love You showed in sending Your Son to die for my sins. I accept the fact that nothing I can do will make You love me more or love me less. Thank You for loving me just as I am, even while You are changing me into the likeness of Your Son and my Savior, the Lord Jesus Christ.*

Is your heart anxious for a loved one, my friend? You've watched them walk farther and farther away from God, away from what they know to be right, away from what they once professed. Believing that they're headed down a path of destruction, you have warned, admonished, pleaded, begged—until you don't know what else to say.

May I suggest you cease striving and simply talk to God about your loved one? You have done all you can do physically, but perhaps you've overlooked the most powerful tool of all. Listen to 1 John 5:14-16:

"This is the confidence which we have before Him, that, if we ask anything according to His will, He hears us. And if we know that He hears us in whatever we ask, we know that we have the requests which we have asked from Him.

"If anyone sees his brother committing a sin not leading to death, he shall ask and God will for him give life to those who commit sin not leading to death."

*Lord, I don't know what to do about _____.*
*Nothing I say or do seems to reach this loved one's*
*heart. I ask now that You will grab hold of this person's*
*heart, mind, and soul, reminding him or her of Your*
*love and bringing this dear one back to You. Thank*
*You for Your promise to hear my prayer.*

Do you want to weep when you see the suffering, the pain, the sin? The abortions performed daily in this nation? When children suffer horrendously because of the sins of their parents?

Are you distressed when you see the corruption in the leaders of our country as they break God's commandments without even a blink of the eye or a blush of the cheek?

Is your heart grieved when you look at the sin, the worldliness of those who enter church sanctuaries week after week and drag the ways of the world in with them, seducing others and despising those who are righteous? Do you ache within?

It's an appropriate response to weep over sin, to grieve over unrighteousness. It means you have God's heart.

"'Yet even now,' declares the LORD, 'Return to Me with all your heart, and with fasting, weeping and mourning; and rend your heart and not your garments.' Now return to the LORD your God, for He is gracious and compassionate, slow to anger, abounding in lovingkindness and relenting of evil. Who knows whether He will not turn and relent and leave a blessing behind Him" (Joel 2:12-14).

*Father, move upon our nation. Reveal to us Your abhorrence of our sin. Bring us to our knees in godly sorrow so that we seek Your face and turn from our wicked ways. May our hearts long for Your pardon.*

How my heart is burdened by the awful harvest so many people are reaping—the pain, the snare, the destruction they've fallen into—and the futility of it all! It is time for each of us to stop and take a good look at what we are doing with our lives, our time, our energies, our bodies. We must become vigilant and walk circumspectly!

Our tendency is to spend our time worrying about how we look on the outside or trying to control what others think about us. But God tells us to watch over our hearts with all diligence—why? Listen to God's word:

"But the things that proceed out of the mouth come from the heart, and those defile the man. For out of the heart come evil thoughts, murders, adulteries, fornications, thefts, false witness, slanders. These are the things which defile the man" (Matthew 15:18-20).

What is hidden in the recesses of your heart, my friend?

*Cleanse my heart, O God. Search my heart, and test my mind. Reveal any hidden sin that could take root and destroy me. Help me to walk in Your way.*

Have you left your heart unguarded? Are you in love with someone you are not married to? Do you think God is in this?

Listen carefully, my friend. You're in great danger. God cannot be tempted by evil, nor does He tempt us—and He has clearly stated in His Word the bounds of appropriate relationships. There are *NO* exceptions; He does not bend the rules for anyone.

Because God is God, altogether holy, He would not tempt you to do evil. And no matter how good, how right it seems to you, this relationship is wrong and you are greatly deceived. You've bought into a deadly delusion that, if pursued, will bring judgment. End the relationship immediately. Listen:

"No temptation has overtaken you but such as is common to man; and God is faithful, who will not allow you to be tempted beyond what you are able, but with the temptation will provide the way of escape also, so that you will be able to endure it" (1 Corinthians 10:13).

*Lord, forgive me for entertaining thoughts of a sinful relationship. Cleanse my mind, and purify my heart. I thank You that by Your Spirit I have the strength to do what is right. I appropriate that strength. Now, Holy One, help me to guard my heart against further temptation.*

Are you suffering, disappointed with life? Things aren't going as you expected. Your dreams are shattered. You're feeling worn out. In fact, you are more than disappointed; you're discouraged, perhaps even depressed.

My friend, you are headed on a downward spiral that will drop you into total despair. If you don't pull out of this tailspin, you're going to crash.

Whether you feel like it or not, whether you think it will help or not, you need to stop right now and, in faith, thank God for this situation. Your trial is not without heavenly purpose. It is not more than you can bear; God cannot lie, and in His sovereignty He has promised to provide a godly way of escape. You can endure. This is a test of your faith. God is refining you as silver.

If you respond in faith and embrace life's disappointment, your obedience will result in praise, honor, and glory.

God guarantees it: "Blessed is a man who perseveres under trial; for once he has been approved, he will receive the crown of life which the Lord has promised to those who love Him" (James 1:12).

*Dear heavenly Father, in the midst of my frustration, I choose to praise You and give thanks for Your unchanging love and sovereignty. Even when I can't see how, I believe You are working on my behalf, molding me into something beautiful. Help me to persevere in faith.*

Do you occasionally wonder if some people are exempt from the trials of life? It sure seems that way, doesn't it?

At times I've wished that my life could be more like someone else's, someone who seems to have everything under control—the perfect marriage, the perfect family. Then the Lord graciously gives me a glimpse backstage, and I find out we *all* have our problems.

The real question is, how can you and I survive and remain strong in our Lord no matter what? The answer is clear. It's not by looking at others and envying them, but by humbly submitting to the Lord, knowing that each of us has our own set of trials crafted by God to chisel us into His image.

Remember that God knows you. He chose you "before the foundation of the world" (Ephesians 1:4), and He also predestined you "to become conformed to the image of His Son" (Romans 8:29). Therefore, "in all these things we overwhelmingly conquer through Him who loved us" (Romans 8:37).

*Thank You for the reminder, Lord, that my outlook on life need not be directed by my circumstances or by comparing them with Your dealings with others. Christlikeness should be the passion of my heart, Your character my goal. Lord, it matters not what You do with others; I will follow You.*

Has hope become a stranger in your life? Do you feel trapped, caught in a quicksand of life's responsibilities?

Maybe hope is gone because someone robbed you of your childhood or your youth. Or maybe you recently realized that one of your lifelong dreams will never come true.

My dear friend, pain is an inescapable fact of life on this earth.

But you're asking, "Kay, where can I find peace? How can I regain hope?" The answer is simple:

At the cross.

Peace is found only in Christ—Christ crucified and resurrected. Christ triumphant over every pain, every failure, every heartbreak, every dashed hope in this life.

Jesus tells us, "If anyone wishes to come after Me, he must deny himself, and take up his cross daily and follow Me" (Luke 9:23).

Oh, beloved, embrace the cross. Only there will you find hope, an anchor for your soul (Hebrews 6:19).

*Lord, You see the pain in my heart. Only You can restore to me "a living hope through the resurrection of Jesus Christ from the dead" (1 Peter 1:3). Thank You for the sacrifice Jesus made so that I might know the joy and hope found only in Your righteousness.*

Is your heart filled with fear? Are you finding it difficult to face the challenges at work, in your family, in life in general?

That's the way it is with fear. Joy, peace, and security are suddenly obliterated by its chilling cloud. But you don't have to live this way, beloved.

In Revelation 1:17, Jesus said, "Do not be afraid; I am the first and the last." When David feared Abimelech, he said, "I sought the LORD, and He answered me, and delivered me from all my fears" (Psalm 34:4).

If you are struggling with fear about a specific situation, ask God what to do and wait to hear His answer. Immerse yourself in the Word of God. If you don't know where to turn in the Bible, go to the Psalms. In them you'll find His consolations. "When my anxious thoughts multiply within me, Your consolations delight my soul" (Psalm 94:19).

When you are afraid, trust in Him. Let your heart find refuge in God and His infallible Word! ✗

*O Father, with David I pray, "Your lovingkindness, O LORD, will hold me up" (Psalm 94:18). Take my fears, precious Lord, and replace them with Your peace. Give me wisdom to respond to my situation with faith and trust in You alone.*

Are you hanging on by your fingernails, precious one? Too worn, too weary, too weak to cry out to God anymore? Are you ready to give up, to stop praying, to stop believing, to walk away? Are you ready to call it quits on trying to live in surrender to Christ?

Do you think, "I can't bear any more. I can't deal with the incessant pain"?

If I didn't know God's Word or hadn't experienced God's marvelous, miraculous love for me, I might tell you to call it quits and get on with your life.

But because God is who He is, because our times are in His hands, and because He's the God of all flesh and absolutely nothing is too hard for Him, I urge you not to give up. I want to encourage you, just as the apostle Paul encouraged the Christians at Colossae: "Therefore as you have received Christ Jesus the Lord, so walk in Him, having been firmly rooted and now being built up in Him and established in your faith" (Colossians 2:6-7).

Keep the faith, beloved. God will take care of you. ✗

*Lord, I'm so, so tired. The pressures of life are over-whelming, and all I want is to give in. Hold me. Sustain me. Help me to walk in a manner worthy of You. By Your grace I appropriate Your strength. I won't let go until I see Your hand working in my life.*

Shall we accept good from God and not accept adversity?

Dear friend, in acceptance lies peace! Not *resignation*, mind you, but *acceptance*.

When you cast yourself on Him, when you respond obediently to God's leading and yet nothing changes, God is still there—and He's adequate!

He is Jehovah-jireh, the Lord who will provide all our needs.

How I wish you and I could sit down together and read some of the letters I receive. You'd be heartbroken over the pain, but you would find yourself awed and encouraged by what God does when we decide to believe Him—and walk in faith's obedience.

"Consider it all joy, my brethren, when you encounter various trials, knowing that the testing of your faith produces endurance. And let endurance have its perfect result, so that you may be perfect and complete, lacking in nothing" (James 1:2-4).

Whatever is happening in your life, God is using it to bring you, His beloved child, toward His personal goal for you: Christlikeness. Your job is simply to trust and obey.

*Lord, once again I surrender to You my disappointment with what's happening in my life. In faith I choose to trust You and to rejoice in the knowledge that You cannot lie and, therefore, You are using my circumstances to transform me into Your likeness.*

Oh, beloved, have you lost your first love?

Was there a time when you were more zealous for the things of God—a time of first love with all its newness, joy, discovery, anticipation, a time when you would have gone anywhere, done anything God asked of you? Have you strayed from the God who loves you?

What happened? If you've strayed from God, if the zeal and passion are gone, something is wrong in your heart.

"I pray that the eyes of your heart may be enlightened, so that you will know what is the hope of His calling, what are the riches of the glory of His inheritance in the saints, and what is the surpassing greatness of His power toward us who believe" (Ephesians 1:18-19).

Nothing is more arresting, gripping, dazzling, and challenging than a heart aflame with love for God. I urge you to pray Psalm 139:23-24 in earnest sincerity:

*"Search me, O God, and know my heart; try me and know my anxious thoughts; and see if there be any hurtful way in me [any way of pain], and lead me in the everlasting way."*

Are you determined to be rich? To have everything you want? All that your mind can conceive or your heart would desire?

Does money—or what it can buy—preoccupy your thoughts? Are you continually thinking about how you can have more? More houses, more furniture, clothes, cars, jewelry, property, businesses, vacations, collector's items? Or perhaps you're focused more on bigger things than what you have: bigger house, bigger boat, bigger car.

Oh, beloved, if this is your focus, be warned: You are in danger.

Listen to the Word of God:

"Those who want to get rich fall into temptation and a snare and many foolish and harmful desires which plunge men into ruin and destruction. For the love of money is a root of all sorts of evil, and some by longing for it have wandered away from the faith and pierced themselves with many griefs" (1 Timothy 6:9,10).

Think about it.

*Lord, forgive me for investing my energy in acquiring material wealth while neglecting the spiritual riches that can be found in pursuing Your heart. Give me strength to flee from the temptation of material things and instead pursue righteousness, godliness, faith, love, perseverance, and gentleness, as Paul admonishes in 1 Timothy.*

Sometimes Satan attacks by way of our regrets, bringing to mind our failures until we find ourselves agonizing over past disobedience, contemplating the "if onlys." "If only I had surrendered sooner." "If only I hadn't been so determined to go my own way." How bitter are the tears of what might have been! I know from personal experience exactly how you feel.

So what should we do? Give up? Weep bitter tears for the remainder of our days?

No, beloved. Consider Lamentations 3:22-23: "The LORD's lovingkindnesses indeed never cease, for His compassions never fail. They are new every morning." Our just, holy, righteous, faithful God is long-suffering and merciful. His righteous anger is slow to kindle against us when we fail to listen to His warnings or obey His instructions.

So dry your tears. If you've repented, acknowledged your wrong and turned from your disobedient ways, He stands there in His mercy, reaching out with open arms saying, "Do not be grieved, for the joy of the LORD is your strength" (Nehemiah 8:10).

*Thank You for redeeming my past, dear Lord. Thank You for Your unending mercy and grace. When Satan tries to distract me with regrets, help me to remember that You have removed my sin as far as the east is from the west. I need not live in the past but press on in hope to the future.*

Getting out of bed is hard when life is overwhelming, when you're battling depression and defeat, wondering if you are going to make it, not certain you even want to.

Everything may look bleak and hopeless, but, beloved, with God nothing is ever hopeless. He is the God of all hope. If you can just believe and cling to this with whatever faith you have—no matter how weak—God will meet you. Remember, "If you have faith the size of a mustard seed… nothing will be impossible to you" (Matthew 17:20).

Cry out, "Lord Jesus Christ, help me." Memorize Isaiah 33:2: "O LORD, be gracious to us; we have waited for You. Be their strength every morning, our salvation also in the time of distress."

If you continue to struggle, ask God to direct you to a doctor who can determine whether a medical problem is causing your depression. But whatever happens, know God is there to sustain you.

*Lord, when no one else notices, You see the struggles of my soul, the sadness of my heart, the darkness of my depression. Give me Your hope, Your strength, Your peace, Your assurance that my life is in Your loving hands. If my struggles are the result of something physical—a biochemical failure, poor nutrition, or a hormonal imbalance—show me. If they're a symptom of warfare, alert me. Whatever the source, may I listen to You—not to my thoughts or my emotions.*

Are you feeling overwhelmed by the pressures of the world? Do you sometimes wonder whether you'll just give in and end up ruining your life—and the lives of others—simply because you don't know how to cope with the stress?

First of all, my friend, please know you are not alone in these feelings. So many of us want to know how to cope when responsibilities weigh heavy, how to stand strong when temptations surround us. We want to be assured that we can make it over the long haul without leaving a disaster area behind.

The New Testament book of Philippians is often referred to as the Epistle of Joy. In four short chapters we find sixteen references to joy or rejoicing, eleven references to mind or attitude, and thirty-six references to Jesus Christ. So what is the theme of Philippians? It is that joy comes from focusing on Jesus no matter our circumstances. "I can do all things through Him who strengthens me" (4:13).

When you are hard-pressed from every side, Jesus will help you cope.

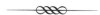

*Lord, thank You for the assurance that what You begin You complete. Thank You for the encouragement to press on toward the goal, to continue living by Your standards even while the pressures of life tempt me to weaken. May Your peace, which surpasses all understanding, guard my heart and mind today.*

How are you responding to the evil in our society? How do you feel when you hear profanity? The blasphemous use of God's name? When you see our nation decaying morally? The destruction of unborn babies, marriages, the family? What do you think about the crudeness, sex, violence, and brutality displayed graphically on television while our crime rate soars?

Do you know that God is watching your heart in all of this? He knows whether you condone these behaviors, whether you see the television programs as entertainment or depravity. He knows whether you are apathetic about the moral condition of our society—or whether your heart is deeply grieved.

Listen: "Go through the midst of the city…and put a mark on the foreheads of the men who sigh and groan over all the abominations which are being committed in its midst…. Utterly slay old men, young men, maidens, little children, and women, but do not touch any man on whom is the mark" (Ezekiel 9:4,6).

Examine your heart and ask yourself, "Would God mark my forehead?"

*Lord, forgive me for my tolerance of sin, for my insensitive, culturally hardened heart. May I so know Your heart, may I be so attuned to You that what breaks Your heart will break mine also. May I weep over sin rather than laugh at it with the world.*

Is hurt and heaviness hanging over you like a dark cloud?

You look at others. They seem so happy. "What's wrong with me!" you cry out. You feel locked away in loneliness, and your heart aches.

I do understand, beloved, because at one time or another I've had to deal with all of this. You're not alone.

Christians aren't exempt from heartache, but we do have the means to endure! For this we have Jesus, His grace, His Word, His promises. "Blessed be the God and Father of our Lord Jesus Christ, the Father of mercies and God of all comfort, who comforts us in all our affliction.… For just as the sufferings of Christ are ours in abundance, so also our comfort is abundant through Christ" (2 Corinthians 1:3-5).

May I urge you today to meditate on verses 3-7 of this chapter? Meditate and take courage, valiant warrior. Fight the good fight of faith!

*O Father, my emotions seem to be controlling me today, and that's not how I want to live. Your Word says that You comfort us in our affliction, and I desperately need that comfort at this moment. Thank You for Your promise to walk with me through every trial of life.*

Are you suffering, my friend? Your faith is being tried, stretched, tested. You're feeling weak, wondering where God is, how long this is going to last—or if it is ever going to end. Sometimes you feel as if you can't endure anymore. You're certain your heart will break. And through it all, you feel alone. You look at others and are convinced they cannot possibly understand your suffering and pain.

Bless your heart. Don't be ashamed. God will give you the grace to endure. He will exalt you at the proper time. As I've reminded you earlier, cast all your care upon God and remember He does care for you.

Don't let Satan devour you with discouragement. Remember, this trial is for a season. It had a beginning; it will have an end. "After you have suffered for a little while, the God of all grace, who called you to His eternal glory in Christ, will Himself perfect, confirm, strengthen and establish you" (1 Peter 5:10).

*Dear Lord, I long for the return of Christ, for the end of suffering on this earth. But I know everything is in Your hands, and I trust that somehow You will use my suffering to mature me, to confirm the authenticity of my relationship with You. I thank You for the promise in Your Word that I will be stronger for it and more established in my Christian life.*

Is life wearing you out, beloved? Are you exhausted? To use an old expression, do you feel like you're just spinning your wheels? When you slow down and take stock, do you find life rather routine, empty?

A familiar promise in the Word of God has taken me through many a wearying situation. It's in Isaiah 40:29-31: "He gives strength to the weary, and to him who lacks might He increases power. Though youths grow weary and tired, and vigorous young men stumble badly, yet those who wait for the Lord will gain new strength; they will mount up with wings like eagles, they will run and not get tired, they will walk and not become weary."

Oh, dear one, go to the Father, hope in Him, claim His promise, and soar above all your difficulties with your eagle wings!

*I am so tired, God. I can't even begin to get through this day without Your strength. What a comfort to know that You never tire and You never sleep. Whenever I need You, all I have to do is call on Your name. Thank You for Your unending care and protection, for bearing me up on Your wings.*

Are you sick and tired of being sick and tired? Have you thought, beloved, of asking God why you're in this wretched state? He is the great physician, and He can bring healing to your soul.

Begin with prayer. Write down anything that comes to mind. Tell God that you want to hear His voice alone and that you refuse to believe any lies the enemy may bring to mind.

Examine your heart, and confess any sin in your life. Be sure that you have forgiven anyone who has offended you. Holding on to your anger is sin that will take root and quietly, gradually destroy you.

Finally, remember that not all weariness is a result of sin. If the Lord brings no sin to mind in the next few days, ask God what medical evaluation you are to seek. Then do as the Bible says: "Call for the elders of the church…to pray over him, anointing him with oil in the name of the Lord…. Pray for one another so that you may be healed" (James 5:14,16).

*Lord, speak to my heart and reveal the source of my weariness. Is hidden sin eroding my heart? Or is it merely a physical affliction permitted by You? If it is, like the apostle Paul I pray that You will take this thorn from me. But if You choose not to do so, I will glory in how Your strength is revealed in my weakness.*

Concern about our view of self seems to be a recurring theme these days. But what does God say about all of this?

Beloved, sometimes we're so introspective and full of self-condemnation we cannot trust ourselves to look at our hearts objectively. First John 3:19-21 says, "We will know by this [that we love in deed and truth] that we are of the truth, and will assure our heart before Him in whatever our heart condemns us; for God is greater than our heart and knows all things. Beloved, if our heart does not condemn us, we have confidence before God."

Perhaps you have a difficult time accepting God's unconditional love and commitment. You feel as if you never measure up to His expectations. Oh, beloved, never fear. Listen to what Jesus, the Good Shepherd, told His disciples in John 10:27-28: "My sheep hear My voice, and I know them, and they follow Me; and I give eternal life to them, and they will never perish; and no one will snatch them out of My hand."

Hallelujah! What further reassurance do we need?

*Dear heavenly Father, I am so grateful for Your unconditional love. So many times I fail to live up to my own expectations; what a relief to know that Your love for me never changes. You have promised to forgive me if only I will confess to You. Thank You.*

# LEAD ME
# TO OBEDIENCE

What do you think it is that makes you acceptable to God? Have you been working yourself to death—doing this, running here, and doing that—trying to earn God's favor? Are you exhausting yourself serving Him, being in church every time the doors are open, saying yes to whatever anyone asks you to do—all because you want to please people for God's sake?

Are you worn out, my friend? If not, you should be. You need to know that doing is not what pleases God; He simply asks for the obedience of faith, for you to order your life according to the Word of God. What pleases God is faith—believing Him, taking Him at His word and then living accordingly.

This, beloved, is what God calls "your work of faith" (1 Thessalonians 1:3). Would Jesus have to say to you as He said to Martha, "You are worried and bothered about so many things" (Luke 10:41)?

Only one thing is necessary: Go sit at His feet and get your work schedule from Him.

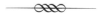

*Lord, I've been so distracted with my "preparations" and service that I've been ignoring the one I claim to serve. Today I place my plans and schedules before You, and I choose to listen for Your guidance and to obey only Your call—not the demands of the world or my own priorities.*

My dear friend, are you struggling with a lack of forgiveness? Are you having a difficult time letting go of an old hurt, a major disappointment? Are you angry?

Oh, beloved, I know what you're going through. I've been there! It's not easy to forgive until you understand that forgiveness is a matter of your will. It's a deliberate choice to obey God—regardless of your emotions. Ephesians 5:1-2 urges us to "be imitators of God...and walk in love, just as Christ also loved you and gave Himself up for us."

Will you cry out to your loving, heavenly Father and tell Him that you choose to forgive those who have hurt you or who have hurt someone you love?

*I've read in Your word that if I do not forgive others, You will not forgive me. God, out of sheer obedience I choose to forgive, to put away that which I hold against this person, even as You have forgiven me. You are God, and I entrust this person to You. As the righteous judge, You will do what is right. I will obey—I will forgive.*

So often in this life we find ourselves being treated unjustly. Perhaps someone in a position of authority over you is simply being mean, harsh, and cruel—unfair and unjustified in his or her treatment of you. What are you to do?

God says Jesus learned obedience through His suffering. He also says, "You have been called for this purpose, since Christ also suffered for you, leaving you an example for you to follow in His steps, who committed no sin, nor was any deceit found in His mouth; and while being reviled, He did not revile in return; while suffering, He uttered no threats, but kept entrusting Himself to Him who judges righteously" (1 Peter 2:21-23).

So what do you do? Follow Jesus' example: Don't sin by acting independently of God. Keep your mouth shut—no deceit, no reviling, no threats. Trust God. He will act with justice on your behalf.

*"In You, O LORD, I have taken refuge; let me never be ashamed. In Your righteousness deliver me and rescue me; incline Your ear to me and save me.... My lips will shout for joy when I sing praises to You; and my soul, which You have redeemed" (Psalm 71:1-2,23).*

Do you know what God's will is for you, but you're having a hard time doing it? How long will you vacillate between two decisions, my friend?

Listen to Elijah's words of old, words still relevant today: "How long will you hesitate between two opinions? If the LORD is God, follow Him" (1 Kings 18:21).

Is God truly God? Then doesn't He know what is going on? Doesn't He know the end from the beginning—and all that goes on in between? Isn't He in charge of the universe? Didn't He number your days "when as yet there was not one of them" (Psalm 139:16)? And aren't you someday going to give an account to Him?

My friend, I urge you to turn to Isaiah 46:9-10 and ponder these words: "For I am God, and there is no other; I am God, and there is no one like Me, declaring the end from the beginning, and from ancient times things which have not been done, saying, 'My purpose will be established, and I will accomplish all My good pleasure.'"

There is no decision to be made. What God says to you, do it.

*God, I choose to follow You today. Even when the path seems dark and treacherous, I know You are here beside me. Thank You for Your promise that Your plans for me, like those for Israel, include a future and a hope.*

Are you withholding yourself sexually from your spouse? Have you pushed him or her away or said no so many times that your mate no longer even approaches you? Or maybe one of you has simply moved to a separate bedroom.

Do you know that when you withhold yourself from your spouse, you are sinning? And you are putting him or her in the path of temptation—an act for which God will call *you* into account.

Listen to the Word of God on this subject: "The husband must fulfill his duty to his wife, and likewise also the wife to her husband. The wife does not have authority over her own body, but the husband does; and likewise also the husband does not have authority over his own body, but the wife does. Stop depriving one another, except by agreement for a time, so that you may devote yourselves to prayer, and come together again so that Satan will not tempt you because of your lack of self-control" (1 Corinthians 7:3-5).

Now then, are you going to be obedient to God and selflessly meet your spouse's God-given needs?

*I repent of the selfishness in my heart, Lord. I confess the self-centeredness, the willfulness that has prevented me from meeting my spouse's needs. Out of an act of love and obedience to You, I will do what You so clearly command. Please meet me at my point of obedience.*

Are you weary, my friend? Tired of the battle? Ready to give up, to walk away?

You say that the sacrifices required of you are too much, too difficult, too costly. You are certain you are going to lose. You feel worn out.

Have you passively given in—resigned yourself to whatever will happen because all your spunk is gone? Have you crawled into the back of the wagon to just go along for the ride?

God doesn't tell you to get in the back of the wagon; He tells you to get to the front, take His yoke upon you, and learn from Him. God hasn't called you to complacent passivity. This is the time to harness up with God. He will pull the load. His yoke is easy; His burden is light. So get on your knees and ask God to hitch you up. Only then will you find rest for your soul (Matthew 11:29-30).

Assure your Master that you are ready to do His will, no matter what. Spend time in the Bible. Don't quit reading until you have God's answer, God's direction.

*Here I am again, Lord, offering myself for Your service. I know that You will not give me a burden greater than I can bear. I'm ready and willing to obey You. Speak to my heart, and show me the first step.*

Do you feel thwarted on every hand? Is everything you do coming out wrong? Have you crashed into one brick wall after another? Does everything you touch turn to dust instead of gold?

What is the problem, my friend? Have you thought about asking God? Or perhaps you already have an inkling. You know that you have not been walking in a way pleasing to God. You have stepped over His line, broken His commandments, ignored Him—all the while thinking you could get away with it. Now deep down inside you are wondering, "Is God behind my recent frustrations?" Maybe He's been trying to get your attention. Are you ready now to listen?

Consider this scripture, my friend: "Yet the people do not turn back to Him who struck them, nor do they seek the LORD of Hosts.... His anger does not turn away and His hand is still stretched out" (Isaiah 9:13,17).

Heed the Lord's call and return to Him—before it's too late!

*You are God. What a fool I've been to think I could sin and escape Your judgment. I will name my sin for what it is. I'll confess it and forsake it and wait for You to graciously remove Your just rod of chastisement. Thank you, Lord, for Your mercy and grace.*

Do you have a friend who has been caught in sin, someone who has strayed from the truth of the Bible? What have you done about it?

If you're typical, the answer is, "Nothing." Why is that? Because we excuse the person, justifying our decision to avoid confrontation by noting that we aren't perfect either. That's certainly true. However, if you are doing what you shouldn't be doing, why don't you stop?

Don't excuse yourself, beloved—or your friend. God expects us to obey Him, to walk in faith by the Spirit, and to hold one another accountable. When we don't, God has to deal with us.

Listen to the Bible: "My brethren, if any among you strays from the truth and one turns him back, let him know that he who turns a sinner from the error of his way will save his soul from death and will cover a multitude of sins" (James 5:19-20).

*O Father, I'm uncomfortable confronting my friend, but I want to obey Your call. Please reveal any areas of sin in my own heart so that I can confess them openly to You. Then, I ask that You would give me wisdom; fill my mouth with the right words so that I can be Your instrument for drawing my friend back to You.*

What do you do when your heart is troubled, beloved? When you've been criticized or misunderstood?

When I find myself in that situation, I stop and remember that I am called to a life of obedience. And I remember that my obedience says to my Father and my Lord, "I love You."

"Love never fails," the apostle Paul wrote in 1 Corinthians 13:8. In verse 7 we read that love "bears all things, believes all things, hopes all things, endures all things." And oh, beloved, as I tell God of my love and deep gratitude to Him for choosing me to be His child, I reaffirm my commitment to obey His call—no matter how my heart is troubled.

And with that, dear one, my heart is quieted and I'm at rest again! Why don't you try it?

*Thank You, dear God, for choosing me before the foundation of the world, for loving me so much that You sent Your Son to die in my place. I commit myself to walking in obedience to You through the strength of Your Holy Spirit. Your approval is really all that will matter when I see You face to face.*

Beloved, how do you suppose God knows you love Him? And what about others? How will they know? It's something to think about.

In the middle of telling His disciples that they could ask what they wanted in His name and describing the future coming of the Holy Spirit, Jesus made this statement in John 14:15: "If you love Me, you will keep My commandments."

I think He wanted His followers to understand that true love for God produces obedience. It's senseless to ask things from God when you don't love Him and therefore have no intention of obeying Him.

If you're a parent, you know how important it is to you for your children to obey you. Oh, beloved, how much more true that is with our heavenly Father! He's omniscient. He sees the danger in the paths ahead, and His loving commandments are intended to keep us safe and unstained by the world.

How about it, beloved? Are you loving God by obeying Him?

*Lord God, I want to show my love for You with all my heart, mind, soul, and strength. When temptation strikes and my flesh wants to live for self, help me remember that words of praise, love, and adoration are empty and useless—a sham—if I don't love You enough to obey You.*

Each of us will encounter trials throughout our lives, moments when our circumstances seem overwhelming, even unsolvable. When this happens to you, beloved, remember that every trial brings a potential for sin, the potential for yielding to the flesh connection.

The flesh wants out of trials. In our human understanding, we think we can't bear anything more. For this reason James warns us to be aware of the temptation that comes with each trial, the temptation to take our own route out of the trial instead of persevering and counting it all joy.

Listen: "Let no one say when he is tempted, 'I am being tempted by God'; for God cannot be tempted by evil, and He Himself does not tempt anyone. But each one is tempted when he is carried away and enticed by his own lust. Then when lust has conceived, it gives birth to sin; and when sin is accomplished, it brings forth death" (James 1:13-15).

Don't yield, my friend. It will only end in death.

*I cannot make it on my own, dear Lord. The weight of my burden is more than I can handle. So I claim the power that comes through Your Holy Spirit. Through Him I can find the strength to endure so that I may be perfect and complete, lacking in nothing.*

Do you think God will tolerate sin in your life? Granted, He's a God of love and of mercy. Even when we fail Him, His compassions are new every morning and His mercies fail not (Lamentations 3:22-23).

However, God is also holy—just and righteous in all His ways. And He bids us remember that God's judgment begins within His own household, with His own children.

"Be sure your sin will find you out," God warned the children of Israel (Numbers 32:23). He was speaking not to the heathen, the unbelieving, but to His own people, those who had promised to follow and obey Him.

Bearing the name "Christian" is a serious thing. It says you're a follower of Jesus Christ, the One who not only paid the penalty for your sin but also was raised from the dead and thus set you free from sin's power. If you tolerate sin in your life, you can be absolutely sure your sin will find you out. You need to repent, which means to change your mind and act accordingly.

*O Father, forgive me for trampling on the blood of Jesus Christ, for sinning against You. Whatever "harvest" I receive, I'll accept it as Your just judgment. I know You love me. Now may I love and honor You as I should.*

Have you gone against the clear teaching of the Word of God? Have you sinned? Are you feeling guilty? What are you going to do?

You can't blame anyone else. You can't say, "The devil made me do it" and escape responsibility. God says you sinned because you allowed yourself to be carried along by your own desires, by your pride. Yes, Satan is the tempter, but he cannot do a thing without your cooperation.

The problem lies within you, beloved. You yielded to lust, choosing to follow the desires of the flesh rather than yielding to God. When lust conceives, it gives birth to sin. And sin kills whatever it touches. Your sin may not necessarily lead to physical death, but it will bring forth death in some form—perhaps the death of a marriage, a relationship, an opportunity, a ministry, virginity, innocence...

However, although you may reap the harvest of your sin, you can have God's forgiveness today. If you confess your sin, call it what it is, you will hear Jesus' words, "I do not condemn you.... From now on sin no more" (John 8:11).

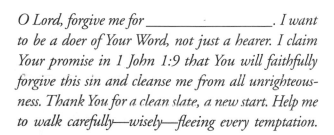

*O Lord, forgive me for _____. I want to be a doer of Your Word, not just a hearer. I claim Your promise in 1 John 1:9 that You will faithfully forgive this sin and cleanse me from all unrighteousness. Thank You for a clean slate, a new start. Help me to walk carefully—wisely—fleeing every temptation.*

One of the characteristics of genuine faith is a life that overcomes the world.

A true Christian is not overcome by the world. Instead, because Christ is in us and because He, by the Holy Spirit, enables us to keep His commandments, we are able to overcome the world.

"For whatever is born of God overcomes the world; and this is the victory that has overcome the world—our faith. Who is the one who overcomes the world, but he who believes that Jesus is the Son of God?" (1 John 5:4-5).

Here's an essential truth you'll want to remember: It is not a burden for a believer to walk in righteousness and to be obedient. We may fail now and then, but it should never be because obedience is a burden! If we fail, it is because we made the choice to walk by the flesh rather than by the Spirit.

*As I look around, the truth of Your Word is so apparent, God—"The whole world lies in the power of the evil one" (1 John 5:19). But I praise You for the wonderful promise that Your Son, who is in me, is greater than he who is in the world (1 John 4:4). Thank You, Father, for Your Holy Spirit, who enables me to resist the pull of the world.*

Do you find yourself desiring something you know is wrong? According to God, the answer to your desire is a firm "no," yet you think that somehow you can have it—and get away with it.

Don't be deluded. The Bible says that yielding to temptation will bring forth sin, and sin will bring forth death (James 1:15). Sin destroys everything in its path, everything it touches.

"God had promised to answer my prayers," you say, "so why isn't He responding to my request in this situation?" You can find the answer in James 4:3—"You ask and do not receive, because you ask with wrong motives, so that you may spend it on your pleasures."

Don't make the deadly mistake, beloved, of thinking of your desires, the cravings of your flesh, as "needs." Recognize your desire for what it is—a temptation leading you to rebel against God—and then let it go unfulfilled. If you don't, someday you'll greatly regret it.

*O Father, You have promised to supply all my needs out of Your abundant riches. Since You have chosen not to fulfill this desire, I must trust that You have another plan for fulfilling my emotional and physical needs. Today I deliberately choose to accept Your answer and let go of my fleshly longings.*

A child of God not only has the power to live differently than the rest of the world but actually is different than the world. What a difference this knowledge can make in our lives! Once you become part of His family, you're no longer a slave to sin. What makes this possible is the Spirit of the living God residing within you. He affirms your salvation—the fact that Christ is in you and you are in Him.

Listen: "By this we know that we abide in Him and He in us, because He has given us of His Spirit" (1 John 4:13). "The Spirit Himself testifies with our spirit that we are children of God" (Romans 8:16).

Do you have His witness within you? Solid evidence that the Spirit is there? The evidence is a changed life. If you don't have it, tell God that you want His salvation, His Spirit. He assures us that those who come to Him He will not cast out.

*God, I don't have total confidence that Your Spirit lives within. I've made a profession of faith and claimed to be a Christian all these years, but deep down inside I have doubts. I lack the power to live as You would have me live, but I want that to change. Jesus, I've believed that You are God, but today I am receiving You, unconditionally, as my Savior. I believe that You died for my sins, that You were raised from the dead. I'm Yours without reservation. Please make my body the temple of the Holy Spirit.*

"Rejoice in the Lord always" (Philippians 4:4).

It sounds ridiculous, doesn't it? A little inane, out of touch. Yet here is a command from the Bible that, if obeyed, will bring victory and peace in the midst of any situation. Why? Because the minute you begin rejoicing, your circumstances cease to control you.

It is crucial to understand, however, that the command to rejoice does not mean rejoicing in your circumstances; it means rejoicing in your Savior, who is Lord over every circumstance of life. "But in all these things [tribulation, distress, persecution, famine] we overwhelmingly conquer through Him who loved us" (Romans 8:37).

You could not be in the predicament you're in without the Lord's foreknowledge. God is sovereign: He rules over all, and nothing happens without His permission. That's why you can rejoice.

So remember, rejoicing is a matter of obedience—obedience that will start you on the road to peace and contentment. What more could you ask for?

*O Father, help me by Your Spirit to remember that You are sovereign and that I can rejoice no matter what. I rejoice simply because I belong to You and You belong to me, for You are my God.*

When you've failed, do you wonder if things can ever be the same between you and God? Do you feel unable to pick up the pieces and begin again? You may even be frightened by the knowledge that God is in control; you're wondering how He'll deal with you.

Beloved, we *all* fail. We've all been at that point when we're certain life is the worst it could possibly be and things will never be the same again with God.

I want you to know that God's *grace* calls you to get up and throw off your blanket of hopelessness, to move on through life in faith. And whatever task His grace calls you to, His grace provides the strength to do!

His grace—through faith—is sufficient for all your failure, for all your powerlessness. It's yours to claim! As Lamentations says, you can have hope. "The LORD's lovingkindnesses indeed never cease, for His compassions never fail. They are new every morning" (3:22-23).

*Great is Your faithfulness, O Lord, my God. You have redeemed my life. Thank You for Your amazing grace and love, for Your readiness to forgive me as soon as I confess and repent of my sin. Thank You that I need not live in the past, but I can look toward the future with hope.*

What a difference it would make if we would learn to simply do what God says!

Try as we might, we cannot change another person's heart, nor can we control our circumstances. Only God can. He alone is our hope, our refuge, our very present help in the time of need and trouble (Psalm 46:1).

If only we'd learn to do as God has instructed us:

- to pray and not faint
- to persist and not quit
- to trust Him implicitly
- to wait upon Him until He brings it to pass

If you're convinced by His Spirit that what you're asking for is in accord with His Word, His will, and His character and you're not asking merely to satisfy your own desires (James 4:2-3), then persist in prayer. Though the answer to your prayer may tarry—even for years—it *will* come!

So, beloved, cease striving and know that He is God—and He is at work!

*Hear my prayer, O Lord. I have nowhere else to turn, nor in reality do I need anyone else. You are my hope and my refuge, and You have promised to answer when I ask in accordance with Your will. I'm claiming that promise today. Thank You, Father. Thank You so much for being there for me.*

When we fail God, does He take back all His promises?

As you read the Old Testament, you'll see no one failed God more than Israel.

- His chosen people broke every commandment.
- They challenged His love.
- They despised and defiled His name.
- They wearied Him with their tolerance of evil.
- They spoke against Him.

Yet there was that faithful remnant, those who clung to His immutable promise: "Behold, I am going to send My messenger, and he will clear the way before Me. And the Lord, whom you seek, will suddenly come to His temple; and the messenger of the covenant, in whom you delight, behold, He is coming" (Malachi 3:1).

How this reminds me of God's promise to us as the church of Jesus Christ. We've been waiting almost two thousand years, but we have His promise, "I am coming," even when He's silent. He will not go back on His word. "The Lord is not slow about His promise, as some count slowness, but is patient toward you, not wishing for any to perish but for all to come to repentance" (2 Peter 3:9).

*Father, thank You that "the gifts and the calling of God are irrevocable" (Romans 11:29). Record my name as I eagerly await Your Son's promised return. May I become pure even as He is pure, so that I won't be ashamed when I see Him face to face.*

Are you on the verge of giving up?

Be courageous, dear one! Face difficulty or danger with the confidence that God is sovereign and He will never permit you to suffer more than you can endure. No matter how violent the storm, Jesus is with you—and able to walk on water!

As Joshua prepared to take Moses' place and lead the children of Israel into the Promised Land, God told him—as he tells us, "I will be with you; I will not fail you or forsake you. Be strong and courageous.... This book of the law shall not depart from your mouth, but you shall meditate on it day and night, so that you may be careful to do according to all that is written in it; for then you will make your way prosperous, and then you will have success" (Joshua 1:5-6,8).

Obedience makes us strong. Faith makes us courageous!

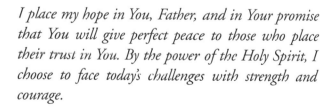

*I place my hope in You, Father, and in Your promise that You will give perfect peace to those who place their trust in You. By the power of the Holy Spirit, I choose to face today's challenges with strength and courage.*

Troubled, beloved? Weary? Groping your way through personal darkness because you're not doing what you ought to do? It has a physically debilitating effect, doesn't it?

Sin affects our spirits and can cause sickness—not only sickness of our emotions but also of our bodies. David knew something about sin's effect! In Psalm 38:18 he said: "I am full of anxiety because of my sin."

Is sin eating you up?

If the Holy Spirit puts His finger on sin in our lives, we must deal with it—thoroughly. Not doing so can stay the healing hand of God. Solomon noted, "He who conceals his transgressions will not prosper, but he who confesses and forsakes them will find compassion" (Proverbs 28:13).

God always meets us at the point of our obedience. When we obey, He comes over to our side, pardons all our iniquities, and heals the diseases of our hearts. So, beloved, if you are troubled and weary, why don't you turn to the One who can take your bitterness and make it sweet?

*Lord, I confess that even my obedience has been tinged with a spirit of arrogance. I find it humbling to face my sins, so I often ignore them until the conviction of the Holy Spirit is more than I can bear. I'm tired of fighting, Lord, and I turn to You once more for cleansing, hope, healing, and help.*

Where do *you* turn for healing, dear friend?

Health, healing, and obedience all go together, according to Exodus 15:26: "If you will give earnest heed to the voice of the LORD your God, and do what is right in His sight, and give ear to His commandments, and keep all His statutes, I will put none of the diseases on you which I have put on the Egyptians; for I, the LORD, am your healer."

Sin affects our spirits and can cause emotional or physical sickness. Personal sin may not always be the cause of the problem or even a contributing factor, but it can be. First Corinthians 11:27-31 and James 5:15-16 clarify this. Therefore we ought to cry, "Search me, O God, and know my heart; try me and know my anxious thoughts; and see if there be any hurtful way in me" (Psalm 139:23-24).

The heavenly Father knows your needs and is responsible for meeting them. To attempt to meet them in your own way and sin in the process is so foolish. Didn't Jesus say, "Seek first His kingdom and His righteousness, and all these things will be added to you" (Matthew 6:33)?

*Once more I surrender my heart to the spotlight of Your love. Please reveal any hidden sins, any secret grudges, any attempt to retain control of my own life. Reveal to me any sin I have nurtured rather than forsaken, concealed rather than confessed. Show me, Father, what I must do to be pure in Your sight.*

Discouragement strikes each of us at various times. We feel alone, abandoned, forgotten by everyone—maybe even by God.

We need something that gives us hope, don't we? We need something to look forward to—the assurance, the promise of someone we can trust. And as Christians we have exactly that: Our God "according to His great mercy has caused us to be born again to a living hope through the resurrection of Jesus Christ from the dead, to obtain an inheritance which is imperishable and undefiled and will not fade away, reserved in heaven for you" (1 Peter 1:3-4).

But how do we keep from being worn down and "distressed by various trials" (1 Peter 1:6)? How can we keep our vision clear in a world that isn't our home? It's by obedience to God's Word, beloved, by meditating on its precepts, by clinging to them in faith—with all of our hearts.

Take Psalm 119:35-37,133 with you, and make it your prayer today:

*"Make me walk in the path of Your commandments, for I delight in it. Incline my heart to Your testimonies.... Revive me in Your ways.... Establish my footsteps in Your word, and do not let any iniquity have dominion over me."*

Another day is before you, precious one, so let me pose a question we should all consider: Will you live by faith today, beloved? Will you believe the Word of God?

When you are in despair, follow the example set in Psalm 42 of the believer who brings his questions straight to God. Run to the living God, your Rock. Cry out to Him. Say a prayer to the God of your life. Seek the help of His presence.

If you feel as if He's forgotten you, then ask Him if He has.

If you feel as if your enemies—physical, emotional, or spiritual—have overwhelmed you, ask Him why.

Pour out your soul to God, dear one. He is your life. You need not live in confusion or despair. Second Corinthians 4:8 tells us that "we are afflicted in every way, but not crushed; perplexed, but not despairing."

Remember, faith consists of three things: first, knowledge; then, surrender to that knowledge; and finally, an act of obedience, to walk in the light of that knowledge.

You have God's Word, beloved. Will you believe it?

*You've revealed Your love for me clearly in Your Word, and I choose today to accept and embrace that love. When problems come my way, remind me by the nudging of Your Spirit to focus on the fact of Your love so that I am free to walk in obedience, undisturbed by the circumstances of life.*

Beloved, sin is never private.

We cover it up, excuse it, rationalize it. We do everything but confront our sin and deal with it honestly and openly. God says, "He who covers his sins will not prosper, but whoever confesses and forsakes them will have mercy" (Proverbs 28:13, NKJV).

The world would have you believe in "victimless" sin, but that's a lie from Satan himself. Sin is never isolated; someone else is always affected. Romans 1:18 says that when we are not living according to what God says is right, we suppress the truth through our unrighteousness. Sin causes repercussions that extend far beyond ourselves, sometimes affecting second, third, and fourth generations.

You cannot cover sin, beloved! God knows it. Others see it and are ready to use your behavior as an excuse for their sin! John 15:22-24 says that the words and deeds of Christ took away men's excuse for their sin. In the same way, when we allow Christ to live through us—when we live righteously and obediently—our behavior takes away their excuse. So determine today to live in faith's obedience.

*Dear heavenly Father, I want my life to be available for Your use so that others will be drawn to You. If anything in my life is creating a stumbling block for others, please bring conviction and transformation. Remind me that my Christianity is on display so that I'll forsake sin for the sake of Your kingdom.*

Dear friend, does the call to take up your cross and follow Jesus strike terror in your heart? I can understand how it could if you don't know God well or you don't know what salvation is all about, but you need not fear.

We who love God are never to fear the cross, which frees us from sin and self. Rather we're to fear its absence! The Bible tells us in Galatians 2:20 that the cross is where the natural dies and the supernatural takes over, because Christ lives through us.

When you want to run, to escape, to save yourself from that call to put aside everything and follow Him, you can be certain that fear is *not* from God! The cross and true Christianity are inseparable.

Fear that keeps you from the cross comes only from Satan. He knows the cross is where we are set free from bondage to death.

Oh beloved, rest securely in Christ's love. The Cross is God's eternal testimony of His immutable love.

*Sometimes my heart quakes at the thought of full surrender, but I know that only in obedience, in taking up my cross, can I find life and freedom.*

*"May it never be that I would boast, except in the cross of our Lord Jesus Christ, through which the world has been crucified to me, and I to the world" (Galatians 6:14).*

It's one thing to suffer when you actually do wrong, but it can be devastating when you suffer for doing right. How do we bear up under the sorrows of unjust suffering?

Dear one, let me share a word of encouragement from Hebrews 5:8-9: "Although He was a Son, He learned obedience from the things which He suffered. And having been made perfect, He became to all those who obey Him the source of eternal salvation."

Suffering—suffering unjustly—teaches us obedience and matures us just as it did Jesus. As His followers, we've actually been called to suffer. Have you ever thought about it in that way, beloved? As we endure suffering, let's learn how by looking unto Jesus, "the author and perfecter of faith, who for the joy set before Him endured the cross" (Hebrews 12:2).

*I thank You, dear God, that Jesus willingly suffered in my place, that He endured to give me salvation. Through Your Holy Spirit, I appropriate the strength to endure, that I may know the fellowship of His sufferings. Thank You for Your promise in 2 Timothy 2:10-13 that if we suffer with Him, we'll also reign with Him.*

Imagine it, beloved! It may be difficult to comprehend, but someday we'll stand before our Savior. Someday we'll see Him face to face!

And on that day, nothing—*absolutely nothing*—is going to matter except our relationship with Him. That's why it's so key, so absolutely crucial, that we understand His eternal ways *now*—including His loving sovereignty over every detail of our lives leading up to that day.

Second Corinthians 5:10 is a great reminder that "we must all appear before the judgment seat of Christ, that each one may be recompensed for his deeds in the body, according to what he has done, whether good or bad." The judgment seat of Christ is not something to dread, beloved—not if we live with eternity stamped on our lives and on our hearts.

Therefore, make it your ambition "to be pleasing to Him" (verse 9).

*O Lord, may I so love You that I truly long to be in Your presence, that I count it far better than anything else. I know that day of accountability is coming, and I want to hear You say, "Well done, My good and faithful servant." As I wait for that day, I am committing myself to a life of obedience. Thank You for Your promise in Jude 24 that You are able to keep me from stumbling and to make me stand in the presence of His glory blameless with great joy.*

MARCH

# SEARCH MY CONVERSATION

If the words of your mouth reflect your beliefs, what do you believe about life? About you? About the future? About God? Do your words reflect faith or unbelief? Are they filled with lies or truths about God? Does what you say and think about God line up with the One described to us in the Bible, the very Word of God?

And what about you, dear one? Are the words you speak about yourself according to what God says about you, how He sees you, what He says about you as His creation, His design, His gifting?

There's a lot of power in the tongue. A person has a tendency to believe what they keep saying, so if you are going to speak, speak according to His Word. God says, "Whoever speaks, let him speak, as it were, the utterances of God" (1 Peter 4:11, NASB early editions).

*O Father, it's so easy to speak without first thinking. I need the help of Your Holy Spirit to curb my natural inclinations. With the psalmist I pray, "Let the words of my mouth and the meditation of my heart be acceptable in Your sight, O LORD, my rock and my Redeemer" (Psalm 19:14).*

Are you catty? Do your words hiss, snarl, and spit? Are you leaving claw marks and scratches on other people's reputations—or worse still, on their character?

Do you know what God says about this? Listen: "A false witness will not go unpunished, and he who tells lies will not escape" (Proverbs 19:5).

But you may say, "I am not being a false witness; it really is true." It may be true, my friend, but why are you repeating it? What is your purpose? God says, "A man's discretion makes him slow to anger, and it is his glory to overlook a transgression" (verse 11).

When someone's actions or words make you want to strike back with swift retribution, hold in view the psalmist's advice: "Rest in the LORD and wait patiently for Him; do not fret because of him who prospers in his way, because of the man who carries out wicked schemes. Cease from anger and forsake wrath; do not fret; it leads only to evildoing" (Psalm 37:7-8).

*Dear heavenly Father, I choose today to walk in Your presence, to wait on You instead of rushing to my own defense. Seal my lips, I pray, and prevent me from speaking any cruel, unloving words. Give me the courage not to enter into gossip but rather to check it with a gentle and appropriate word from You.*

Would you like to be known as a man or woman of understanding? Would you like to build people, to contribute to their character and their success? Do you want to positively impact the lives of your spouse, your children, your friends, your associates, the people you work with or come into contact with?

Then learn to listen carefully to people. Get them to express themselves, to open their hearts. Then respond properly, wisely. Reflect upon these proverbs of life and wisdom: "A plan in the heart of a man is like deep water, but a man of understanding draws it out…. A soothing [healing] tongue is a tree of life, but perversion in it crushes the spirit…. The spirit of a man can endure his sickness, but as for a broken spirit who can bear it?" (Proverbs 20:5; 15:4; 18:14).

Use your ears to listen, beloved, and your tongue to strengthen another's spirit.

*In my conversations today, Lord, speak to my heart and remind me that the world does not revolve around my needs and interests. Prompt me to ask only kind and thoughtful questions and to spend more time listening than talking.*

Have you been kicking yourself around the block since you got up this morning? What you did was dumb! You wish you hadn't made that cruel comment, responded in frustration, reacted in haste. You wonder if you will ever learn to do things right.

I understand exactly how you feel, and I urge you not to give up.

Listen to God's Word: "The steps of a man are established by the LORD, and He delights in his way. When he falls, he will not be hurled headlong, because the LORD is the One who holds his hand.... The LORD loves justice and does not forsake His godly ones; they are preserved forever" (Psalm 37:23-24,28).

If you can right your wrong, then do so. Humble yourself and seek forgiveness. But whatever the circumstances, don't be defeated.

God still has you by the hand.

*I'm so sorry, Lord. So many times I've said something thoughtless, even cruel, only to regret it for days. I want my life to be a reflection of Your love, but I'm not sure I'll ever get it right! Thank You for Your mercy and patience—and for never letting go!*

What is it like around your house? Is it a place of peace, joy, acceptance, security? Or is your home a place of pain? Is there bickering? Hounding? Yelling? A rehearsal of the faults, failures, and faux pas of various family members?

I'm sure you would prefer to achieve peace, security, and acceptance without anyone having to move out of the house—including you. But how?

Notice what God says: "Let all bitterness and wrath and anger and clamor and slander be put away from you, along with all malice. Be kind to one another, tender-hearted, forgiving each other, just as God in Christ also has forgiven you" (Ephesians 4:31-32).

Each member of your household must be willing to let go of bitterness, deal with anger, bring his or her tongue under control, and forgive. (And if your children refuse to do so, they need to be called to account.) That's not easy, but my, how it changes the atmosphere.

Will you take the first step in transforming your home?

*Lord, I'm sick and tired of the atmosphere in my house, and I am willing to do whatever it takes to make a change. With the help of the Holy Spirit, I want to follow Your instruction to let my speech always be seasoned with grace (Colossians 4:6). Let me set the example in our home.*

Have you ever stopped to listen to how you talk to people? Do you find that people have a hard time when they listen to you? Do they get angry or walk away absolutely crushed? Have you ever thought that the problem might be in the way you respond—the tone of your voice, the way you choose your words? Perhaps you speak without thinking about the effect your words will have.

I urge you to turn to the book of Proverbs and do a little "wisdom check."

"A gentle answer turns away wrath, but a harsh word stirs up anger" (15:1). Are your words gentle or harsh?

"The tongue of the wise makes knowledge acceptable" (15:2). Try choosing your words more carefully

"A soothing tongue is a tree of life, but perversion in it crushes the spirit" (15:4).

Watch your words, beloved, and the way you say them. The Bible says, "Your gentleness makes me great" (Psalm 18:35). Follow God's example.

*O Lord, thank You for Your Word, which points me in the way of wisdom. I pray now for the strength and discretion to act on Your instruction so that my words will reflect Your love and wisdom to those around me.*

Are you constantly demeaning your husband, tearing him down behind his back or even shaming him to his face? Do you correct him in public? Do you treat him like a son rather than a husband, calling him into account as a mother would?

Or are you a wife who builds him up, who looks for the good, who cheers him on rather than booing and hissing from the bleachers?

You know, don't you, that the way you treat your husband says quite a bit about you, and it may determine his success on the field of life. The Word of God says, "An excellent wife is the crown of her husband, but she who shames him is like rottenness in his bones" (Proverbs 12:4).

What kind of a wife do you want to be?

*Convict me, Holy Spirit, every time I'm inclined to say something negative to or about my husband. Remind me of my commitment to respect him in every situation. Remind me to appropriate Your wisdom and the self-control of the Spirit, to close my mouth and cut off those demeaning words.*

You may be right, but are you kind? Does your tongue wound or heal? Does it spark strife or is it a mediator of peace? The words that you speak, that pour from your mouth, reveal much about the kind of person you really are, for "the things that proceed out of the mouth come from the heart" (Matthew 15:18).

Listen to the Word of God from the book of Proverbs: "There is one who speaks rashly like the thrusts of a sword, but the tongue of the wise brings healing.... A soothing tongue is a tree of life, but perversion in it crushes the spirit.... A perverse man spreads strife.... A fool's mouth is his ruin" (12:18; 15:4; 16:28; 18:7).

Now then, by the very words you speak, what is your tongue saying about you, beloved? What does it tell others about your character? The motives of your heart? The way you view others?

Give a good listen to yourself, my friend, for a worthwhile analysis.

*Lord, I cringe when I think of the thoughtless words that pour from my mouth on any given day. How many people have I driven from the truth by my callous comments? I ask You to cleanse my heart and to give me the strength to bridle my tongue.*

Do you love to talk? Do you find it stimulating to get into a good discussion? Are you invigorated by explaining and defending your stand on various issues?

That's great! When you communicate, people really get to know you. The ability to converse, to think together, to set, propose, and postulate plans are part of being human—a gift from our creator. But how do you live? What are your deeds like? Can people tell what you believe by watching the way you live?

Talk is great, but it can be cheapened by the way we conduct ourselves.

Listen to what God says: "It is by his deeds that a lad distinguishes himself if his conduct is pure and right" (Proverbs 20:11).

If your talk is good, let your walk match it. Distinguish yourself, beloved. Our world desperately needs to see someone like you.

*O Father, thank You for the opportunities You provide for me to discuss my faith with those around me. I choose today to walk in the power of the Holy Spirit so that my lifestyle will reflect what I claim to believe.*

Did you say something you wished you hadn't said? Did you speak too quickly, and now you regret your impulsive response?

Are you concerned that your words are going to reach ears you don't want them to reach? Or are you worried that your comments are going to push a situation in an awkward or potentially destructive direction? I understand. It's painful to face the consequences of our shortcomings, isn't it? Once something is said, we can't take it back. Our words are out there—for good or for bad.

Personally, situations like this make me fall on my face before God, plead for forgiveness, and ask God to help me learn to control my tongue.

The book of Proverbs offers such good insight for us in this area. Think upon this: "He who guards his mouth and his tongue, guards his soul from troubles" (21:23).

*O God, help me to guard my mouth. It would deliver me from so many problems and hurts. Give me the wisdom to consider my comments before I speak them aloud, and grant me the humility to ask forgiveness whenever I speak impulsively.*

Have you found yourself telling jokes that demean our politicians? Or have you joined your friends in just generally badmouthing our nation's leaders? It's easy to mock someone in a high-profile position, especially when we don't admire that person's lifestyle or disagree with his or her stand on various issues.

But what does God think about your comments? Does He become your companion in derision or do your words grieve Him?

Consider this instruction from the Bible: "Remind them to be subject to rulers, to authorities, to be obedient, to be ready for every good deed, to malign no one, to be peaceable, gentle, showing every consideration for all men. For we also once were foolish ourselves, disobedient, deceived, enslaved to various lusts and pleasures, spending our life in malice and envy, hateful, hating one another" (Titus 3:1-3).

Only through God's kindness have we been saved from our own enslavement to sin. Without His merciful cleansing, we are no better than the leaders we mock.

Are you going to join the crowd or obey God by showing respect to our leaders?

*Forgive me, Lord, for deriding those in leadership when I should be on my knees in prayer for them. Thank You for this reminder that the hallmark of Christianity is love—desiring another's highest good.*

Rude. Crude. Defensive. Inconsiderate. Are these words fairly accurate descriptions of people whose paths you cross day in and day out? Sometimes such people are hard to take, aren't they?

I understand. I am appalled at how people behave. Appalled by how they treat others. Their lethargy at work, their carelessness in their relationships, and their negative attitude in general are distressing. And how are we to respond? Certainly not in like manner or they will never have an example of what it is to live on a higher plane.

Let's look at how the Word of God tells us to behave: "So, as those who have been chosen of God, holy and beloved, put on a heart of compassion, kindness, humility, gentleness and patience; bearing with one another, and forgiving each other.... Put on love.... Let the peace of Christ rule in your hearts" (Colossians 3:12-15).

*Thank You for Jesus' example of how to respond when others behave rudely or unjustly. Help me resist the anger that crops up at each perceived offense and instead reply in a way that glorifies Your name.*

How do you talk at home to your mate and your children? Do you use the same tone of voice at church—or do you put on your Sunday-go-to-church muzzle before you step out of the car?

And how do you talk around the guys or the gals at work? Would you talk that way, use that kind of language at church? Are you like a Pharisee who outwardly appears righteous to others, but inwardly you're "full of hypocrisy and lawlessness" (Matthew 23:28)?

God tells us, "You are a holy people to the LORD your God; the LORD your God has chosen you to be a people for His own possession" (Deuteronomy 7:6).

Should God's people talk the way you talk? If not, beloved, you had better clean up your speech.

*Help me, dear Father, to see the impact of my words, to realize that what I say can have a devastating effect—or it can make a wonderful difference in someone's day. The choice is mine, and I choose to walk in the power of the Spirit, selecting my words carefully so that Your love and holiness are reflected in my conversation.*

When people speak against you or misjudge your motives, it really hurts. Often there's no opportunity to explain or defend yourself. I have found that you can't be in leadership and not experience this kind of trouble. Sometimes even your own family can misunderstand your intentions.

Sometimes what people say is so wrong and hurts so badly that I want to vindicate myself, to cry out, "Don't you know my heart? Has one statement, one misunderstood action nullified everything that I am or have stood for? Isn't there grace on your part to cover rather than condemn? Love that covers…believes…hopes…endures?"

So what do we do, precious one, when this happens? We can cry, "Lord, teach me to act rather than react. Help me respond in meekness."

Oh, beloved, the meek believe that God is at work in everything, and they live accordingly. Explain, if you can, what you meant, said, or did—and then go forward. Don't become discouraged and allow your joy to be squelched or your life to be dictated by those around you. Like Jesus, simply focus on the works the Father has given you to accomplish and speak the words He has given you to say (John 5:36; 14:10,24).

*Lord, may any rebukes about my words, actions, or intentions be brought to You for Your analysis. When others misjudge my motives, teach me to respond in love—carefully and thoughtfully.*

Beloved, do you ever wonder what our purpose is on this earth? Why God doesn't simply take us out of this world with all of its pain and suffering?

According to the Bible, one of our purposes for remaining on earth is to be the light of Jesus Christ in the midst of a crooked and perverse generation (Philippians 2:15).

We are commanded to walk just as He walked—in complete, absolute submission to the will of God, without grumbling or disputing. In the Gospels you'll never read of Jesus complaining, arguing, or resisting, even when He faced the cross.

Isaiah 53:7 says, "He was oppressed and He was afflicted, yet He did not open His mouth.... Like a sheep that is silent before its shearers, so He did not open His mouth."

You know, when you grab hold of a sheep to shear its wool, it doesn't utter a sound. But when you go after a hog, it squeals to high heaven. Which do you resemble in times of affliction: a squealing pig or a silent lamb?

*O God, I'm so ashamed about my attitude. I've made a covenant with You, a promise to serve You faithfully, but so often my service is filled with resentment and grumbling. Please forgive me for resisting Your will and help me to walk with a spirit of surrender.*

Do you demonstrate the glory of Christ through the way you talk and the way you treat others?

Beloved, to honor the Lord means to value Him in every area of your life: in the way you spend your time, in the way you conduct the details of your life, in the way you use your energy and your talent, and last but not least, in what your lips bring forth.

When we mumble or complain about our lot in life, we're certainly not bringing glory to the name of God.

Compare your actions and words with the instructions in Matthew 5:16: "Let your light shine before men in such a way that they may see your good works, and glorify your Father who is in heaven."

Take a few minutes today to examine yourself. Are your life and your words an expression of the truth that Jesus Christ is worthy of honor, of glory, of blessing?

*You have blessed me in so many ways, Father, that I cannot possibly count all of them. So what right have I to complain? Let my words and my actions reflect the attitude of the apostle Paul who said, "For momentary, light affliction is producing for us an eternal weight of glory far beyond all comparison" (2 Corinthians 4:17).*

Do you find yourself snapping at people? Are you quick with a crushing, cutting retort? Are you the king or queen of put-downs? Do you find yourself hurting others, casting off any concern for their feelings?

If this is so, have you wondered why you are the way you are? Have you thought about the condition of your heart?

Consider the words of Proverbs 14:30: "A tranquil heart is life to the body, but passion is rottenness to the bones."

Could something be wrong with your heart? Is some damaging passion, some harmful emotion seething within? Perhaps you're allowing yourself to be controlled by this passion and it is ruining you, eating away at your gut. What are you going to do?

You must make the decision to say no—a once-for-all, final no—to it and put it away. Confess the passion to God for what it is: sin. Then put it out of your thoughts. If you don't confess it now and repent, this passion will destroy your heart—and your life.

*I confess that I have been harboring bitterness and anger in my heart toward certain people, and my resentment has at times led me to be cruel and vindictive—even toward those who aren't involved. Dear Lord, help me to discover and cut out the root of this bitterness. Lead me back to Your way.*

Have you ever heard the expression, "I am so angry I could spit nails"? Heard it or not, does it describe how you felt at some point recently?

Anger is a valid emotion. In fact, if you study biblical references to anger, you'll find out that the one who's angry most often is God. He has much to be angry about, and it is good for us to be angry about the things that anger Him.

However, you cannot allow your emotions, including anger, to control you. Anger not handled God's way will give the devil a stronghold in your life. Let me share what the Word of God says on this subject: "Be angry, and yet do not sin; do not let the sun go down on your anger, and do not give the devil an opportunity" (Ephesians 4:26-27).

When you are angry, let God have control. "For the LORD loves justice and does not forsake His godly ones" (Psalm 37:28).

*Dear Father, I thank You for Your promise to defend me. When my flesh is crying out for revenge or retaliation, I will choose instead to trust in Your justice. So far as it depends on me, I will strive to be at peace with those around me.*

How do you respond to people with whom you do not agree doctrinally, those you think are going against the Word of God?

Your response tells much about your character and maturity as well as your knowledge of and obedience to the Bible.

Sometimes Christians can become quite vicious, can't they? Do you think this accomplishes anything? And how do you think God feels about your response to others? Remember what His Word says: "The Lord's bond-servant must not be quarrelsome, but be kind to all, able to teach, patient when wronged, with gentleness correcting those who are in opposition, if perhaps God may grant them repentance leading to the knowledge of the truth, and they may come to their senses and escape from the snare of the devil" (2 Timothy 2:24-26).

Could your wrong response be a hindrance to someone seeking truth?

*Lord, You have promised that, if I only ask, You will give me wisdom. Oh, how I need Your wisdom when I speak to people with whom I disagree. Give me words that are gentle, kind, and patient, and help me to resist the fleshly urge to quarrel. May I always be governed by that one quality that distinguishes Christians from the world: Your love.*

Has someone recently blasted you? Cut you down? It's hard to handle, isn't it—especially when it happens in front of other people! By the way, how did you handle it—or are you still trying to decide what to do? Have you repeatedly rehearsed the situation, thinking of what you could have or should have said? Maybe you've even considered how you could have nailed them to the wall, giving them, as the proverb says, a good dose of their own medicine?

Before you say another word, my friend, reflect upon God's Word:

"[Let] all of you be harmonious, sympathetic, brotherly, kindhearted, and humble in spirit; not returning evil for evil or insult for insult, but giving a blessing instead; for you were called for the very purpose that you might inherit a blessing" (1 Peter 3:8-9).

Could this incident be God's opportunity to let this person see Jesus in you?

*Lord, how do You want me to respond in this situation? What can I say that would allow Your love and holiness to shine through me—or should I say anything at all? I want to walk in obedience to You. Please show me the way.*

This week, in all probability, someone is going to push your hot button. They'll trip your anger switch, and the whole system will be ready to blow. Are you going to let that happen, or are you going to handle the control box?

When someone pushes your hot button, remember that to get angry is human but controlling one's emotions is divine. The Bible says, "The anger of man does not achieve the righteousness of God" (James 1:20).

If you're a Christian, the Spirit of God lives within you. The fruit of the Spirit in your life includes peace and self-control. So when something sets you off, turn from your anger and walk by the Spirit. God says, "A man's discretion makes him slow to anger, and it is his glory to overlook a transgression" (Proverbs 19:11).

When the situation is volatile, phrase your response carefully, for "a gentle answer turns away wrath, but a harsh word stirs up anger" (Proverbs 15:1).

And whatever the circumstances, no matter how provoking, never take your own revenge, but leave room for the wrath of God. Do this and you'll delight your God.

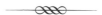

*God, You know better than anyone else what my temper is like. You know exactly how I feel inside and how I sometimes struggle to contain my anger. And You know that I want my life and my conversation to glorify You. This week I choose to walk in the power of the Holy Spirit and resist the temptation to respond in anger.*

Are you angry? Determined to get revenge if it's the last thing you do? Are you planning how to get back at someone? Are you itching to see them suffer as you have suffered? To see them be rejected as they have rejected you? Destroyed as you have been destroyed?

If you're thinking this, I know you've been greatly wounded. Your heart is bruised and sore. I'm so sorry. No person has the right to treat others so cruelly.

God wants us to love and care for one another, to be our brother's keeper. But for the most part, that hasn't happened has it? And it grieves our Lord.

Do you realize this is the reason Jesus came to earth—to release us from our sins and restore us to the image of God? Jesus Christ suffered, died on the cross, and rose again to give us new life so that we can love one another as He loves us—unconditionally, without getting even (1 John 3:16).

*I cannot thank You enough for the incredible sacrifice Jesus made on my behalf. How I rejoice in the love You have shown for me! Help me, Lord, to walk in the light of this love, to let go of my anger and respond in a way that pleases You.*

Are you hateful toward others? Or are you known for the love you show toward the people around you, especially believers? Love and hate help us distinguish where we stand in relationship to God. One of the evidences of genuine Christianity is that we love one another.

Listen to the Word: "The love of God has been poured out within our hearts through the Holy Spirit who was given to us" (Romans 5:5). "We know that we have passed out of death into life, because we love the brethren. He who does not love abides in death" (1 John 3:14).

Love is an attribute of God, and because a Christian is indwelt by God, it is only logical that love is an attribute of Christians. John, in his short epistle, makes it clear that if you have no love for others, you do not belong to God!

"Everyone who hates his brother is a murderer; and you know that no murderer has eternal life abiding in him.... Whoever believes that Jesus is the Christ is born of God, and whoever loves the Father loves the child born of Him" (1 John 3:15; 5:1).

Where do you stand, my friend?

*God, I don't want to be deluded, thinking I belong to You, that I'm a true child of Yours, when I'm not. Show me where I stand so that I am assured that I have a relationship with You rather than a religion.*

Are you judging others by your standards? Maybe criticizing them or condemning them because they don't adhere to the same "dos and don'ts" you hold to? Their hair, their dress, what they drink, where they go all seem "unspiritual" to you. Or maybe you disagree with the Bible translation they use or the way they worship or the type of songs they sing in church.

Have you written them off as unsaved, unspiritual, or simply guilty of not loving God?

Before you do, beloved, maybe you should examine your heart. Read Romans 14 very carefully. Then check out your "dos and don'ts" and make sure they are in line with the whole counsel of God's Word, which says, "Why do you judge your brother?... Why do you regard your brother with contempt? For we will all stand before the judgment seat of God" (Romans 14:10).

*Lord, even when I don't agree with the choices of other Christians, I know that You have called me to love them as You love them. Instead of wasting time in pointless arguing, show me how to invest my time in pursuing the things that make for peace and the building up of the body of Christ.*

My dear one, is your life an expression of the truth that Jesus Christ is worthy of honor, glory, and blessing? Do your conversations each day demonstrate His worthiness? Do your words bring value to His name?

Revelation 5:12 says, "Worthy is the Lamb that was slain to receive power and riches and wisdom and might and honor and glory and blessing."

Dear friend, to honor the Lord is to value Him in the way we talk. His name deserves our praise and respect. "Then those who feared the LORD spoke to one another, and the LORD gave attention and heard it, and a book of remembrance was written before Him for those who fear the LORD and who esteem His name. 'They will be Mine,' says the LORD of hosts" (Malachi 3:16-17).

The way we live our lives, including our daily conversations, demonstrates the worthiness of our Redeemer! Oh, dear one, I urge you to give that kind of value to Him now so that your new song in heaven might be merely an echo of your life here on earth.

*Lord, You are indeed worthy of all praise. You reign in righteousness and justice, and my heart rejoices in Your presence. Today, through my words and actions, I want to let the whole world know how wonderful You truly are.*

Dear one, I know just how you feel when someone you love discredits you, when you find yourself wrongly accused. It's so agonizingly painful! How are you and I to act when this happens?

Just remember, precious one, God is your defender! You may be despised and rejected now, but someday you'll sit with Him on His throne. We never have to defend ourselves, justify ourselves, or retaliate.

Consider this promise in 2 Thessalonians 1:6-8: "For after all it is only just for God to repay with affliction those who afflict you, and to give relief to you who are afflicted and to us as well when the Lord Jesus will be revealed from heaven with His mighty angels in flaming fire, dealing out retribution to those who do not know God and to those who do not obey the gospel of our Lord Jesus."

Remember, beloved, you don't have to fight your own battles! Jesus is your kinsman-redeemer and, therefore, your avenger.

*"Be gracious to me, O God, be gracious to me, for my soul takes refuge in You; and in the shadow of Your wings I will take refuge until destruction passes by"* (Psalm 57:1).

I see so many Christians today taking a stand for godliness, which is wonderful. But so often they do it in a way that appears ungracious, even mean. If our efforts to stand for righteousness are not rooted in love, we negate whatever we're trying to accomplish publicly as Christians.

So often the focus is on who *I* am instead of who *God* is!

And, beloved, meekness is *not* weakness. You need to thoroughly understand the difference. In Psalm 37:3 we see that those who trust in the Lord don't run away from their enemies. They "dwell." They "cultivate faithfulness." They keep their vows, their promises, their commitments—and they do it in the character of their Lord, who is meek and lowly of heart.

How about you today, beloved? Are you taking your stand graciously, lovingly, with meekness before the Lord, knowing that He will act as His holy and just nature requires? "Commit your way to the LORD, trust also in Him, and He will do it" (verse 5).

*Lord, even though I long to lash out with cutting words to defend Your honor, to bring low those who oppose You, may I realize they only behave this way because they do not know You. Help me at all times to be constrained by Your character so that in defending the truth I won't disgrace Your name and drive others from You rather than draw them to You.*

Where are the watchmen Ezekiel 3:17 speaks of, those who are to sound God's trumpet and warn the people of the enemy on the horizon? What are you doing to let people know who God is and what His Word says so that they might be rescued from destruction?

May I make some suggestions?

- Be zealous about pursuing moral purity in your life and your church as we're admonished in 1 Corinthians 5 and 6. Don't cover sin, but expose it.
- Fast and pray consistently for the moral situation in our nation.
- Write letters to newspapers and local government, graciously reminding them of what God says on the subject.
- Make your concerns known to advertisers and those who create television shows and movies that undermine biblical values.
- Prayerfully seek what else God would have you do.

Remember, beloved, we're called to be God's watchmen on the wall!

*Here I am, Lord, ready and willing to do whatever You ask. I want to be used by You to call our nation to repentance. Speak to my heart, and let me know exactly what You want me to do.*

Dear one, we each must ask ourselves some challenging questions: How does my life express the worthiness of the One who conquered sin and death by redeeming me with His own blood? How does my life express the worthiness of the One who brought me from impotence to power, from abject poverty of spirit to a heavenly inheritance? How does my life express the worthiness of the One who brought me from utter weakness to strength, the One who brought me to the place where I can stand alone, if necessary, for His truth?

Oh, beloved, as I see the word "worthy" repeated over and over in Revelation 4 and 5, my mind races to Ephesians 4:1 where it says to "walk in a manner worthy of the calling with which you have been called."

Why don't you sit quietly for a few minutes and ask God to show you how your life reflects His worth.

*Lord, forgive me for responding to the wisdom of men more quickly than I respond to the call of Your heart. You alone are worthy of my devotion, and I long to worship You with every aspect of my life.*

Have you ever been frustrated because you've been unexpectedly detained? Somehow you've been held up or prevented from carrying out your plans? And so you've become agitated, impatient, irritable, even angry. Your frustration is clear in your response to people around you.

I've been there and done that, as they say. And each time I do, I get so impatient with myself. Oh, beloved, why do we get all upset? Are not the steps of a righteous man ordered by the Lord, as we're reminded in Psalm 37:23? We don't need to let frustration direct our response, and we don't need to understand exactly why our plans have been sidetracked. Our job is simply to walk by faith and know that the Lord is our Shepherd and we shall not want. Our times are in His hands.

What a comfort it is to read 1 Thessalonians 5:18: "In everything give thanks; for this is God's will for you in Christ Jesus."

*I confess that sometimes I am so focused on my own personal to-do list that I totally ignore Your plans for my day. Open my eyes, dear Father, to the tasks You have for me and to the people You want me to reach with Your love—people of immeasurable, eternal worth. Help me to see the interruptions as coming from Your sovereign hand.*

Precious friend, are you experiencing the incredible joy of being a living epistle?

Most of the world doesn't read the Bible. So what does God do? He shows the world pictures of Himself and the sufficiency of His grace—through you and me!

There are times, beloved, when God will place you in the middle of trials—a hospital stay, rejection, a financial blow. He lets you hurt as others hurt, knowing that the way you handle it will be a testimony, that your response will show others that there's something awesomely different about you.

This is where Romans 8:36-39 comes in: "We are being put to death all day long…as sheep to be slaughtered. But in all these things we overwhelmingly conquer through Him who loved us. For [we are] convinced that [nothing] will be able to separate us from the love of God, which is in Christ Jesus our Lord."

Think about that, precious one!

*It's easy to become so caught up in myself that I forget others are watching me, looking to see what difference Your presence makes in my life. Thank You for this reminder, Lord, and for Your continual mercies toward me. Help me walk today in a manner worthy of my calling, with all humility, gentleness, and patience.*

# APRIL

# LEAD ME TO WISDOM

How finite man is, how lost he is without God! Man apart from God is governed only by his emotions, his desires, his own knowledge and understanding, which are limited by his own reasoning powers and his exposure to truth. And while man can try to predict the future, it remains only an uncertain guess. Man is not in charge of today—let alone tomorrow! He may do what he wants, but he's bound by the actions of others. Man is finite.

"We are but dust" (Psalm 103:14).

God, however, is infinite and eternal, the Alpha and Omega, the beginning and the end. He sees all and knows all—your past, your present, your future.

Therefore, beloved, if you are going to live in confidence and peace, you need to embrace in faith the fact that "the LORD is in His holy temple" and "be silent before Him" (Habakkuk 2:20). Quit your futile reasoning and get into God's Word. You will find His Word to be words of life—and in them, precious one, you'll discover godly wisdom that you might know how to live.

*O Father, forgive me for leaning on my own understanding, for putting my trust in the arm of flesh when You are God and have given me "Christ Jesus, who became to us wisdom from God" (1 Corinthians 1:30). Thank You for Your Word, my daily bread, in which I can find the answers I need for today and the reassurance that You are always in control.*

Whose wisdom dictates your life? When you need answers, where do you turn? Who advises you? And where does their wisdom come from?

And what do the people you consult think about God? About the Bible? About what God says in respect to the condition of man, the need of man, the solution to the problems of man?

Do you realize that, when it comes to ordering the decisions of your life, you either have or can have the mind of Christ? According to 1 Corinthians 2:16, the mind of Christ—insight into truth and life—is what God gives to every true child of God. It's access to the wisdom of God.

The Bible says God has "made foolish the wisdom of the world" (1 Corinthians 1:20). So the next time you lack wisdom, beloved, ask of God. He says He'll give it to you, generously and without reproach. It's yours for the asking—if you belong to Him.

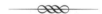

*O Lord, I confess that I often lean on the wisdom of men rather than turning to You. Forgive me. How foolish that is! Today, dear Father, by an act of my will I choose to walk by faith and by the precepts of Your Word. Make me sensitive to Your leadership. I ask for Your wisdom and do not doubt you will give it to me, for You know the sincerity and intent of my heart.*

Is your life in a state of controlled frenzy, my friend? You're looking calm, being attentive and civil to those around you. But on the inside it's different. You're hanging on by your fingernails, wondering how to not blow it. Your self-control dangles from a fraying thread.

You know those who are watching think you have it all together, but all you want to do is escape!

Do it. For the next seven days escape once a day, in the morning before anything diverts you and the day bombards you with its demands. Begin your day asking God for divine wisdom as you lay your day and its cares at His feet. Open the New Testament. Read one chapter a day.

"In the morning, O LORD, You will hear my voice; in the morning I will order my prayer to You and eagerly watch" (Psalm 5:3).

If you'll do this, the frenzy will slip quietly away.

*You know the burdens of my heart, the fears I face today. Right here, right now, I cast all my cares on You, dear God, and by an act of my will I choose to take refuge in You. As I read Your Word day by day, speak to my heart. Give me Your understanding and wisdom for the tasks ahead.*

If I told you I knew the secret to a successful life, would you be interested?

It's spending consistent time with God in His Word—knowing Him and His ways and understanding what He's said—being quiet, waiting, and listening. This, beloved, will bring you stability and intimacy you've never known.

You will know where to run for refuge, where to rest your burdens, "casting all your anxiety on Him, because He cares for you" (1 Peter 5:7).

As you read and study His Word, bring every dilemma you have and lay it at the feet of God.

There is no other foundation for success, beloved. No other is needed, because the Word of God is totally sufficient!

Remember, "How blessed is the man who finds wisdom and the man who gains understanding" (Proverbs 3:13).

And now you know exactly where to find it!

*My beloved, all-sufficient God, thank You for the gift of Your Word, which is food for my soul and hope for my future. Forgive me for so often taking it for granted, for being too busy with the things of this world to spend quality time with You.*

What *kind* of a Christian are you, beloved? Are you a follower of God or of men, of certain teachers from certain theological camps?

The answer to these questions can be found by examining your spiritual diet. Do you like only milk? Do you love to watch Christian television—the short, attention-getting, miraculous, "wow" kind of stuff? Or perhaps you love the church meetings and the music, but you aren't into serious Bible study?

If so, it is likely that you are still a babe in Christ. Examine your spiritual maturity in light of Hebrews 5:12-14: "For though by this time you ought to be teachers, you have need again for someone to teach you the elementary principles of the oracles of God, and you have come to need milk and not solid food. For everyone who partakes only of milk is not accustomed to the word of righteousness, for he is an infant. But solid food is for the mature, who because of practice have their senses trained to discern good and evil."

It's time to change your diet, beloved, to move from milk to meat as you "press on to maturity" (Hebrews 6:1).

*Father, sometimes I feast on fluff rather than on the meat of Your Word. It's so much easier to watch TV or listen to the radio than to study Your Word for myself. I want to mature, to change my appetite, so that I can say with Job, "I have treasured the words of His mouth more than my necessary food" (23:12).*

Are you troubled, my friend, because you just don't know what to do? Your heart is set on being obedient to God. You have done everything you know to do, but it doesn't seem to be enough. You've cried to God, asking what more you should do, what direction you should take—but heaven is silent, and you have received no specific instruction from the Spirit of God. You feel like you are groping your way along in the dark.

So what do you do? Does God have any word for you today? Yes, beloved. Listen and think on this: "Who is among you that fears the LORD, that obeys the voice of His servant, that walks in darkness and has no light? Let him trust in the name of the LORD and rely on his God" (Isaiah 50:10)

One of God's names is Jehovah-shammah—the God who is there. God has not forsaken you. You are precious to Him, as costly as the life of His only begotten Son. Wait patiently for the Lord. In time you'll know what He wants you to do. He's your Lord; He'll make it clear.

*At this moment I feel abandoned and uncertain, but I know, Father, that You have promised never to leave me nor forsake me. So by faith I choose to walk in that knowledge today. I will trust in You. With the psalmist I will say, "My soul waits in silence" for You, for my hope comes from You alone (Psalm 62:1).*

Does the future frighten you? Are you scared because of what might come—or what you have heard is going to come? Or are you so scared you don't even want to hear about it? Oh, dear one, do you think ignorance of the future will alter or stop what is coming, make it go away? It won't, beloved. That is wrong thinking. Don't be unwise and close your eyes to what's coming.

God does not want you to be frightened about what is coming, nor does He want you to be ignorant of it or unprepared. Read what He says in Amos 3:7— "Surely the Lord GOD does nothing unless He reveals His secret counsel to His servants the prophets."

The future is as certain as God, and you can be prepared for it. Read the books of the prophets in the Bible. Know for yourself. Learn for certain what is coming and how God plans to care for you. You'll be so excited about and comforted by what you learn.

*I've read in Your Word that You have plans to give Israel a future and a hope. Thank You for revealing Your plans, for Your promise to take care of Your chosen nation and me, Your chosen child. Thank You for making it clear that You will triumph in the end, no matter how dark the future seems. Work in my heart, Lord, so that through Your Word I will be prepared for that moment when You and I stand face to face.*

Are you an information junkie? Are you into news—radio, television, magazines, the newspaper? Do you love to get on the Internet and communicate with others of like mind? Do you like to wrestle with the issues, explore topics in depth? Maybe you're suspicious of bullet points that march to the bottom line; you want the big picture—the story behind the story—so that you can understand the issue from beginning to end.

Are you also concerned with your inner life and the needs of the people around you?

Have you ever read the Bible? I mean, have you read it in a meaningful way, determining to find out what it is really saying? It would be terrible to be an information junkie yet miss out on the Book that gives you the story behind the story, the book that has the answer to all man's social issues.

Make it your goal to say with the psalmist, "From Your precepts I get understanding" (Psalm 119:104).

*Lord God, I confess that I have spent my time studying the words of men and dallying with everything else before meditating on the precepts of Your Word. Today I make a commitment to set aside time to become a student of the Bible. I want to be prepared to compare the words of men against the words of the Bible, so that I can wisely discern truth from lies.*

Are you continually running out of money before you run out of month? What do you do when this happens? Charge your purchases? And when the next month comes, are you able to pay off in full whatever you charged?

If you keeping running out of money, I'll bet your debt is accumulating. Do you realize that charging your purchases costs much more than the price of the item? Even if you got it on sale, it was not a bargain because you didn't have the money to pay cash and still cover other expenses.

Something is drastically out of order. You're headed for a financial crisis. You're not living within your means, and you're not trusting God to meet your needs.

The Bible tells us, "My God will supply all your needs according to His riches in glory in Christ Jesus" (Philippians 4:19).

Learn discipline, beloved, and practice denial. Portion out your money every month. Don't spend beyond your income; then you can hold God to His promise. And just watch how He takes care of you—better than you could possibly take care of yourself!

*Thank You, Lord, for Your promise to supply all my needs. Forgive me for my lack of faith, for my tendency to get ahead of You and purchase things You've not provided for. Help me distinguish my needs from my wants and trust You to supply both as You see fit.*

Where do you run when you're in trouble, beloved? Where do you seek counsel when you're gripped with worry?

Not long ago I found myself in a situation of deep distress. I felt at times as if the pressure was going to push me right through the floor. My husband was away, so I couldn't turn to him. I couldn't go to my friends. I couldn't go to anybody but the Lord.

Alone and on my knees, I cried out to God in my anguish.

And, beloved, He heard my cry. Before I got up from that place of prayer, the fog of anxiety lifted from my heart. In place of distress, I felt peace.

John 14:27 says: "Peace I leave with you; My peace I give to you."

Where do you run when you need peace? He is peace, precious one!

*You have promised in Isaiah 26:3 to give Your perfect peace to those who trust in You. You told us in Isaiah that Jesus' name is "Prince of Peace." O Father, I need that peace more than ever. Protect and comfort me today. Wrap me in Your everlasting arms of strength.*

Success, the password of the nineties, didn't go out of style with the coming of the new millennium! We're consumed with the idea of success in our businesses, our marriages—even for our children. Beloved, what rules your life?

The only way to truly succeed is to maintain a true and vital relationship with God. And how do we do this? By loving God with all our heart, soul, mind, and strength. Under the Old Covenant, God set before Israel blessing or cursing, life or death, and then left the choice to them. Deuteronomy 30:19-20 says: "So choose life in order that you may live, you and your descendants, by loving the LORD your God, by obeying His voice, and by holding fast to Him; for this is your life and the length of your days."

That's not what the world would tell you, beloved! It would claim that you have the power to choose your own destiny. True, you can choose your way, but you cannot choose the consequences of your actions.

Choose wisely, precious friend. Choose His abundant life by loving your God, by obeying His voice, by following His Son.

*Father God, more than anything I want to succeed in Your eyes. Today I surrender my heart to Your wisdom, and in obedience I hold fast to You, no matter what temptations come my way that would lure me to trust in something or someone other than You.*

Are you thinking of marriage? In God's eyes marriage is permanent, so you had better do some thinking and talking before you say, "I do." Find out whatever you can about your potential spouse's relationship with God and with his or her parents. Is it a respectful and obedient relationship? How does your spouse-to-be respond to discipline and a disciplined life?

Proverbs 15:5 says, "A fool rejects his father's discipline, but he who regards reproof is sensible." Are you about to marry a fool or a sensible and prudent person? Remember, it's unwise to walk into marriage with the intention of reforming your spouse. Only the individual and God can do the reforming.

Proverbs also says, "He whose ear listens to the life-giving reproof will dwell among the wise. He who neglects discipline despises himself" (15:31-32).

Is your potential mate wise? If not, don't get married even though your heart is full of passion. Night is shorter than day—and life gets terribly dreary when you're living day in and day out with a fool.

*Open my eyes, dear Lord, to see what You see. Give me Your wisdom as I make decisions that will impact the rest of my life. Admonish me to overrule my emotions; help me to walk instead by the light of Your Word.*

Are you pleased with the way your children are turning out? Are they disciplined? Of strong moral character? Are you raising children with integrity?

Of course your children are not perfect; they're still maturing. But are you proud of them—not because they excel in sports, academics, the arts, or are simply very good-looking, but because they are pleasant to be around, gracious, generally obedient, and polite?

How many children do you know like that?

It's time we went back to parenting God's way. Time we embraced His Word as our plumb line in child rearing. The Bible says, "You shall therefore impress these words of mine on your heart and on your soul.... You shall teach them to your sons, talking of them when you sit in your house and when you walk along the road and when you lie down and when you rise up" (Deuteronomy 11:18-19).

How will you pass on to your children today the wisdom found in the Word of God?

*Thank You for entrusting me with the soul of this child. It's a wonderful but frightening privilege, and I cannot do it without Your guidance. Help me watch and listen today for opportunities to teach biblical principles that will last a lifetime.*

When you are crossed by another person, does your anger immediately show? Does your smoke alarm go off, letting everyone know there's a fire blazing in your emotions? That someone has hit your hot button and you're anything but happy?

Oh my friend, how a person reacts in aggravating situations reveals much about his or her character. Notice what is written in the book of Proverbs: "A fool's anger is known at once, but a prudent man conceals dishonor.... He who is slow to anger has great understanding, but he who is quick-tempered exalts folly" (12:16; 14:29).

Nothing is worse than a fool in his folly. Rude behavior is embarrassing for everyone around. Instead of reacting immediately to some perceived offense, take time to cool down. If you are a genuine Christian, the Spirit of God lives within and can overcome your flesh. The fruit of the Spirit includes peace and self-control. The choice is yours, and you are responsible for the consequences.

*Father, I stand amazed when I read of how Jesus responded with grace when others deliberately provoked Him. Oh, how I long for the wisdom and self-control to speak only the words that You give me. O Lord, work in my heart today through Your Holy Spirit, and give me the grace to respond wisely to aggravating situations.*

What kind of people hold positions of leadership in your church? Are they people whose lives you can emulate? And what is your plumb line for measuring what is taught and who is allowed to be an authority in the church? Do you pride yourself on the broadness of your views, your willingness to accept everyone?

Dear one, God is not broadminded. He has clear standards—rather strict standards—for those in positions of leadership. To congratulate yourself on being broadminded and all-encompassing is to walk in disobedience to the Word. God and His precepts are supposed to govern our churches. God says rebellious men, empty talkers, and deceivers are to be silenced, reproved severely so that they may be sound in the faith (Titus 1:10-13). Factious men are to be rejected after two warnings (3:10).

Have you ever thought about what might happen if the church listened to God instead of following the precepts of men? Christianity might become far more respected.

*Forgive me, God, for embracing the worldly emphasis on tolerance and ignoring Your standard of holiness. Your Word clearly states the qualities that I should value in a person, especially a person in leadership. I ask for Your wisdom and discernment—both for my church and for myself—as we pursue Your will for our future.*

America is into real estate. We're building, buying, selling houses—or longing to do so. Everyone seems to be striving to move into something bigger and better. All the while, the families who inhabit these houses are falling apart.

Wouldn't you like to build a house that would last beyond your lifetime and be a refuge for successive generations? The house I am talking about bears your family name, and it includes your children and the generations that will follow. This is the house you need to devote your energies to. God tells you how: "By wisdom a house is built, and by understanding it is established; and by knowledge the rooms are filled with all precious and pleasant riches" (Proverbs 24:3-4). By walking in God's ways today, you are building an inheritance for your children and their children—an inheritance of spiritual riches.

The family is falling apart because we have embraced the world's wisdom while ignoring God's. Get into the Bible; it's the Architect's plans. I especially urge you to spend time in the book of Proverbs; it's God's blueprint for wisdom.

*Thank You, Lord, that You have not left me to flounder in the dark. You have given me all the direction I need, if only I will humble myself and go to Your Word for the answers. Help me not only to read and study the truths You have laid out, but also to incorporate them into every aspect of my daily life.*

Are you surrounded by skeptics? Overwhelmed and oppressed by their godless lifestyle? Does their brashness shock you? Do you shudder at the way they speak about God? Do their questions intimidate you? "If God is God," they ask, "where is He when bad things happen?"

What do you do? How do you answer? Man's inhumanity to man is taking place all the time in every corner of the world. Why doesn't God intervene? Perhaps you even wonder sometimes, Why doesn't He do something?

The Word of God says, "Look among the nations! Observe! Be astonished! Wonder! Because I am doing something in your days—You would not believe if you were told" (Habakkuk 1:5). God is at work.

So don't argue with the skeptic. Simply do what Paul did: present the gospel. The skeptic can come to God through the Cross and confess that Jesus Christ is God. Or he can stand before God's Great White Throne to be judged according to his deeds and spend eternity in hell (Revelation 20:12-15).

The choice you present in love to the skeptic is his. You're clear. You've done all God requires.

*Give me wisdom today, dear Lord, as I encounter those who mock my faith. May I water in prayer what has been sown in word until You tell me to cease and rest in the fact that Your sheep will hear Your voice.*

Do you worry about how you're going to defend God?

The skeptic's problem is twofold: He sees evil triumph over good, and he doesn't see God intervening to stop it. In the skeptic's logic, if God is who he thinks God ought to be, then He wouldn't allow things to be the way they are.

Skeptics don't understand why God allows such things even though He is sovereign and can intervene at any time. They are blind to the certainty of God's just judgment. Yet the Bible tells us the day is coming "when the Lord Jesus will be revealed…in flaming fire, dealing out retribution to those who do not know God" (2 Thessalonians 1:7-8).

Another thing skeptics don't understand is that God is not ruled by love alone. God is also holy, and He acts in accordance with the sum total of all His attributes.

You need not defend God, beloved; simply explain Him and the Cross. Paul wrote in 1 Corinthians, " I determined to know nothing among you except Jesus Christ, and Him crucified" (1 Corinthians 2:2). Determine to do the same, pray, and watch God work.

*With Your servant Job I say, "I know that You can do all things, and that no purpose of Yours can be thwarted" (42:2). Almighty God, You don't need me to defend You—explain You, yes! Defend You, no! All You ask is that I boldly proclaim Your truth. Give me the words to do exactly that today.*

Have you ever had anyone tell you you're absolutely stupid to believe the Bible? Caustically challenge you to grow up and get a mind of your own? Have they laughed at your beliefs? Belittled you? Called you narrow-minded or maybe simple-minded? Perhaps someone has poked fun at your innocence—mocked you for being prudish, straight-laced, inexperienced, naive. Or maybe they've pulled out their degrees and tried to disparage your intellectual skills.

Did you shrivel up inside and long to slink out of the room—embarrassed, hurt, chagrined? Did the verbal tirade intimidate you?

Oh, beloved, throw those shoulders back and hold your head high. Your critics are natural men, men devoid of God's spirit. In 1 Corinthians 2:14, the apostle Paul explained that "a natural man does not accept the things of the Spirit of God, for they are foolishness to him." He cannot understand them. But you have the mind of Christ; you're the appraiser (1 Corinthians 2:16).

Don't be distracted by the comments of natural men; continue to pursue wisdom by seeking the mind of Christ.

*Thank You, Father, that "the foolishness of God is wiser than men, and the weakness of God is stronger than men" (1 Corinthians 1:25). Whenever I am criticized for my beliefs, help me remember that my faith rests not on the wisdom of men but on Your unfailing power!*

In the days of the prophet Malachi, God was calling His people to return to Him. They had done things that were displeasing, so He withheld His hand of blessing. Their intimacy with Him was dulled. One of the root problems was that the priests were not giving God's people the right instruction.

It's an awesome thing, a serious matter, to speak for God. James 3:1 cautions us: "Let not many of you become teachers, my brethren, knowing that as such we will incur a stricter judgment."

If you advise someone else, make sure you're giving true instruction in accordance with the whole counsel of God's Word. We need to be careful not to make allowances for a person, excusing sinful behavior because of unique circumstances. Instead we are to say, "As the LORD lives, what my God says, that I will speak" (2 Chronicles 18:13).

*Fill my heart, dear Lord, with Your wisdom so that the words of my mouth will glorify You and point others to You. Rather than leaning on my own understanding, I want to acknowledge You in all my conversations so that You will direct not only my paths but also my words.*

Is counseling wrong? Should one Christian not seek counsel from another?

The problem doesn't lie in seeking counsel, my friend. In fact, the book of Proverbs teaches: "In abundance of counselors there is victory" (11:14; 24:6).

Actually, the danger lies in seeking or giving counsel that is not rooted in the wisdom of the Word of God.

If you give counsel that contradicts God's Word, then unrighteousness is on your lips and you could cause other people to turn aside from God's will for their lives. The responsibility for their sin lies heavily on you. "As for you, you have turned aside from the way; you have caused many to stumble by the instruction.... So I also have made you despised and abased before all the people, just as you are not keeping My ways but are showing partiality in the instruction" (2:8-9).

Make sure that the counsel you give is "true instruction" (2:6)—instruction that is in accordance with the whole counsel of God's Word.

*O Father, before I offer advice, let me pause to seek Your heart and make sure my words are in alignment with the plumb line of Your Word. May Your Holy Spirit work in me so that I may speak Your truth in love, building up the body of Christ according to Your wisdom.*

What do you do, my friend, when you're suddenly confronted with an insurmountable problem?

The situation looms over you like a hungry giant, and you can't help but tremble. Fear pierces your heart. Where do you turn for answers? How do you keep from completely falling apart?

When life takes a totally unexpected turn, we have to make a choice.

We have to decide whether we will allow our hearts to be ruled by panic or whether we will choose by faith to walk in the light of what we know about God, what we've studied in His Word, and what we've proclaimed with our mouths.

The sky may be absolutely black, yet you can rest in Him. Don't leave the place of your appointment. Stay on your face before His throne. He can bring to pass what He wills. His Word remains true.

"Commit your way to the LORD, trust also in Him, and He will do it" (Psalm 37:5).

*Whom have I in heaven but You? And besides You, I desire nothing on earth. My flesh and my heart may fail, but You, O God, are the strength of my heart and my portion forever. I have made You my refuge, that I may tell of all Your works (Psalm 73:25-26,28).*

Sometimes just a word, a thought, or an unexpected call or visit can strike panic in your heart. One minute everything's bright and sunny, and in the next black clouds have obliterated the sun.

What do you do when fear strikes? How do you handle it without falling apart?

When fear hits, our first tendency is to react, to run, to do *something!* But the Christian life is supposed to be a life of rest. We're told to rest in who God is, in what He has promised: "Cease striving [let go, relax] and know that I am God" (Psalm 46:10).

The psalmist declared, "When I am afraid, I will put my trust in You" (56:3). He knew that panic is foolish and fruitless. How about you?

*O Lord, You know exactly what I'm feeling. You see the waves of panic rolling over me. By an act of my will, I give all of my fears to You, and I ask You to replace them with Your perfect peace as I cease striving and put my trust in You.*

What kind of child are you raising? Do you want a fool or a child who is wise? You may not have given this much thought, as busy as you are. Your days are spent just trying to hold life together—to feed your children, clothe them, get them to school and every place else they need to be.

Kids just kind of grow up on their own, don't they?

Yes, but you are greatly responsible for *the way* they grow. That's why Proverbs is in the Bible, that we might know wisdom and receive instruction in wise behavior. Thus the author of Proverbs wrote to his son, "I have directed you in the way of wisdom; I have led you in upright paths.... A wise son accepts his father's discipline" (4:11; 13:1).

If you want a child who will bring you joy, not shame, do your part as a parent. Start with Proverbs as your parenting manual. It has one chapter for each day of the month.

*Sometimes the weight of my responsibility as a parent is overwhelming. Thank You, Lord, that I don't have to face this task alone. You are the Father of fathers, the Parent of parents. Help me grab hold of the wisdom of Your Word and find ways to pass that wisdom on to my children.*

Do you hate reproof? Perhaps you can't stand to be wrong—or to be corrected when you make a mistake?

Oh, my friend, don't you realize that no one is perfect? There is room for all of us to grow, to improve. Correction is all part of the maturing process. And while you may not be perfect, you can still be wise. "How?" you ask. Remember that a wise man is teachable. King Solomon, the wisest of men, wrote in the book of Proverbs that if you reprove a wise man, he will love you. If you give instruction to a wise man, he will be still wiser. The wise of heart will receive commands, but he who hates reproof is stupid (9:8-9; 10:8; 12:1).

Think about that the next time someone corrects you or gives you instruction. Act like a wise man or a wise woman and accept their words with humility.

*Thank You for the people You have placed in my life, dear Father, people who love me enough to correct me. Open my ears to their reproof, to listen in grateful humility and then take it to the plumb line of Your Word. If the two match, then may I be wise and do what is right, making the necessary changes.*

Do you remember the childish trick of substituting salt for sugar in the sugar bowl? Remember how you snickered and watched with wide-eyed delight as the unsuspecting spooned salt onto their cereal or into their coffee! Such impish but innocent pranks may cause some sputtering and spitting, but they don't cause serious harm.

Sadly, however, as adults we sometimes make spiritual substitutions—with dangerous consequences.

The Word of God says, "Woe to those who call evil good, and good evil; who substitute darkness for light and light for darkness; who substitute bitter for sweet and sweet for bitter! Woe to those who are wise in their own eyes and clever in their own sight!" (Isaiah 5:20-21).

Those who are wise in their own eyes play God, substituting their evaluations for the sweetness of God's truth. Don't be guilty of such foolishness. Learn the Bible; it's where true spirituality is found.

*You have warned us, Lord, that we are as sheep in the midst of wolves. Knowing my weakness, I choose today to walk in Your wisdom, shrewd as a serpent. Through the power of Your Holy Spirit, help me also remain innocent as a dove, unmoved by the lies of the world.*

Are you suffering right now? Has your life been going badly because of some bad choices made in the past? Have you ever stopped to consider why the little nation of Israel, the people chosen by God and in covenant with God, has suffered so much and has had to fight just to survive? It's worthwhile to think it through. When we watch Israel, we not only see what God is doing, but we can learn valuable precepts for our own lives.

According to the prophet Isaiah, Israel is suffering and has suffered because "they do not pay attention to the deeds of the LORD, nor do they consider the work of His hands. Therefore [God's] people go into exile for their lack of knowledge.... They have rejected the law of the LORD of hosts and despised the word of the Holy One of Israel" (Isaiah 5:12-13,24).

Some of the pain and suffering in your life may be for the same reason: your refusal to acknowledge God's authority in your life. It's worth your time and could transform your future to check it out.

*Forgive me, Lord, for my spirit of rebellion, for reject-ing Your truth and authority. Teach my to do Your will, for You are my God. Let Your Holy Spirit lead me on level ground, for I am Your servant (Psalm 143:10,12).*

So often, after telling others about some positive event in their lives, Christians will say, "The Lord has been so good to us."

That is true, but when I hear an expression like this, I wonder, *Would they still consider God good if something bad happened instead?*

So often we associate the goodness of God only with His blessing. However, to do so is to be ignorant of the purpose of the trials—the difficulties, hardships, and testings—that suddenly invade our lives. We see trials as robbers, bent on stealing our joy or our sense of God's blessing and goodness.

How earthbound we are! How temporal our perspective!

The Word of God says, "Consider it all joy, my brethren, when you encounter various trials, knowing that the testing of your faith produces endurance. And let endurance have its perfect result, so that you may be perfect and complete, lacking in nothing" (James 1:2-4).

Are you prepared to praise God for His gifts, even when they take the form of trials?

*Dear heavenly Father, help me to adopt Your perspective about the problems in my life. Your Word clearly says that You are sovereign and that You have a purpose in permitting these trials. I choose to believe that, and I rest in You.*

Have you ever wondered why, before you were saved, the Bible seemed boring and difficult to understand, but after you were saved, you couldn't get enough? Finally you could understand it! And it was interesting and exciting!

The apostle Paul offered an explanation: "For what man knoweth the things of a man, save the spirit of man which is in him? Even so the things of God knoweth no man, but the Spirit of God. Now we have received, not the spirit of the world, but the spirit which is of God; that we might know the things that are freely given to us of God" (1 Corinthians 2:11-12, KJV).

Now you understand, don't you? Without God's Spirit inside us, we cannot understand the things of God! In fact, to the natural (unsaved) man or woman, the things of the Spirit of God are foolishness (1 Corinthians 2:14).

You can tell the saved from the lost because the saved are hungry for His Word and His righteousness. How is your appetite today?

*I confess, Father, that my passion for Your Word has faded. Remind me of the days when Your words were for me a joy and the delight of my heart. Today I commit myself to delving into Scripture, making the study of Your Word a priority in my life.*

What do you do, beloved, when you find yourself in need? Is your first impulse to turn to man or to God?

In recent years we've watched various nations and people endure persecution, natural disasters, political unrest, and other disturbing events. The headlines are filled with despair and turmoil. But so much of that feels removed from our everyday lives.

Sometimes I think we in the United States are plagued by too much material wealth and security—so much that we see no reason to call upon God. In these relatively prosperous times, we need to claim the promise of Jeremiah 33:3: "Call to Me and I will answer you, and I will tell you great and mighty things, which you do not know." If we practice calling on God now, we'll know exactly where to turn when trouble strikes.

Oh, beloved, what will be your prayer today?

*Father, teach me to run to You in childlike faith, to call for You in any and every situation. Thank You for Your promise that my times are in Your hand.*

# SEARCH MY PRIORITIES

What's important to you, beloved? What things do you value most? Why don't you pause and jot them down on a piece of paper.

Now then, are these priorities reflected in your daily life?

If you want an accurate picture of your present values, analyze how you spend your time each day. Ask yourself if your activities reflect the things that are—or should be—closest to your heart.

Then measure your priorities against Philippians 3:7-8: "But whatever things were gain to me, those things I have counted as loss for the sake of Christ. More than that, I count all things to be loss in view of the surpassing value of knowing Christ Jesus my Lord, for whom I have suffered the loss of all things, and count them but rubbish so that I may gain Christ."

Are you gaining Christ? Is He such a high priority that you long to know Him better and better? If not, ask yourself and God what is keeping you from that.

*Dear Father, teach me to seek Your heart above all else. I want to know Jesus so intimately that everything else fades into the background. As I think about all I've written down, please show me where my priorities need to change for the sake of Christ.*

Have you been working hard, just trying to make ends meet? Does life lack a sense of fulfillment or accomplishment? Are your days spent in the search for real love, genuine happiness, or at least a little peace—and some pleasure along the way?

And where is God in *your* portrait of life? In the shadows? The foreground? Or is He completely absent?

Let me ask you some further questions in light of Matthew 16:26. What will it profit you if you gain the whole world and lose your own life? What will you give in exchange for your life?

If you choose to lose your life—give it to the Lord Jesus Christ to do with as He pleases—then you will really find life. Why? Because life and Jesus Christ are synonymous.

If you'll believe God, if you will surrender yourself to the Lord Jesus Christ, then, beloved, you will find a deep inner peace and a quiet satisfaction.

*Lord, today I present myself to You as a living sacrifice. I long to be a vessel of honor, sanctified for Your use, so today I surrender to Your transforming, all-encompassing love. I commit myself to live in obedience to Your will.*

It takes money to survive in this world. We need it to put bread on the table, clothes on our backs, and gas in our cars.

Money! We all have to have it.

Yet what headaches money brings. Every day some people go to jobs they hate just because they have to have money. In most families both parents work outside the home just to bring in enough money, and that brings guilt because the kids are home alone or in day care. Issues of money often cause tension in marriages.

Yet we have to have money.

So what can you do? I urge you to take a good look at your lifestyle. Could you do with less? God's Word says, "If we have food and covering, with these we shall be content" (1 Timothy 6:8).

Be content. It will take off the pressure—and restore you to your proper, God-ordained place in the family.

*Father, You have promised to supply all my needs. Forgive me for being anxious about my financial state, for giving in to my desires and worldly ambitions, for letting society dictate my values and needs. Through the strength of Your Holy Spirit, I determine today to reexamine it all and then make Your priorities my priorities. In faith I'll fulfill the role You've determined for me and trust You to supply all my needs.*

Has life become one ongoing beauty contest? Are you constantly comparing yourself with others? Every time you step in front of a mirror, especially after showering, do you look at your thighs, arms, torso—and sigh? The little collections of fat are beginning to show, your skin's not smooth and supple like it once was, your muscles are sagging. You dread being seen in a bathing suit or shorts, especially when you measure yourself against the ads on billboards, on television, and in magazines.

Before you think about surgery or start buying every piece of workout equipment advertised on television, before you deem yourself inferior, consider this: Maybe you are miserable about what God never intended you or anyone else to expose.

If you have been more concerned with your appearance than with the condition of your heart, it's time for you to confess your pride and let go of worldly things. Remember, a gentle and quiet spirit is more precious in God's sight than any outward appearance (1 Peter 3:3-4).

*O God, I pray that You will teach me to rest in the confidence that I belong to Christ. Rather than comparing myself to others—or even to what I used to be—let me glory in the work You have done in me. May my inner beauty far outshine my physical appearance.*

Dear one, when was the last time you took a few minutes just to smell the roses?

We're a swarm of stressed-out people living in a stressed-out world, aren't we? But shouldn't being a child of God make a difference in our outlook on life?

I believe a major cause for our stress is that we react rather than act. I struggle in this area myself. I want to do everything, to take advantage of every opportunity. But when we're moving so quickly, we don't stop to consider the consequences of our actions. What will this action demand of us? What will it cost? We simply move on impulse, reacting to the immediate.

Just stop, beloved! God knows what we're dealing with. He knows the pressures we face, and He has made provision for each and every one of them. In Matthew 11:28 Jesus says, "Come to Me, all who are weary and heavy-laden, and I will give you rest."

Yoke up with your Lord. Then you won't run ahead or lag behind—and He'll pull the load.

*Lord God, in Your Word You tell me, "In repentance and rest you will be saved, in quietness and trust is your strength" (Isaiah 30:15). Teach me to ask You what I should or should not say yes to. Teach me that saying no to even a good or "spiritual" opportunity is not sin. Help me to walk under Your leadership and rest in Your approval alone.*

Dear friend, how much time are you setting aside to having fellowship with God? How much time are you spending in His Word?

Think with me a moment. If you tithed the hours of each day, you'd owe God two hours and twenty-four minutes a day. That puts a new perspective on things, doesn't it?

Oh, beloved, how we need to be serious about knowing God. We need to spend the kind of time that we invest in learning our profession or our job.

Won't you press on to know the Lord?

In John 14:6, Jesus said, "I am...the truth." He is the truth, and He is the Word. To know and embrace and live by His Word is to build a solid, unshakable structure in the midst of life's earthquakes. Precious one, take the time to go deeper into His Word!

*I confess, dear Lord, that I have allowed the busyness of life to push You and Your Word out of first place in my life. I repent of my selfish ways. I consciously commit to making time in my schedule just to be with You and to study Your Word, which You say is the very bread by which we live.*

Do you ever feel out of focus? Deep down inside, are you dissatisfied or even downright miserable? Have you ever thought that misery comes when we are the focus of our lives?

However, when God rather than self becomes the focus, everything takes second place to His will for our lives. In essence, nothing else really matters. He is the only one we have to please. He is the only one to whom we are truly and rightly answerable. The Bible urges us to make it our ambition to be found pleasing to God (2 Corinthians 5:9).

When we are set free from the bondage of pleasing people, including ourselves—of currying others' favor and approval—then no one will be able to make us miserable or dissatisfied. Only what pleases God will please us. If you will begin each day by making the will of God your focus, if you will seek to please Him alone, then you'll find yourself satisfied with life. Misery will slip away like a scolded puppy with its tail between its legs. Life will take on purpose.

*O Father, I long for the love of Christ to control my life to such an extent that I always do the things that are pleasing to You. Help me to break free of the false notion that I must have the approval of others. Give my life a purpose that is rooted in You.*

Suppose, just suppose, you knew the coming of the Lord Jesus Christ was near. Suppose you knew for certain that by this time next year you would be standing before your God and your Lord, giving an account of how you have lived as His child (Romans 14:10-12; 2 Corinthians 5:10).

Would it make a difference in the way you live today? This month? This year? Are you prepared to see Jesus?

God says that everyone who has the hope of being like Jesus purifies himself even as He (Jesus) is pure (1 John 3:3). The days ahead should become days of cleansing as you examine yourself and put away those things—sins, habits, weights, possessions, activities, excesses—that keep you from pursuing His holiness (Hebrews 12:1-2,14).

*Dear heavenly Father, You have made it clear in Your Word that each of us will one day stand before You to give an account of our deeds, good or bad. On that day how I long to hear from You, "Well done, good and faithful servant. Enter into the joy of your Lord." Oh, please, please reveal to me anything that holds me back from serving You. Show me what needs to be purified in my life so that I can glorify You in all I do, in all I say, in all I am.*

Do you ever get nauseated by all the corruption in this world, sickened by the untold pain it brings? In the midst of all the ugliness of this world, as we witness lives disfigured and distorted by sin, we long for beauty.

Dear friend, I want you to know the beauty that comes from being alone with God. Lines of stress, wrinkles of frustration, creases of bitterness are lifted from your face as you quietly, unhurriedly sit before your God, reading His Word, stopping to pray as He speaks to your heart, sorting things out, confessing, unloading all of your burdens, and listening. There in His sanctuary, you gain assurance of His unlimited sovereignty and unconditional love, and with that assurance comes beauty—to life and to you.

Then you can walk out to meet the day, knowing that whatever happens you can say with the psalmist, "But as for me, the nearness of God is my good; I have made the Lord GOD my refuge" (Psalm 73:28).

*Thank You, dear Father, that You are not far from each one of us (Acts 17:27). What a wonder that You want to have an intimate relationship with me! In a world made ugly by sin, thank You for the unspeakable privilege of beholding Your beauty and meditating in Your presence.*

Do you realize that the way you spend your time reflects your values? Think for a moment about how you spend your days.

So many who name the name of Christ do not have time for God—time to get to know Him, to meet with Him daily. They don't have time to pray, to study His Word, to share His love with others. Each moment of the day is consumed by self, and then it's gone, never to be redeemed because it wasn't spent on eternal values.

God urges us to redeem the time—buy it back, take charge of it, make the most of it—"because the days are evil" (Ephesians 5:16). He wants us to invest our time and energies in things that have eternal value, not in that which is useless, temporal, self-centered, or destructive!

If you don't have time for God, beloved, what does that say about the value you place on your relationship with Him?

*Forgive me, O God, for wasting time, for allowing my day to become so full of things that have no eternal value. How could I be so foolish as to forget that only in You do I live and move and have my being? Restore to me, I pray, the joy of Your salvation.*

What are you doing with your money? Are you spending it on earthly pleasures—or are you making eternal investments? Are you laying up treasures on earth or in heaven?

God's Word teaches that we'll be held accountable for our investments. He also will call us to account for those times we see a brother in need but don't use our resources to help. And while spiritual rewards and losses are apportioned now, "in the present age" according to the gospel of Mark (10:28-31), these will not be known fully until it is too late to change the course of our lives.

When death comes, what has been done is done. We'll receive no second chances. Our Lord will come quickly, and "render to every man according to what he has done" (Revelation 22:12).

Examine your life, beloved. Haven't you invested enough in yourself? It's time to share God's blessings with those in need.

*Thank You, God, for all the ways You have blessed me, even above all that I have asked or imagined. Forgive me for being stingy where You have been abundantly generous. Show me how to honor You by giving out of the monies You have enabled me to earn and out of the things with which You have blessed me.*

Do you find yourself so preoccupied with the present business and pressures of life that you are always in a hurry, even with God?

There's no time—when you're not tired—to let go, to relax, to simply be still and know that He is God (Psalm 46:10, NKJV). I understand. The pace of life for most of us breaks the speed limit.

But is that a legitimate excuse? Will it hold with God? Not really.

If you're going to please God, you need reexamine your priorities and make some choices. It means that some things will not get done and some people may not understand. But didn't Jesus say that sitting at His feet and hearing His Word was the one thing that was needful— the thing which could never be taken away from us (Luke 10:42)?

You've heard the words, "Take the world, but give me Jesus?" Oh, that this were the heart cry of all of us so that at every moment, in every place in which we find ourselves, He would abide as our everlasting portion.

*Lord, I've been so busy, so worried and bothered with many things. I've even been distracted from You by serving You and Your kingdom. Thank You for this reminder that the only thing I need, the one thing that will bring true joy, is to grow closer to You, to have intimacy with You as my first priority.*

What is your relationship to the Word of God? How well do you understand it? What is life like when you're not in it? Could you live without it? Would it make any difference in your life if the government took away your Bible?

Let me put it another way: Have you ever wondered why people would risk their jobs, their freedom, their relationship with their loved ones, even their very lives for the Word of God? This happened for years behind the Iron Curtain and is still happening today in many countries around the world.

Why is the Word more precious than freedom?

Because within the soul of every genuine child of God there is a spiritual craving, a hunger and thirst for righteousness. "Man does not live by bread alone, but man lives by everything that proceeds out of the mouth of the LORD" (Deuteronomy 8:3).

Let me ask you again: What is your relationship to the Word of God?

*O Holy Father, I confess that often I find myself spending more time in reading material about Your Word than in going directly to the Bible and reading it for myself. Help me to give Your Word its proper place in my heart, treasuring its nourishment more than food for my body.*

Our enemy, the devil, will do anything he can to prevent us from living a godly life! You need to know how to recognize his strategies. One of them is deceptively simple: distraction.

That's right, distraction! He wants us to focus on anything except what is truly important. How often are you and I drawn away and distracted from what Luke 10:42 says is the one thing that is necessary?

It's needful, beloved, to sit at His feet and learn of Him, yet the pressures and pleasures of life can so easily distract. Even the busyness of serving the Lord can get in the way. I think this is why we've seen many prominent Christians fall.

The dangers of our time should put a holy fear in us! Dear one, I urge you to let God and His Word block out the temptations of the flesh and the distractions of the world.

*O God, let my driving passion once more be the pursuit of You and Your Word. The lure of my desires, the worry of this world, and the deceitfulness of wealth have consumed my thoughts, and I've lost sight of what's important. Plow the soil of my heart, dear Lord, and sow precious seeds of truth so that my life can once again bear fruit for You.*

How much time do you give to your loved ones? What comes first: you, your career—or your mate, your children, your family?

Granted, you have to earn a living, but does work consume all of the hours in your day? Is getting ahead, earning the approbation of your colleagues, your boss, your peers, more important than fulfilling those God-given roles to which you've committed? Do you take time to be the father, mother, husband, or wife you should be? Is your time spent in serving self, pursuing your pleasures, your career, your goals, and your interests?

God commands us to redeem the time—to buy it back, to control it and not to let it control us—because the days are evil (Ephesians 5:16). In a later passage (Ephesians 5:21–6:9), He also sets before us our responsibilities in our relationships. Why don't you take a few minutes today and read these verses? Underline each one that pertains to you, and then list what God tells you to do.

Now then, beloved, how do you measure up? What is to be your course of action?

*Lord, give me a heart that reflects Your own. Help me to base my priorities on the priorities You have set. Help me to love others with a pure, unselfish heart, giving generously of my time and Your love, fulfilling the duties You've given me in my relationships.*

Is happiness achieved through "things"? Through pleasant circumstances? Or does it come with a sense of knowing everything is right between you and God?

So often we think, *If I only had that car (house, job, dress size), I'd be happy. Successful. I'd win the attention of others.*

At least that is what the media tells us every day as we watch and listen to the advertisements, drawn by the lust of the eyes, the lust of the flesh, and the boastful pride of life to the appeal of things, success, and power (1 John 2:16).

We're tempted on every hand. The world is appealing and life is hard—full of disappointments, discouragements, defeats, difficulties.

And so we turn to "things," to achievements, to people to ease the pain or to bring us joy. Why? Why don't we turn to God? Are we so blind, so deluded that we don't realize that only by focusing on Him and ignoring the distractions of the world can we discover true happiness?

*O God, forgive me for every time I filled my desperate need with the chaff of the world. No matter what it takes, remind me that You alone can fulfill the longings of my heart. Help me to believe You when You say that in Your presence is fullness of joy and at Your right hand are pleasures forever.*

God is setting a choice before you. What will it be, dear one? The world and you—or Jesus and you?

In Philippians 3:8-11, Paul describes the one goal for which he is willing to give his all: "That I may gain Christ, and may be found in Him, not having a righteousness of my own...but that which is through faith in Christ...that I may know Him and the power of His resurrection and the fellowship of His sufferings, being conformed to His death; in order that I may attain to the resurrection from the dead."

What does this mean? What does this cost? It's the discipline of counting all things as loss—as dung—for the excellency of knowing Him. The simple truth is that your self must be put to death before you can join Paul in saying, "to live is Christ" (Philippians 1:21).

How about it, beloved?

*Lord, today I choose not to love the world or the things that are in the world. You alone are worthy, and I commit today to love You with all my heart, with all my soul, and with all my might.*

Dear one, has your relationship with God become ho-hum? Are you wondering how you can bring the spark back into your spiritual walk?

You begin, beloved, by being in His Word consistently, day in and day out. Three minutes and a cup of coffee isn't going to do it!

But you say, "How can I possibly find time for that?"

Beloved, seeking God and having an intimate relationship with Him may mean you'll have to set aside some of your activities and maybe some of your ambitions. Try giving God even a minimum amount of time—say, thirty minutes to an hour. That's not even a full tithe of the twenty-four hours that make up your day.

Psalm 34:10 says, "They who seek the LORD shall not be in want of any good thing."

Is an hour of each day too much to give, beloved?

*You have promised to listen to me when I call upon You and come to You in prayer, to be present when I search for You with all my heart. Lord, show me how to schedule this time with You and keep it as a priority rather than an obligation.*

Intimacy with God must be your priority.

You're probably overwhelmed simply trying to meet the demands of your day. How can you possibly make knowing God intimately a priority? Well, you're not alone in your struggle! We all deal with the same thing. It's called the "tyranny of the urgent."

Placing a priority on your relationship with God is going to take faith and discipline on your part. It doesn't mean you're to stop earning your living, but it may mean laying aside some of your time-consuming activities—and yes, maybe even some of your ambitions. Seeking God may mean learning to be satisfied with less rather than working longer hours in order to have more.

"Less" is a concept totally foreign to our era. The world tells us it's not smart thinking. But, dear friend, Matthew 6:33 promises that if you first seek His kingdom and His righteousness, the basics of life will be provided.

God keeps His promises!

*O Father, I want to love You more. I want to know You and Your Word intimately. As I pause before You, show me the areas of life where I need to be satisfied with less. Show me where I need to let go and what I need to change.*

Have you experienced a time when God seems distant? The intimacy, the fellowship is gone. Oh, you still talk the talk and go through the motions. Everyone at church thinks you're fine. They talk about the Bible, you talk about the Bible. They talk about prayer, you talk about prayer. They talk about intimacy with God, you do the same. But you know it's just a charade.

So what do you do, beloved?

Let me ask a few questions. First, are you so busy that you don't have time to be still before God, immersing yourself in the Word and in prayer? If so, this is where to begin.

Second, has there been partial obedience in your life? Remember when God told Saul to destroy everything after Israel's victory over the Amalekites (1 Samuel 15)? Instead of obeying completely, Saul spared the king along with the best of the animals and all that was good. Saul was not willing to destroy everything as God said, and he suffered greatly.

Is there some area of partial obedience in your life, beloved? If so, this could be the reason God seems distant. Ask God to forgive you, then prove your genuine repentance by doing what you know to be right. "Draw near to God, and He will draw near to you" (James 4:8).

*O Father, I long for the comforting sense of Your presence. Show me where I need to reorder my life or where I have resisted Your instruction. Help me to draw near to You by following Your heart's desire for me.*

Have you ever looked in the mirror and thought, *I'm not as attractive as I once was?*

Perhaps you don't feel old, but the lines in your face contradict your feelings. And when you step into bright sunshine, it's evident that time has stretched your skin, your contours, your waistline.

The reality of getting old can be difficult to face, especially since we live in a society captivated by external appearance. So how do we handle it biblically? Consider the message of the apostle Paul: "Therefore we do not lose heart, but though our outer man is decaying, yet our inner man is being renewed day by day" (2 Corinthians 4:16).

The next time you pass a mirror ask, "Am I as pretty, as handsome as I want to be spiritually?" Then look into the mirror of God's Word and behold the glory of the Lord. You'll become more attractive than you thought you could be!

*Father, thank You for this reminder that outward appearances are of little importance. May I ever be cognizant of the fact that, because Christ Jesus has abolished death and brought life and immortality, death has no hold over me and the aging of my earthly body has no impact on the state of my eternal soul. May I seek the beauty of Christ.*

Many today don't recognize the nearness of our Lord's return. Have you given thought to the fact that what you do today will not go unnoticed by the Lord? We must not be caught sleeping!

Only one thing will matter on "that day"—the same thing that mattered to Jesus when His life was over. He could honestly say, "I glorified You on the earth, having accomplished the work which You have given Me to do" (John 17:4).

How should you live so you won't be ashamed when you see Him face to face?

Get alone with Him, take pen and paper, and ask your heavenly Father that very question. Honestly deal with those things in your life that would keep you from looking unashamedly into His face. Then live accordingly.

Remember, you're accountable only to an audience of One.

*Let it be the cry of my heart to follow You faithfully and obediently all of the days of my life. I long for Your return, and I pray that, through the indwelling Holy Spirit, I may conduct myself in a manner worthy of the gospel of Christ.*

What difference can it possibly make to be in the Word every day?

You read the Word of God a little. You read a verse here and there in the Bible, but you don't get much out of it.

I can tell you, from my own experience, that once you're in the Word consistently, once you've learned how to dig out its treasures of truth for yourself by moving through it book by book, you'll experience the incredible, revolutionary difference.

It's the difference between a "Hi! How are ya?" relationship with God and a deep intimacy with your heavenly Father. It's the difference between a panic attack in the unexpected jolts of life and a supernatural peace in the midst of the worst storm.

The Bible says, "The fear of the LORD is the beginning of knowledge" (Proverbs 1:7). If we really respect God for who He is, then we'll make listening to Him a priority.

*My heart stands in awe of Your words, Lord. Whenever I spend time in the Bible—contemplating what You have said and then listening for Your voice as truth is applied to my life or You provoke me to prayer—I am amazed by the difference it makes in my perspective. Thank You for the marvelous gift of Your Word. Teach me to cherish it more with each passing day.*

How would you describe your relationship with God? Are you like two friends walking side by side? Or would He need to shout to get your attention?

Any relationship takes time and an investment of energy. Spending time with others assures them of their importance in our lives. If you've ever had a friendship that gradually unraveled, chances are it was because the two of you spent less and less time together until eventually you had little or nothing in common.

I know that your life is filled with pressures and ongoing demands, but I urge you to weigh your choices carefully. Don't exchange what's temporal for what pays eternal dividends. If you do, you're a fool.

Intimacy with God and holiness come when you make God your priority, when you spend time with Him, praying and waiting on Him to speak to you. Waiting until, as Scripture says, you hear Him saying, "This is the way, walk in it" (Isaiah 30:21).

*Holy God, I come to You today seeking refuge from the pressures of my life. Soften my heart. Make me sensitive to the voice of the Holy Spirit. Speak to me today as I quietly wait on You.*

Heaven is silent. Winter has set in. Your heart shivers. The warmth of intimacy is gone. You try to rekindle a fire, but your efforts are useless. Your spirit reaches out in the cold darkness to touch Him, only to confront lonely, numbing, confusing, discouraging silence.

Your heart cries out, "Why?" Where can you find the answer to heaven's silence? First, beloved, consider the following. Is God silent because He has spoken and you did not respond in obedience—so He waits?

Or are you so busy that you haven't been quiet enough to hear His "still small voice" in the recesses of your heart?

If neither of these fits your circumstances, then consider that God may be silent because it is His time to be silent. God's silence may simply be a test of your faith. This verse may just what you need: "Who is among you that fears the LORD, that obeys the voice of His servant, that walks in darkness and has no light? Let him trust in the name of the LORD and rely his God" (Isaiah 50:10).

*I will trust in You. I will cling to You, my Father and God. Even though You seem far away and I don't know what to do, I won't let go of what I know about You. The heavens may seem as brass, but I will trust You. You have promised You would never leave nor forsake me, and I know You cannot lie.*

Make time "in the sanctuary" a priority, beloved. According to the writer of Psalm 73, this is where we learn God's ways. He was troubled by the inequities of life, the prosperity of the wicked and the problems of the righteous. He couldn't understand why God didn't intervene— "until I came into the sanctuary of God; then I perceived their end" (verse 17).

Oh, how we need to see that "Thy way, O God, is in the sanctuary" (Psalm 77:13, KJV).

In the sanctuary we receive strength to go on. Have you ever thought, "It would just be easier to die"? One day everything seemed so overwhelming that such a thought entered my mind. But because I live in the Word, I knew that the thought was not from God; it was Satan's subtle seduction, his tactic as a murderer (John 8:44).

In the sanctuary of God's presence I received strength to resist, to persist, and to continue to be productive as a servant of the Most High God, El Elyon!

Do you need strength, beloved? Make it your priority to spend time in His presence and in His Word.

*It is a battle, Lord. So much to do, so many distractions. Yet I know that if I want the comfort of Your counsel, I must seek Your presence by spending time with You, unhurried and quiet. Strengthen my confidence in You, my understanding of what is transpiring— and my resolve to not neglect my "sanctuary time."*

What are you willing to settle for, beloved? Exactly how contented would you say you are?

First Timothy 6:9 warns, "But those who want to get rich fall into temptation and a snare and many foolish and harmful desires which plunge men into ruin and destruction."

One of our greatest problems is our lack of contentment. God's Word says, "Godliness...is a means of great gain when accompanied by contentment" (1 Timothy 6:6). When we take our focus off Christ and put it on the world, that's when we get into trouble. Oh, beloved, if there's even one thorn of the deceitfulness of riches in your heart, it can cause you to wander away from the faith. And this very thing has kept many a man and woman from holiness.

Leave behind your love of money, which is "a root of all sorts of evil" (1 Timothy 6:10). Live not by the standards of the world but by every word that proceeds out of the mouth of God. Dear one, are you going to settle for anything less?

*I refuse to settle for what little this life has to offer. You alone offer true peace and contentment, and I choose to live by the precepts of Your Word—not by the standards of this materialistic world.*

Are you living life in overdrive? Do you feel like running away, checking out, giving up? Life is filled with pressure.

Pressure to be.               Pressure to do.

Pressure to perform.        Pressure to produce.

And with the pressure come anxiety and stress. Realistically, the pressure is part of our lives. And stress? The stress will always be there in one form or another.

So what are you going to do about it? Tough it out until you break? Jump into some ungodly escape hatch? Give up? Check out?

None of these provide the answer, dear one. In Ephesians 5:18-19, we're instructed to "be filled with the Spirit." God tells us to sing! Make melody in our hearts to the Lord. Singing spiritual songs and making melody in your heart is God's way of delivering you from the stresses of the world. If you do this, you will find it possible to fulfill the instructions of next verse: "Always [give] thanks for all things in the name of our Lord Jesus Christ to God, even the Father" (verse 20).

*O Lord, You are my hiding place. You preserve me from trouble, and You surround me with songs of deliverance (Psalm 32:7). Thank You for showing me how to not only endure the pressures of life but to come through them with a heart full of grateful praise.*

Beloved, if you knew a very important guest was coming to your house today, what kind of meal would you prepare? What kind of special touches would you add? How much time would you spend in preparation?

Most of us would cancel whatever appointments we had. We'd be scurrying around, trying to get the house cleaned. We'd wipe off the best china, polish the silver, wash the crystal, and make sure everything was just right.

And what about God? Do you consider Him a special guest worthy of your best efforts, or does He get your leftovers? Do you give Him the first hours of the day or the last few sleepy moments? How much of your gifts and abilities are devoted to Him? Your possessions? Your service?

In Malachi 1:6 God is admonishing His people for their improper attitude toward Him. They were offering God less than their best, and they refused to admit they were wrong.

How about you, beloved? Do you give God your leftovers or your best?

*O Father, why am I so foolish to forget that You are worthy of my highest praise and my faithful obedience? Forgive me, I pray, for all the times I fail to give You my best. Help me to remember that I was created for Your pleasure, not my own.*

Do you ever find yourself caught up with desiring more and more? Do you feel as if you can't get enough of material things? And how much time do you invest in temporal pleasures? Perhaps your days are filled with going to the mall, eating out, overeating—whatever it is *you* like to do, even if it's sitting in front of television.

Is this what life is all about? Focusing on things and on self? May I suggest you take time to think about Titus 2:11-13: "For the grace of God has appeared, bringing salvation to all men, instructing us to deny ungodliness and worldly desires and to live sensibly, righteously and godly in the present age, looking for the blessed hope and the appearing of the glory of our great God and Savior, Christ Jesus."

Remember, beloved, our Savior is coming again and then you and I will have to give an account for the way you live. How will you answer?

*Thank You, Father, for the wonderful promise and hope of Christ Jesus' return. As I wait, help me to live a life that is pleasing to You. I ask You to convict me greatly whenever I stray from the protection of Your loving hands and draw me back to fellowship with You, no matter what it takes.*

If the Word of God does not take priority in your life, how can you expect to run to God and ask for whatever you wish? So often we claim the truth that God answers prayer, but perhaps we're not reading Scripture closely enough.

John 15:7 says, "If you abide in Me, and My words abide in you, ask whatever you wish, and it will be done for you."

The Christian life is to be lived in total dependence on God. We should go to Him for all that we need. But He has set one condition: abiding in Him. Our life is to be spent dwelling in Him, absorbing Christ's character until we become so one with Him that His life fills and permeates every cell of our being.

And you know what? When we do abide in Him, our requests will be in accordance with God's will, God's desire, and God's character.

*Precious Savior, I want to live every moment of my life conscious of You. Through the presence of Your Holy Spirit, show me what it means to truly abide in You. Fill my heart with Your love and my life with Your words. May my priority always be You—being like You, bringing You glory and pleasure, giving You preeminence in all things.*

---

# LEAD ME
## TO TRUTH

What are you going to do with your sin, my friend? Or do you even know what sin is? If you don't have the right perspective on sin, it could cost you your life. You need to be aware of God's perspective.

How does God define sin? He informs us in Romans 3:23 that "all have sinned and fall short of the glory of God." The word *sin* means to miss the mark, to fall short of God's standard. God tells us that "whatever is not from faith is sin" (Romans 14:23). And what is faith? Faith is taking God at His Word.

In other words, you sin when you don't believe God and when you don't believe in Jesus Christ. Sin is knowing to do right but choosing not to do it. Sin is transgression of the law; it is crossing over the line drawn by God. It is willfully doing your own thing, choosing your own way.

Although no one is sinless, God has offered to take away your sin. The question is, would you like to be set free from sin's power and penalty—or do you love sin and the company of sinners?

*God, thank You for sending Your Son, Christ Jesus, to pay the penalty for my sin and set me free from its power. I pray You will make sin absolutely abhorrent to me. By Your grace I choose to flee temptation and reject the company of sinners.*

Have you ever thought that the crucifixion of Jesus Christ was an absolute tragedy? At one time Peter, one of Jesus' followers, would have agreed with you. When Jesus told His followers about His impending death, Peter said, "God forbid it, Lord! This shall never happen to You" (Matthew 16:22).

Does your heart echo Peter's response? Then you need to discover the truth about Jesus' death: It was God's plan. He sent His Son, Jesus Christ, to earth for this specific purpose. My friend, you are a sinner (a person who has your own rules for life), and Jesus Christ took the death penalty for your sin. Jesus died in your place. Did you know that?

Far from being a tragedy, the crucifixion of Jesus is good news. It means you can be set free from slavery to sin. It is called salvation. Just tell God that is what you want, now. He will see that it happens.

*God, help me understand the full import of the death of Your Son—why He had to die and what His death and resurrection accomplished. I believe in You, and I want to fully comprehend the good news of Jesus' crucifixion.*

Do you feel as if God could never accept you, after all you have done? You believe He's written you off, given up hope. After all, a holy God would have to reject you, wouldn't He? You're unacceptable, a sinner. When it comes to doing right, you are absolutely helpless. You couldn't be a good person if you tried—and you have tried. You are nothing like God and could never hope to be.

You are wrong, beloved. The Word of God says, "While we were still helpless, at the right time Christ died for the ungodly.... God demonstrates His own love toward us, in that while we were yet sinners, Christ died for us" (Romans 5:6,8).

The truth of the matter is, God already loves you and is calling you into relationship with Him. If you will respond to His call, He will give you the righteousness, the purity of His own Son.

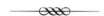

*God in heaven, I feel so unworthy to even approach You. But You have promised in Your Word that through the righteousness of Your Son, I can find redemption—full forgiveness of my sin. In my own strength, I am helpless against the power of sin, but I claim Your promise and believe that through the strength of Your Holy Spirit, I can live in freedom.*

*Thank You for the gift of new life, which gives me a new beginning, and the power of Your Spirit, who now resides within—the guarantee of my redemption.*

Are you living contrary to the Word of God? When people question your salvation because of your lifestyle, do you disregard their comments saying, "Look, everything's fine between God and me—I know I am a Christian"?

Are you sure?

True Christians are painfully aware of the awfulness of their sin because they have seen the holiness of God. They have witnessed God's justice in dealing with sin at Calvary, and they value the price paid by Jesus on their behalf.

Genuine Christians—the real thing—are people who have repented of sin and turned from it. They've seen sin for what it is: willful rebellion against the rulership of God over their lives. In turning from their sin, they have embraced God's only means of dealing with sin, which is the death and resurrection of His Son, the Lord Jesus Christ, on their behalf.

Therefore sin brings conviction to the Christian—justified guilt that prompts us to confess and repent. First John 3:8 says that the one who practices sin, who habitually violates God's principles, is of the devil. Whose team are you on?

*God, show me the truth about the condition of my soul. I don't want to be deceived into thinking I'm Your child, when in reality I'm still a slave to sin. I want to truly surrender to You as Lord of my life.*

If you think you're a child of God yet you're still living just as you did before you got saved, before you declared yourself a Christian, you may be greatly mistaken, my friend. If you think you can get away with sin because you and God have an "understanding," that it doesn't matter how you choose to live on earth since you have the promise of life in heaven, you are deceived.

Listen to what God says: "But immorality or any impurity or greed must not even be named among you, as is proper among saints; and there must be no filthiness and silly talk, or coarse jesting, which are not fitting, but rather giving of thanks. For this you know with certainty, that no immoral or impure person or covetous man, who is an idolater, has an inheritance in the kingdom of Christ and God. Let no one deceive you with empty words, for because of these things the wrath of God comes upon the sons of disobedience" (Ephesians 5:3-6).

Are you sure you haven't been deceived?

You need to repent, my friend. Tell God you want Him to set you free.

*Lord, I want to be set free from the bondage of sin. Through the blood of Jesus, cleanse me from immorality and impurity. Blot out all my iniquities, and create in me a clean heart. I give myself to You and surrender my will to You as my God, my Savior, and my Lord.*

Are you dealing with a sense of worthlessness? Feeling lower than a third-class citizen? Perhaps you see yourself as an alien who sneaked into the Kingdom of God, unwanted and undetected. Maybe you even doubt whether anyone loves or wants you. In other words, you are down—on yourself.

You'll probably stay there unless you believe the Word of God: "Blessed be the God and Father of our Lord Jesus Christ, who...chose us in Him before the foundation of the world, that we would be holy and blameless before Him. In love He predestined us to adoption as sons through Jesus Christ to Himself, according to the kind intention of His will" (Ephesians 1:3-5).

God chose you, beloved. In love He made you His. God chose you. He does not lie. Now are you going to live according to your feelings, or will you walk by faith?

*Thank You for the wonderful truth that You chose me to be Your child. In faith I believe and embrace this comforting evidence of Your unconditional love.*

Do your feelings dictate to you what is truth? When you read the Bible, do you say to yourself, "That verse can't be true because it doesn't match my feelings about my situation?" Do you find yourself saying, "I know what God's Word says, but—"

Oh, my friend, you're in a royal battle, and you will lose if you abandon truth for a lie. The feelings that seem so real are leading you to embrace Satan's deception. If you are justifying actions that clearly violate God's principles, trying to rationalize your choices because your situation is "different," you have already fallen into his trap.

Now is the time to repent. You must obey the Word of God, "casting down imaginations, and every high thing [thought, feeling] that exalteth itself against the knowledge of God" (2 Corinthians 10:5, KJV). You must bring every feeling, every thought, captive to the obedience of Jesus, who is the truth and in whom there is no lie.

*Lord, my feelings are so real, my thoughts so convincing. Show me how to constantly measure the truthfulness of every thought and emotion against the plumb line of Your Word. And if I have believed a lie, may I reject it, refusing it until I wear down the enemy and he leaves me alone.*

Are you dealing with rejection? Someone has hurt you, criticized your efforts, ridiculed your opinions, or maybe even walked away from you, indicating they'd be happy to never see you again.

You're demoralized. Your thoughts mow you down like a machine gun, riddling you with guilt, condemnation, and a sense of worthlessness. You feel drained of life and of hope. You're beginning to question the value of your life.

Oh, precious one, don't listen to the father of lies. The Bible exposes his tactics. He's the thief who comes to steal, kill, and destroy (John 10:10). He is a murderer and a deceiver. Block your ears to his destructive lies and listen instead to God, "who is at work in you, both to will and to work for His good pleasure" (Philippians 2:13).

Take courage. You have great value in the eyes of God.

*O Father, thank You for showing me in Your Word how to respond to the lies of Satan. Whenever rejection comes, in any form, help me to remember that You, the God of the universe, are for me. With You on my side, whom shall I fear? Thank You that Christ Jesus, Your Son, stands at Your right hand, interceding on my behalf.*

Do you realize that you are not to walk by your feelings but simply by the naked, unadulterated truth of what God says?

Feelings play a powerful role in our lives, but they must be weighed against the reality of God's Word and His wisdom. Trusting our feelings, which can shift like waves in a wind-tossed storm, can destroy relationships, take lives, and render a person impotent and unable to cope with the everyday situations of life. Feelings can keep you from attaining the calling God has on your life. They can keep you from stepping out in faith.

Perhaps your feelings are out of control because of a hormonal or chemical imbalance. Or perhaps you have believed one of Satan's lies. Check with your doctor, and check with the Word of God.

Whatever the cause, God tells you to bring every thought, every feeling captive to the obedience of Jesus Christ (2 Corinthians 10:5). If you will believe God's Word—no matter what your feelings—victory will come.

*Father, teach me to greet every emotion with Philippians 4:8, to frisk every thought at the door of my mind. If it doesn't meet the criteria—of being true, honorable, right, pure, lovely, of good repute, excellent, or worthy of praise — may I vehemently refuse to think about it.*

Have you ever noticed how easily people are swayed by what they "suppose" without ever having concrete evidence of the fact?

Are you suffering right now, my friend—maybe taking a beating because people have supposed something wrong about you? It's difficult to defend yourself, isn't it? What are you going to do?

The Bible tells us in Acts 11 that the apostle Peter also endured unjust criticism. What did he do? He trusted God. Remember Jesus' words: "Woe to you [beware] when all men speak well of you" (Luke 6:26). "Blessed are you when people insult you and persecute you, and falsely say all kinds of evil against you because of Me" (Matthew 5:11).

So pray and wait for God's opportunity to set matters straight. While you are waiting, rehearse all that God has done for you in the past and remember that His calling on your life does not change. Jesus suffered, and as His follower, you will too. But take heart; you're in good company (John 15:18-25; Hebrews 5:8).

*In You, O Lord, I take refuge; let me never be ashamed. Be to me a rock of strength, a stronghold to save me. You are my strength. You have ransomed me, O Lord, God of truth. Save me in Your lovingkindness, and let me not be put to shame.*

Tolerance. That's the buzzword of our day. It sounds good, nice even.

But what does it mean? To many tolerance means that no one has the authority to say anything is right or wrong. If we claim there is an immutable standard, we will be condemned for being intolerant.

We live in a day when no believes in absolutes. Thus, in man's eyes sin is no longer sin. But God has not changed. What He defines as sin is still sin, and whoever does not obey Him will someday reap the consequences.

So what does God define as sin and therefore unacceptable behavior? Listen: "Do you not know that the unrighteous will not inherit the kingdom of God? Do not be deceived; neither fornicators, nor idolaters, nor adulterers, nor effeminate, nor homosexuals, nor thieves, nor the covetous, nor drunkards, nor revilers, nor swindlers, will inherit the kingdom of God" (1 Corinthians 6:9-10).

The God we serve is not tolerant of sin—and neither should you be.

*O God, teach me to hate the things You hate. Teach me not to compromise truth for the sake of society's acceptance and approval. Help me to be as Joshua 1:7-9 instructs: strong, courageous, and knowledgeable about Your Word.*

Are you walking around lost in the maze of the enemy's lies? Blocked at every turn by thoughts and feelings that lead you down dead-end paths? Are you confused, not knowing where to go, where to turn, or what to do because you are being led by your emotions, your feelings, and your suppositions? Or are you living by the evaluations, the opinions, and the counsel of others rather than by the absolute truth of God's inerrant Word?

Our peace, our happiness, our well-being, our soundness of mind, our effectiveness all go back to what we believe—and whom we believe.

It does not matter what you experience, what you feel, what you think or hear. If it does not agree with the Word of God, then it is a lie and has its origin with the great deceiver, "the father of lies" (John 8:44)—the one who is a murderer.

Don't miss the knowledge of your worth and your purpose in this life by believing his lies. Choose to believe God, no matter what.

*O Lord, the entire Bible speaks of Your holiness and Your love. It offers words of hope and life. No matter my circumstances, I choose to reject the lies of Satan, clinging instead to You and to the truth of Your inerrant Word "as the waistband clings to the waist of a man," so that I might bring You praise and glory, as Jeremiah 13:11 says.*

Are people questioning the reasonableness of your faith? Are they calling you a fool for believing that the Bible is inerrant and that Jesus Christ is the only way to God? That, beloved, is the reasoning, the wisdom, of the world.

In 1 Corinthians 2:11, the apostle Paul tells us, "For who among men knows the thoughts of a man except the spirit of the man which is in him? Even so the thoughts of God no one knows except the Spirit of God. Now we have received, not the spirit of the world, but the Spirit who is from God, so that we may know the things freely given to us by God."

Dear one, whatever may come along to trouble your heart, turn it aside. As God's child, you have the Holy Spirit. You've been given the mind of Christ. The Spirit will guide you into all truth—He is the truth! What a promise! Don't be intimidated by the world, "for the word of the cross is foolishness to those who are perishing, but to us who are being saved it is the power of God. For it is written, 'I will destroy the wisdom of the wise, and the cleverness of the clever I will set aside'" (1 Corinthians 1:18-19).

*O Father, when I encounter people like this, may I determine to proclaim nothing but Jesus Christ and His crucifixion for their sins—and leave the rest up to You.*

Have you heard of people who at one time had a zeal for God, were excited about the Word of God, just couldn't get enough of Christianity, and then they walked away from it? Are you confused when people turn away from the Word of God? Do you wonder how they can become so caught up in the worries of life, the deceitfulness of riches, that they suddenly don't have time for God?

Can a person who is truly saved habitually walk where Jesus would never walk? Can a person say that he doesn't believe the Bible anymore and still be saved?

Listen to what God says: "By this we know that we are in Him: the one who says he abides in Him ought himself to walk in the same manner as He walked" (1 John 2:5-6).

According to the Word of God, there are ways you can tell the professors—those who merely name the name of Christ—from the possessors—those who are truly indwelt by Him. True Christianity brings forth lasting fruit—the evidence of salvation. What would a fruit inspection reveal?

*Lord, I'm concerned about my loved ones who seem to have abandoned their faith. Only You can see the condition of their hearts, but I am certain that these people need to have a biblical understanding of true Christianity. Confront them with truth in Your way and Your time, and help me to live in such a way that they will see the difference Your indwelling presence makes in my life.*

Have you ever said, "I sinned because God didn't deliver me"? Perhaps you justified your actions by saying, "It was too tempting, too hard. Anyone in my circumstances would have done the same thing."

That, my friend, is not true. You may get others to go along with your excuse, and your rationalization may soothe your conscience temporarily—but it won't get past God. The book of James assures us that we cannot blame God when we are tempted:

"Let no one say when he is tempted, 'I am being tempted by God'; for God cannot be tempted by evil, and He Himself does not tempt anyone. But each one is tempted when he is carried away and enticed by his own lust. Then when lust has conceived, it gives birth to sin; and when sin is accomplished, it brings forth death. Do not be deceived, my beloved brethren" (James 1:13-16).

*Forgive me, Lord, for yielding to the lust of my flesh. I know that when I walk in the authority of the Holy Spirit instead of relying on my own strength, He gives me the power to resist temptation. I failed, God. I have no excuse, for You promise that You will not allow me to be tempted beyond what I am able to handle. Forgive me and cleanse me from all unrighteousness.*

Have you ever felt like a loser? Sometimes life is painful, isn't it?

Don't forget: When God called you, He called you to deny yourself, take up your cross, and follow Him (Mark 8:34). You've died to self and you've died to the opinions of others. No matter how often you're thought to be a loser, Jesus is to be your one desire. His life, lived through you, is all that counts.

Hanging on the cross, suspended between heaven and hell, Jesus found neither comfort nor comforter. He didn't look like the King of kings that day. He looked like the loser of losers! But the story didn't end there.

I don't know what your pain is, beloved—what failure you're facing, what inadequacies you wrestle with, what shattered hopes or dreams plague you, what wrong judgments haunt you. But I can tell you this: If you belong to Jesus, you may be despised, rejected, laughed at, scorned, talked about, and deemed a loser, but you're not!

The final chapter hasn't been written yet!

*O Father, thank you for the reassurance that I have worth and value, even when I feel despised and rejected. In my times of despair, help me remember that Jesus endured all this and more—and He is Your beloved Son. Remind me to focus on You instead of my circumstances so that I can have victory in the end.*

Is it hard for you to imagine God judging His own people? Bringing down the rod of correction, letting them reap the harvest of their willful disobedience? Many people think of God as a God of love—and He is. However, man's definition of love many times is a figment of his imagination, rather than a description of the real thing.

A description of real love is found in the Bible, as we read of God's relationship with His chosen and beloved people, Israel. God's judgment of Israel reveals many lessons for our lives today. Notice particularly this passage in Lamentations: "Jerusalem sinned greatly.... Her uncleanness was in her skirts; she did not consider her future. Therefore she has fallen astonishingly; she has no comforter" (1:8-9).

How this describes so many people today! Our uncleanness is our immorality. Multitudes live for the passion of the minute, not realizing that their sin can bring a lifetime of pain, not only to them but also to others. Yet when God's judgment comes—and, according to Hebrews 13:4, it will come—God's primary intent is to bring the sinner back to the safety of His arms. How much more loving could He be?

*You have made it clear in Your Word that those whom You love You reprove and discipline (Revelation 3:19). Give me wisdom not to rescue those You are judging, but simply to pray as You direct.*

Just stop for a moment, beloved, and consider this question: How much do you value God's Word? There's a growing trend—even among Christians—to treat God's Word as irrelevant. If there's one message I'd like to get across to you, it's this: God's Word is true!

Psalm 138:2 tells us God has magnified His Word together with His name. The Word stands because God stands. He is ever God, never changing. I don't know about you, dear one, but I find that comforting in times like these. We want our ears tickled, we seek the exciting and the miraculous, but too often we turn our backs on the pure, unadulterated teaching of the Word.

Speaking through Jeremiah, God said: "Let him who has My word speak My word in truth" (23:28). The Word of God is not to be treated casually, my friend.

*I praise You, dear Lord, for being the same yesterday, today, and forever. Forgive me for being more impressed with signs, miracles, and the dreams, visions, and prophecies of men than with Your Word, holiness, righteousness, sacrifice, and suffering patiently in the trials of faith. Forgive me for always looking for that new thrill, that new experience, and following the latest teaching fad rather than adhering unswervingly to Your Word.*

Which do you prefer: messages about health, wealth, healing, and miracles or teaching that walks you through a book of the Bible? Do you like to listen to the Word with pen in hand, ready to learn who God is and what He has to say? Or would you rather sing…and sing…and testify?

And what about teachers? Are you a follower of a specific man or group? Do you accept the teachings of a certain television preacher, a particular ministry, or even your own pastor without question? Or are you able to listen to a variety of teachers and examine whether they're teaching from the whole counsel of the Bible?

Those who cannot digest truth for themselves, those who have to be given predigested milk, are described as "fleshly" and "infants" (1 Corinthians 3:1-4; Hebrews 5:13). "But solid food is for the mature, who because of practice have their senses trained to discern good and evil" (Hebrews 5:14).

It's time to grow up, beloved—to go on to maturity. It's an adulterous nation that seeks signs and wonders. Get off the milk and into the solid food of God's Word.

*O God, forgive me for being swayed by my emotions, for loving the sensational and neglecting Your Word. I have left myself open to be deceived by a false gospel. Today as I delve into Your word, open my heart to Your truths so that my faith will be based on a firm foundation.*

At this moment you may be facing a crisis. Perhaps you're asking, "Doesn't God care about what happens to me? Why did He allow this in my life?"

God is sovereign! Nothing happens without His permission. "The LORD has established His throne in the heavens, and His sovereignty rules over all" (Psalm 103:19).

I don't believe there's a more reassuring message in all of Scripture than the sovereignty of God. Neither necessity nor chance nor Satan's malice controls the sequence of events or their causes. God rules supremely over all.

If we're to truly walk in the peace that passes all understanding, we must understand His character and nature—how God works in our lives. I know of so many who have been able to pass through trials as "more than conquerors" (Romans 8:37, NIV). They know that, because of His sovereignty, all things in our lives will eventually work together for good. It's all part and parcel of God's foreknowledge, and He's going to use every circumstance to make us more like Jesus (verse 28-30). Are you ready to embrace this truth for yourself?

*Father, in faith I bow my knee to You in total submission. Your Word declares that You alone control the universe and everything in it. You are Lord over this crisis. Every circumstance of my life has been sifted through Your loving hands, and today I will rest in that comforting truth.*

Beloved, it's the most powerful, liberating, peace-giving truth I've ever learned in God's Word.

God is sovereign! It's been a mainstay in my life. Resting in the sovereignty of God has held me through all the trials, all the pain—everything life has thrown my way! God is in control, and in everything I can give thanks, not because of the situation but because of the One who directs and rules over it.

Remember, God is even sovereign over your mistakes, your wrong choices. He will hold you accountable for them, but His sovereignty will not be limited by them. Hallelujah! "His sovereignty rules over all" (Psalm 103:19).

So when the pain is deepest and sharpest, engulfing the world around you and infiltrating your heart, when your failures overwhelm and threaten to paralyze you, remember: This is a testing and proving ground for your belief in the sovereignty of God and for your understanding of His heart and His omniscient omnipotence to bring good out of your pain. Forget those things that are past and press on. There's a good ending to your story (Philippians 1:6).

*Father, I believe...help my unbelief. As I faithfully read Your Word, confirm this powerful truth over and over: You are sovereign. Don't let me forget it.*

Do you ever feel as if you're groping in the dark, squinting your eyes, searching for the path as you stumble through life? Are you confused by what you hear and what you see? Sickened and discouraged because of the way life seems to be going?

Are you groping for answers to life's terrible complexities, searching for security as you look toward the very uncertain future?

Oh, beloved, the light of life is found in the Bible—the very Word of God, in whom we find light and life. You may have heard that it's full of errors, myths, and folklore, but that is a lie designed to keep you from truth. Don't succumb to finite man's judgment of God.

Listen to His Son: Jesus said, "You will know the truth, and the truth will make you free" (John 8:32). As He spoke to God in prayer, He affirmed it again for all His disciples to hear: "Your word is truth" (John 17:17).

Quit groping your way through life, beloved. You have all the light you need. Turn it on; discipline yourself to read the Bible.

*Heavenly Father, You say that Your Word is a lamp unto my feet, a light unto my path, and that those who follow You will not walk in darkness. As I anticipate each new day, may I arise before dawn and cry for help and wait for Your words (Psalm 119:147).*

We're in the midst of spiritual warfare, precious one! How well do you understand the ways of the enemy?

God's Word offers a description of the enemy's weapons, and deception looms large in that picture. This is why you find it a battle to be in the Word of God consistently. In John 8:44 Jesus said that the devil "does not stand in the truth because there is no truth in him. Whenever he speaks a lie, he speaks from his own nature, for he is a liar and the father of lies."

But, oh, dear child, you don't have to lose the battle. Remember that "greater is He who is in you than he who is in the world" (1 John 4:4). Jesus said in John 8:36, "If the Son makes you free, you will be free *indeed.*"

He has given you all the armor you need for victory. Read Ephesians 6:10-17—it's all connected with the Bible, the Word of truth. So put it on and know that God will never send you into a battle you can't win.

*O Father, thank You for Your precious Word, the sword of the Spirit. As I study the Bible and absorb its riches, show me how to clothe myself as a warrior so that I might resist the devil, standing firm in the victory You've won for me.*

Do you think you can change or alter things simply by refusing to acknowledge them? We find reality so hard to deal with. Does that describe you today, beloved? Are you afraid to go to the doctor? Or maybe to talk to a friend or family member and find out what's wrong? Or to look at your finances? Or to_____? You fill in the blank, beloved.

Somehow we think that if we ignore the problem, maybe it will go away. We try to find our own way of coping rather than crying out for help from the God of all wisdom, power, and truth. Isn't His name Jehovah-jireh—the Lord our provider—and Jehovah-shammah—the God who is there? Isn't He our ever-present help in the time of need (Psalm 46:1, NIV)?

Oh, beloved, go to the One who freely gives us all things and ask Him for the strength and wisdom to face your problem. He'll give it to you just as He promises. He's simply waiting on you.

*O Father, forgive me for burying my head in the sand. May I learn that this doesn't solve a thing—and it leaves me vulnerable to attack. You're my problem solver. Lord, work with me until I am so dependent on the Holy Spirit that at the first sign of trouble, I turn to You.*

When you channel-surf, do you find yourself stopping on various Christian television programs, amused, curious, maybe a little scornful of what you see? Hands are raised, eyes closed, bodies swaying. Maybe the congregation is laughing, jumping, carrying on while the preacher shouts his message or someone sings. Do you watch with curiosity, fascination, or possibly skepticism as people line up for healing?

Do these programs create confusion for you? Maybe you wonder, "Should that be happening to me? Am I less than spiritual if I am not doing those things or responding in that way?"

Oh, my friend, don't let television like this be the plumb line by which you measure true spirituality or the moving of God's Spirit. Listen carefully to the content of the message—if there is one. Then get in the Bible and compare the message with God's Word, which is pure truth, preserved by God and unadulterated by men. Check the message against the context of the Bible. Don't be "tossed here and there by waves and carried about by every wind of doctrine, by the trickery of men" (Ephesians 4:14). Compare the content of Christian television with 1 Thessalonians 2:3-14 and the rest of God's Word.

*O Father, help me to see the folly of not studying the Bible for myself so that I can discern true Christianity from the false messages I may see elsewhere. May the truth of your Word be my passion, my plumb line.*

Beloved, is today one of those times when you feel you're at rock bottom? Has your life become a major disappointment? So what can you do? Your first response, my friend, must be an act of pure obedience. You must believe God, no matter how you feel or what you think, no matter your circumstances.

Tighten that belt of truth. Recognize and acknowledge that every disappointment is God's appointment. God doesn't say the situation is good, but He does promise in Romans 8 that, because He's your God and you're His child, He will bring good from it.

Read James 1:2-4 with a fresh, child-like faith: "Consider it all joy, my brethren, when you encounter various trials, knowing that the testing of your faith produces endurance. And let endurance have its perfect result, so that you may be perfect and complete, lacking in nothing."

*Thank You, Lord, for the good You promise to bring from my circumstances. Make me alert to it as I bow before You with my face on rock bottom. By an act of my will, I thank You in faith and count it all joy.*

Doesn't your heart grieve when you read news reports about people suffering enormous loss in earthquakes, floods, and other cataclysmic events? It's a terrible thing to watch as villages and towns are suddenly wiped out by natural disasters over which they have no control. Man is impotent to stop the wind, floods, droughts, or plagues that ruin crops.

No one can stay the hand of God, who is behind these events.

"Not a loving God!" Yes, beloved, a loving God who uses these disasters to turn us to Him in reverential fear and respect. Consider the words of the prophet: "At night my soul longs for You, indeed, my spirit within me seeks You diligently; for when the earth experiences Your judgments the inhabitants of the world learn righteousness. Though the wicked is shown favor, he does not learn righteousness; he deals unjustly in the land of uprightness, and does not perceive the majesty of the LORD" (Isaiah 26:9-10).

Perhaps we need to redirect our grief and mourn the tragic state of our souls more than the material losses prompted by such disasters.

*God, remove our blindness. Help us to recognize that You will not allow us to continue in our sin. Open our eyes to the truth of Your holiness and majesty so that we will turn to You in fear and respect.*

Precious one, God's Word is either true or it is not true! It's as simple as that!

I don't mean to sound harsh, but when you look at all the unspeakable tragedies that people must endure, you either believe that God is in control or you don't.

Oh, beloved, how you need to see this for yourself in the Bible. As you read through the Word of God, put a mark (I use a triangle) beside every reference to God that tells you something about Him or His ways, His power and control over nature, man, and nations. Then record in the margin of your Bible what you learn about God and His sovereignty. Proverbs 23:23 says, "Buy truth, and do not sell it. Get wisdom and instruction and understanding."

Oh, beloved, thank Him for the power of His Word!

*Almighty God, although I don't understand it all, I stand amazed as I read of Your sovereignty, holiness, and love. What a privilege it is to read Your words with my own eyes and to learn for myself what You are really like! May I not stop until I've read Your book from cover to cover, learning all I can about You.*

Are you rejoicing in your salvation? Even when circumstances prompt you to ask "Why?" are you rejoicing?

Remember, precious friend, it is God's right to do with us as He pleases. He's God, and therefore we never have the right to chafe at His decision. Paul said in Romans 9:20-21, "Who are you, O man, who answers back to God? The thing molded will not say to the molder, 'Why did you make me like this,' will it? Or does not the potter have a right over the clay?" God's sovereignty is always something to ponder and study. Even more important, it's something to acknowledge before Him.

Whether you've got it all figured out or not doesn't matter. We don't have to understand it all. All we have to do, beloved, is submit to the truth of God's sovereignty.

So, little pot of clay, don't argue with God. Simply bow the knee and in perfect confidence say, "If it pleases You, it pleases me."

*Father, You are the Potter; I am the clay. Mold my life as You will so that Your Son will be glorified in me. I trust Your sovereignty, O God. I surrender to Your control, and I rejoice in You.*

Do you know what being a Christian is all about in the day-to-day situations of life?

If you're a child of God, He has given you spiritual gifts for the edification of other believers. These gifts reveal Jesus living in you, making you an extension of His hands, arms, and feet. You can see with His eyes. Listen with His ears. Speak His words.

First Peter 4:11 says, "Whoever speaks, let him speak, as it were, the utterances of God; whoever serves, let him do so as by the strength which God supplies; so that in all things God may be glorified through Jesus Christ, to whom belongs the glory and dominion forever and ever" (NASB, early editions).

Beloved, look for opportunities today to listen, to care, and to share the truths of God's Word so that others can cope with the traumas of this life. Listen for God's quiet urging to walk alongside some hurting soul, just as Jesus would if He walked upon this earth today.

*Use me today, Lord, to reach out to someone in need of Your love. Help me to watch and to listen with a heart in tune with Yours, so I won't miss a single opportunity to serve someone in Your name.*

# SEARCH MY RELATIONSHIPS

As we begin this month of examining our relationships, we must begin here: When it comes to God, where do you stand? Do you have a religion or a relationship? There is a big difference between the two, and which one you have will determine what happens to you after death. You don't want to be deceived. Whether you believe it or not, there is life after death, but it will not be a pleasant life for everyone. Despite all the stories about "seeing the light," not everyone will go to heaven. The Bible tells us that many will spend eternity in a lake of fire, including those who depended on religion in this life.

The only guarantee of heaven, clearly defined in the Bible, is a relationship: "Christ in you, the hope of glory" (Colossians 1:27).

And how can you be sure you have this relationship? How can you know Christ is in you? By the change in your life once you invite Jesus to move in and take control. "Anyone who does not practice righteousness is not of God" (1 John 3:10).

*Thank You for the promise of eternal life for those who choose to follow You. And thank You for the Holy Spirit, who not only is given as a pledge of our inheritance but is the One who enables me to conquer the desires of my flesh (Ephesians 1:14; Galatians 5:16).*

Is there someone you flat out refuse to forgive? The hurt runs deep, doesn't it? They must have done something fairly cruel or damaging if you're clinging to your anger.

May I ask how your relationship is with God?

"Fine! Fine!" you say. My friend, it cannot be fine because of the simple fact that God will not condone unforgiveness in a person's life. No matter what was done, beloved, no matter how greatly you were injured, God demands forgiveness. Matthew 18:21-35 makes that very clear. In that passage Jesus tells the story of a man who was forgiven a debt of more than ten million dollars. Afterward he refused to forgive someone who owed him the equivalent of a day's wages. When his hypocrisy and cruelty were revealed, the man was turned over to the torturers.

What is the point? Jesus says, "My heavenly Father will also do the same to you, if each of you does not forgive his brother from your heart" (verse 35). Why? Because you've been forgiven by God, you're obligated to forgive. It's part of genuine Christianity.

*O God, You know my pain. You know that I've been clinging to my anger, feeding my resentment of this person. In my own strength, I cannot possibly forgive what was done to me. Help me, Lord, to let go of my bitterness.*

God will not forgive us if we don't forgive others! That's about as plain as it gets, my friend.

In all the history of mankind, there's only one man who's never sinned and needs no forgiveness: our Lord Jesus Christ. And even totally innocent as He was, He forgave those who beat Him, mocked Him, and killed Him.

What right, then, do we as forgiven people have to withhold forgiveness from others?

First John 1:9 says, "If we confess our sins, He is faithful and righteous to forgive us our sins and to cleanse us from all unrighteousness." Accept His forgiveness and be generous in giving it to others.

Be sure your actions today match these words in Ephesians 4:32: "Be kind to one another, tender-hearted, forgiving each other, just as God in Christ also has forgiven you."

*How arrogant of me to hold a grudge against someone else after all You have forgiven me! Soften my hard heart, Lord, and replace my bitterness with Your love. Through the power of Your Holy Spirit, give me the courage and strength to forgive.*

On this Independence Day—a time when so many families gather together—do you wonder why some families seem so successful while others are falling apart? Do you want to know what you can do to assure the stability of your family and home? God has provided a plan—a co-operative plan—to help every member of your family find unity, respect, and love.

Read carefully what God says to you about your particular role: "Wives, be subject to your husbands, as is fitting in the Lord. Husbands, love your wives and do not be embittered against them. Children, be obedient to your parents in all things, for this is well-pleasing to the Lord. Fathers, do not exasperate your children, so that they will not lose heart" (Colossians 3:18-21).

Can you imagine, beloved, what would happen if each of us listened to God and did what He told us to do? What changes might take place in your home if you followed God's plan for the family?

*Lord, You have provided a clear plan for my family, a role for each of us. Now I ask that, through Your Holy Spirit, You would also provide the wisdom and love we need to follow Your plan and bring unity to our household.*

Is your marriage stale? Does your spouse seem a little distant? He rarely says he loves you. She doesn't show interest in holding your hand, and the kisses you share are mechanical, lacking the passion of your earlier years of marriage.

The tenderness, gentleness, and caring are gone. You no longer have someone with whom to share the burdens of life. You rush here, run there. No time for talking, too much to do. Both of you are trying hold down jobs, trying to keep the house neat and still find time to eat—and it's all on the run.

That, my friend, is part of the problem. Relationships, especially marriages, cannot deepen, let alone survive, "on the run." If you're always in a rush, it's hard to hold hands, enjoy a kiss, or share a moment of conversation.

It's time to make some choices about what's important to you. Can you make do with less, cut out some unnecessary activities, reduce your workload? Whatever it takes, you need to invest yourself in your marriage—before it's too late.

*I don't want to lose my marriage, Lord. Show me how I need to change my attitudes, my habits, and my priorities. I'm willing to sacrifice my personal ambitions so that we can work together to strengthen and build our relationship.*

Has your child wandered away from everything that is decent and right in God's eyes? Do you feel you've absolutely failed? You wonder what will become of her, where he will end up, and what you did wrong. Wherever you go, whatever you do, you can't get your child off your mind. His or her sins are ever before you, and you feel absolutely impotent to help.

You may feel that way, beloved, but you're not impotent. Like Moses, you have the recourse of prayer. In Psalm 106 we read of Israel's rebellion: "Therefore [God] said that He would destroy them, had not Moses His chosen one stood in the breach before Him, to turn away His wrath from destroying them" (verse 23).

The intercession of Moses prevented God's punishment. You have that same recourse, dear parent. Don't cease to pray.

*God, You brought my child into being. I may have failed, but You are greater than my failures. As Abraham put his son Isaac on the altar, so I put my child there in perfect trust. You must work Your work in my child. I trust You. I trust You because You are God and not willing that any should perish. Thank You. In faith I leave my child in Your hands.*

Do you wish you could be a perfect parent so you would have perfect children?

Know what? Being a perfect parent does not guarantee perfect children. Think with me: Who is the perfect parent? There is only one, and He's mentioned in Ephesians 3:14-15: "For this reason I bow my knees before the Father, from whom every family in heaven and on earth derives its name."

What a comfort when God reminded me that even His children are not perfect. "Foolishness is bound up in the heart of a child" (Proverbs 22:15). While we're all born in sin, the ability to live righteously is a God-given option. Ultimately each of us must choose for ourselves. No one—not even our parents—can make that choice for us.

Measure your parenting decisions against the plumb line of God's Word. Then rest in the confidence of your obedience, remembering, beloved, that the rest is up to your child.

*Sometimes being a parent is so hard, Lord. I guess You know that better than anyone else. Thank You for the assurance that I don't have to bear the full weight of this responsibility. Sometimes I need to be reminded that my child is also accountable, that one person can never set another's destiny. O Father, may my child choose to love and follow Jesus.*

Oh, beloved, sometimes we can feel so alone—even with others around us. I know. I've been there. It's not a pleasant situation, is it? You want to give up, to die—but that's not the solution because you are not alone, even if you feel like it.

You are not an orphan abandoned by your heavenly Father or your Lord! John 14:23 says you have the Father and the Son. Be at peace. Let not your heart be troubled. Jesus has given you a helper. Listen: "I will ask the Father, and He will give you another Helper, that He may be with you forever; that is the Spirit of truth.... You know Him because He abides with you and will be in you. I will not leave you as orphans; I will come to you" (John 14:16-18).

Feeling and fact can be two different things. Turn to your Helper, and know you are precious to Him.

*Thank You for the comforting presence of Your Holy Spirit, who walks with me when I pass through floodwaters and through the fire. When troubles come my way, let the Spirit bring to remembrance Your promise of peace for those who pursue a relationship with You.*

Are you feeling friendless, precious one? You're not. Jesus says, "You are My friends if you do what I command you.... I have called you friends, for all things that I have heard from My Father I have made known to you" (John 15:14-15).

You have a friend who will stick closer than a brother, and that friend—Jesus—connects you to others. I believe this is one of the reasons God lets us know in His Word that we're part of His body—members of one another. It's why we're instructed to be part of "the church," to assemble together, not only for the purpose of worship but also for fellowship.

Each of us needs a friend—a friend who is the friend of Jesus.

So turn to the people of God around you, beloved, both to find strength and courage and to *give* strength and courage!

*Lord, I want to be an instrument of Your love, and I long to receive love from You. Open my eyes to those around me who need to hear a word of encouragement. And please send someone who will give me renewed strength and hope, someone who will be the flesh-and-blood, here-and-now friend I need.*

Have your circumstances been difficult lately? Are you feeling uptight about everything that's going wrong?

When you let the worries of life get to you, it can affect your relationships with others. You become frustrated, pound things, set them down hard, or slam them! You're tempted to vent the frustration of difficult circumstances in one way or another on a person or an object. You find yourself wanting to chew out the kids, kick the cat or throw out the dog, hide and glare behind the newspaper, or just tune out the family and turn on the TV—loud! Or perhaps you only want to slam the bedroom door, crawl into bed, and pull the blankets over your head.

Beloved, this is not the way to handle frustration! When things are difficult, God says, "Let your gentle spirit be known to all men. The Lord is near" (Philippians 4:5).

God is there, my friend. Shut your mouth, and willfully give your frustrations to Him. Then take a deep breath and let the Spirit take control.

*Today, Father, I take all my frustrations and worries and drop them at Your feet. Breathe Your peace into my heart so that I can respond in love to those around me rather than letting circumstances rule my life.*

Do you angrily jerk your children around when they misbehave? Spend the majority of your time screaming at them or talking to them through clenched teeth? Or have you thrown up your hands in defeat? They're impossible to contain or restrain without a fuss, so you let them go their merry, willful, and oftentimes rude way.

If this is the situation in your home, you have a problem and so do your children. Children are a trust from God. The Bible tells us we are to "bring them up in the nurture and admonition of the Lord" (Ephesians 6:4, KJV). Admonition means "putting in mind." What do you want to put into the minds of your children? What do you want them to know, to believe, to understand about God and about life? What kind of characters do you want your children to develop?

If the future generation is to honor God and carry on the goals, values, and missions of their families, we need to give our children the time and parenting they need. Good kids don't just happen!

*Dear God, I need an outpouring of Your patience and wisdom. Help me model Your love for my children and teach them biblical principles for life. Show me what I need to do today to nurture within my children reverence and love for You.*

Someone to talk to. Someone who will listen. It's what we all need, isn't it?

The Lord is the Someone who's always there, but sometimes it helps to have a person who stands beside us to physically give us support and encouragement.

How desperately we need to understand our place in the body of Christ, to accept our responsibility to be God's "someone" in the life of one of His children.

If neighborhood children or teenagers hang around your house, you have a wonderful opportunity for ministry. Listen to them, love them, and model for them what Christianity is all about. You could be God's "someone," the person He uses to draw them to Himself.

Showing Christ's love to those around us—it's what being a believer is all about!

"As each one has received a special gift, employ it in serving one another as good stewards of the manifold grace of God" (1 Peter 4:10).

Be God's "someone" today!

*I surrender my day to You, Lord—my plans, my goals, my time—to be used as You see fit. Fill my heart with Your compassion and my mouth with Your healing words. Point me toward that person who needs someone to talk to today. Let me invest myself in another's welfare and Your kingdom.*

Are you in a difficult marriage, beloved? Does it seem as if your spouse will never come around? He or she is not brutal or mean—simply content to let things stay as they are. But you are desperate for a change. Years have dragged by as you wait for your dreams of a happy marriage to be fulfilled. Have others mentioned divorce as an option? Did they suggest that you deserve better than this?

Before you take their advice, you had better get God's.

Jesus said, "He who created them from the beginning made them male and female, and said, 'For this reason a man shall leave his father and mother and be joined to his wife, and the two shall become one flesh.' So they are no longer two, but one flesh. What therefore God has joined together, let no man separate.... And I say to you, whoever divorces his wife, except for immorality, and marries another woman commits adultery" (Matthew 19:4-6,9).

Are you going to listen to mortal man above God, beloved? Don't—you'll regret it.

*My marriage isn't what I had hoped for, Lord. I'm beginning to lose hope that it ever will be. I so desperately want to be loved and in love! I need Your strength to endure and Your wisdom to know exactly what to do. I'm willing to obey, no matter what You ask of me.*

Have you been going to bed after your mate is asleep or perhaps lying on the edge of your side of the bed, pretending to be asleep? You say you have a headache…you are tired…maybe later—but later seldom comes. Oh, my friend, let me share God's Word on this critical subject.

"The husband must fulfill his duty to his wife, and likewise also the wife to her husband. The wife does not have authority over her own body, but the husband does; and likewise also the husband does not have authority over his own body, but the wife does. Stop depriving one another, except by agreement for a time, so that you may devote yourselves to prayer, and come together again so that Satan will not tempt you because of your lack of self-control" (1 Corinthians 7:3-5).

Are you going to disobey God and put your mate in the path of temptation?

*Work in my heart, Father. Help me to love as an act of my will, to conquer my selfish desires and fulfill my duty to my spouse regardless of whether I have pleasure or not. Revive the dying embers of love as, in obedience to You, I give my spouse priority in my life, second only to You.*

What are you looking for that you cannot find? Are you saying to yourself, "If I only had the right person, the right relationship, things would be different"?

Trust me, beloved, there's only one relationship that will bring the lasting love, peace, and contentment you're longing for. You need a Father—a Father who not only promises to supply all your needs through Jesus Christ, His Son, but One who's capable and willing to do so.

"And my God will supply all your needs according to His riches in glory in Christ Jesus" (Philippians 4:19). No single person can meet all of your physical and emotional needs; only by accepting God's invitation to join His family will you find the peace, love, and satisfaction that are missing from your life.

Oh, I can't promise your circumstances will change, but this relationship will be unlike anything you've experienced before. Why? Because you'll no longer be looking to another human being to meet your needs; you'll be looking to God. And He never fails!

*Thank You, Lord, that at the cross of Christ I can find life, peace, and purpose. I praise You for Your ability to meet all of my needs, and I recognize that, because You are "Father God," You are all I need—and You are always there!*

How do you view your relationship with God? Is He simply your friend, someone to run to when things are difficult? If so, you need to examine your heart.

Do you remember what Jesus said in His Sermon on the Mount? "Why do you call Me, 'Lord, Lord,' and do not do what I say?" (Luke 6:46).

God is not merely a buddy with whom we walk down the road of life, someone to whom we just shout praises in soul-stirring songs. Our relationship with God must acknowledge His lordship in our lives. As Adonai, our Lord and Master, He has a right to expect obedience!

If you claim God as your Father, then He must also be Adonai, Master. Do you need to make some changes in your relationship with Him?

*O Lord, forgive me for failing to give You the reverence due Your name. Don't let me simply be emotionally stirred; may my worship also be that of willing service, as Your Word teaches. Search my heart and reveal all the areas I have not surrendered to You, areas in which I fail to serve You. I acknowledge You again as Lord and Master of my life, and I commit myself in obedience to You.*

Dear friend, the Bible tells us that we manifest our love to the Lord by loving those who are His. With this in mind, ask yourself how deeply you love those whom the Lord loves. Have you neglected Him by neglecting others?

The message of Matthew 25:40 is clear: "Truly I say to you, to the extent that you did it to one of these brothers of Mine, even the least of them, you did it to Me." First John 5:1 says, "Whoever loves the Father loves the child born of Him."

The world is watching to see whether Christians truly are different. Jesus said, "By this all men will know that you are My disciples, if you have love for one another" (John 13:35).

Next to loving God, it's the most important part of being a Christian. Are you loving your neighbor as yourself, beloved?

*Heavenly Father, I ask You to transform my attitude toward my neighbor through the indwelling of the Holy Spirit. Give me a heart full of Your love, eyes that see the pain You see, and a willingness to show Your love in tangible ways rather than in mere words.*

Is your life working, beloved? Are your relationships just what you want them to be? Are you getting along with your spouse, your children, your coworkers?

Precious one, when we sin we know it—and God knows it! If sin has damaged your relationship with someone, then confess it. Don't gloss over it or sugarcoat it. Call it by name. Say, "Lord, this is how I failed you. I lied. I responded cruelly. I ignored a plea for help." Then tell Him you're willing to do whatever is necessary to mend the relationship if He will simply show you what to do.

Remember, if you're receiving a message from God, it will be in keeping with His character and with His Word. Philippians 3:15 tells us He "will reveal that also to you."

Go to Him, beloved! Make it right. Then observe, listen, and do according to all He tells you!

*Instead of letting Your love rule in my heart, I acted out of selfishness. I wounded one of Your children, and I failed You. I confess my sin, Lord, and I humbly ask You to show me what I need to do to make amends.*

There always will be some people you and I just can't please. No matter how hard we try, there's just no satisfying them.

Don't despair, beloved. Jesus understands your frustration. He lived among the same type of people. Read what He said in Luke 7:31-32. It's written just for you:

"To what then shall I compare the men of this generation, and what are they like? They are like children who sit in the market place and call to one another, and they say, 'We played the flute for you, and you did not dance; we sang a dirge, and you did not weep.'"

No matter what Jesus or His disciples did, they couldn't please some men. So you can be sure that Jesus understands your frustration.

Make your one goal to please God. If you do that, you've done all you can because you will respond to others as He would have you respond. And if they still complain, remember Romans 8:31: "If God is for us, who is against us?"

*Forgive me, Father, for losing sight of what's most important, for focusing my efforts on pleasing others rather than on pleasing You. Thank You for Your unconditional love, which doesn't depend on my feeble efforts but on Your unbreakable covenant promise. May I focus on that and extend it freely to others— even to those who won't be pleased!*

Do you know how to love your spouse? From the womb, women differ from men because God made them different.

If you are a married man, it is your responsibility before God to love your wife God's way—sacrificially. And if you are a married woman, it is your responsibility to fulfill your role as a wife.

Consider the Word of God: "Wives, be subject to your own husbands, as to the Lord. For the husband is the head of the wife, as Christ also is the head of the church.... As the church is subject to Christ, so also the wives ought to be to their husbands in everything.

"Husbands, love your wives, just as Christ also loved the church and gave Himself up for her.... Husbands ought also to love [nourish, cherish] their own wives as their own bodies.... Nevertheless, each individual among you also is to love his own wife even as himself, and the wife must see to it that she respects her husband" (Ephesians 5:22-33).

If God commands you to love your wife, then it is a matter of your will, not your emotions. Will you?

And will you allow your husband to be the head? Will you respect him as God commands?

*Dear Lord, help me to love You so much that I fulfill the responsibility You have given me, regardless of the response of my spouse and regardless of the changing values of this world.*

Beloved, what does God's grace mean to you? How is it impacting your life? Your marriage? The difficulties you face every day?

Meditate on these comforting words in 2 Corinthians 12:9-10: "And He has said to me, 'My grace is sufficient for you, for power is perfected in weakness.' Most gladly, therefore, I will rather boast about my weaknesses, so that the power of Christ may dwell in me. Therefore I am well content with weaknesses, with insults, with distresses, with persecutions, with difficulties, for Christ's sake; for when I am weak, then I am strong."

God's grace offers all the strength you need: strength to persevere in a difficult marriage; strength to be a faithful and consistent witness in your workplace; strength to face temptations and trials.

Oh yes, my dear friend, God's grace is sufficient!

*I bow my knees before You, Lord, and ask You to strengthen me with power through Your Holy Spirit, so that I can be rooted and grounded in the love and grace of Christ. I thank You that grace is power—power to be all I ought to be.*

Are you suffering because someone is on your case? He or she is dealing harshly with you, and you cannot walk away because that person is also your boss.

What does God say to do?

"Be submissive to your masters with all respect, not only to those who are good and gentle, but also to those who are unreasonable. For this finds favor, if for the sake of conscience toward God a person bears up under sorrows when suffering unjustly. For what credit is there if, when you sin and are harshly treated, you endure it with patience? But if when you do what is right and suffer for it you patiently endure it, this finds favor with God" (1 Peter 2:18-20).

Continue to be respectful and patiently endure the wrong. Jesus will show you how because He's been there, done that (verses 21-25). Simply allow them to see Christ doing it again through you.

*Help me to do my work as though I were working for You, my Lord. Because I value Your favor above all else, I will endure through these unjust circumstances, trusting that You are working Your good purpose in my life and in the life of the person who is behaving this way. Let my actions and attitude bring glory to Your name.*

Beloved, do you know that the more you comprehend the greatness of God's forgiveness, the more you'll love? And the more you love, the easier it will be for you to forgive others?

Ephesians 5:2 says, "Walk in love, just as Christ also loved you and gave Himself up for us, an offering and a sacrifice to God as a fragrant aroma."

Love is an action word. Loving someone you have forgiven may be hard, but true forgiveness will make that kind of sacrifice. Jesus not only forgives you, He treats you as if you had never sinned against Him. That's God's type of forgiveness, and your forgiveness is to be just like His!

"And this commandment we have from Him," 1 John 4:21 says, "that the one who loves God should love his brother also."

*Thank You, precious Lord, for Your example of genuine love and forgiveness. Despite my fleshly desire for revenge, I choose today to act in love toward those who have hurt me. Instead of protecting myself, I trust You to defend me.*

What about the children in your life? Are you careful with them? Do you give them time and attention?

Remember Jesus' words in Matthew 18:5-6: "Whoever receives one such child in My name receives Me; but whoever causes one of these little ones who believe in Me to stumble, it would be better for him to have a heavy millstone hung around his neck, and to be drowned in the depth of the sea."

I'm sure the children who surrounded Jesus on this occasion were wide-eyed in amazement, their little elbows poking one another. "Hey! We matter! We're no bother! See, Jesus is not too busy for us because we are important!"

Beloved, will your children find it natural to go to Jesus because they've lived tucked under your loving arm?

*O Lord, when I become impatient, remind me that children are precious in Your sight. Help me abide in You to such an extent that my children see Your love in my eyes, hear Your love in my words, and feel Your love in my touch. May I remember that what I'm sowing now will bring a harvest later.*

Beloved, what's your marriage like? If you're a man, are you fulfilling your role as a husband should? What about you, my woman friend, are you submitting to your husband as to the Lord?

As a husband, God demands in Ephesians 5 that you not only assume the responsibilities of headship but that you live in the attitude of Christ as the sacrificial lover of your wife. Does that describe you? Nowhere does the Word of God say that you are to command obedience from your wife; rather, you are to win it with love.

As a wife, are you a sensible and pure woman, a faithful keeper of your home as we're instructed in Titus 2:5 (KJV)? Are you a woman of great worth, as described in Proverbs 31:10-31, one who brings her husband praises?

As old-fashioned as these words may sound, precious one, to do these things as a husband or wife means you're faithful to the covenant of marriage—that you're not seeking to deal treacherously with one another.

What I'm saying is not popular, but it is biblical!

*Thank You for the wonderful gift of my spouse. I believe You placed us together so that we could bring each other comfort and strength as You refine and mold each of us into the image of Your Son. Help me today to be sensitive to my spouse's needs and to meet them with gracious selflessness.*

Wouldn't it be great to have a family you could always depend on? A family of such closeness that if one member suffers, they all suffer and if one rejoices, they all rejoice?

One day when Jesus was told that His mother and brothers had arrived, He said, "Who are My mother and My brothers?... Whoever does the will of God, he is My brother and sister and mother" (Mark 3:33,35).

When you enter into relationship with God, you are joined in covenant with all the other members of the body of Christ—your brothers and sisters.

The book of Acts tells us that "all those who had believed were together and had all things in common" (2:44). They shared their possessions with anyone in need. They shared meals together "with gladness and sincerity of heart, praising God and having favor with all the people" (verses 46-47).

Think about it, dear one. If you were to live this way, how would it revolutionize your relationship with other Christians? Would it dispel the loneliness so many feel?

*Let Your love reign in my heart, God, so that I can obey Your instructions to Your church to encourage one another, build up one another, appreciate one another, live in peace with one another, and esteem one another in love. Remind me to be given to hospitality—to shut off the TV and open my home to Your family.*

Are you always striving to do the right thing, to make yourself acceptable to your friends, your family, to everyone?

Beloved, when God is our focus, everything else—including "self"—has to take a back seat. He's the only One we have to please! Galatians 1:10 says, "For am I now seeking the favor of men, or of God? Or am I striving to please men? If I were still trying to please men, I would not be a bond-servant of Christ."

When we are set free from the bondage of trying to please others, no one will be able to make us miserable or dissatisfied.

Oh, dear one, if you know you have pleased God, contentment will be your consolation, for what pleases God will please you. If it doesn't please others, that's their problem, not yours.

Isn't that refreshing?

*What a relief to know that I can cease striving and rest in You! The longing of my heart is to walk so closely with You that all other concerns fade into the background. Purify my heart until Your image is reflected in me and I am content and freed in my obedience to You—the only One who is to be my God.*

Wouldn't you love to be the life-giver to someone else? I don't mean simply being a mother or father; I'm talking about giving *real* life!

Oh, beloved, when we're willing to die, to lose our lives for Christ's sake, it brings life to others. John 12:24 says: "Truly, truly, I say to you, unless a grain of wheat falls into the earth and dies, it remains alone; but if it dies, it bears much fruit."

Jesus was born to die so that we could live—that was His purpose. Oh, that we would be willing to be poured out for others! Will you share His life with someone else today in word and in deed so they can see your good works, hear your words of truth, and then, hopefully, desire to be an imitation of you—and of Christ (1 Thessalonians 1:1-10)?

*I am not ashamed of the gospel of Christ! Use me today, Lord, to spread the light of Your truth to those in darkness. I'm willing to be poured out as a sacrifice of faith to bring life to others.*

Are you married to an unbeliever? Are you thinking of leaving? There's no evidence he or she will ever accept God's lordship, and you're wondering if you and your children might be better off if you weren't living with an unbeliever. Before you go any further, take time to contemplate God's Word on this subject:

"If any brother has a wife who is an unbeliever, and she consents to live with him, he must not divorce her. And a woman who has an unbelieving husband, and he consents to live with her, she must not send her husband away. For the unbelieving husband is sanctified through his wife, and the unbelieving wife is sanctified through her believing husband; for otherwise your children are unclean, but now they are holy" (1 Corinthians 7:12-14).

Be encouraged, beloved. Something about your presence as a believer sets your family apart for God. Christ living in you can work a miracle in your spouse's heart.

*Thank You for this encouraging reminder that You have a special purpose for me in my marriage. Give me the strength to live in consistent obedience so that, through my example, my spouse may be drawn to You.*

How committed should we be in our relationship with other members of Christ's body?

When Paul wrote to the believers in Corinth, he reminded them that as Christians they were to abound in the gracious work of giving. He wrote in 2 Corinthians 8:7, 13-14: "But just as you abound in everything, in faith and utterance and knowledge and in all earnestness and in the love we inspired in you, see that you abound in this gracious work also.... For this is not for the ease of others and for your affliction, but by way of equality—at this present time your abundance being a supply for their need, so that their abundance also may become a supply for your need."

Beloved, think what it would mean to the body of Jesus Christ—and to the work of Jesus Christ—if we were to live in the fullness of our covenant with God, remembering that as Jesus gave up riches and became poor for our sake, so we are to share our lives, possessions, and monies with others.

*In entering into covenant with You, I committed my whole life, including all of my possessions, to Your service. All that I have is a gift from Your hand, and I willingly offer it up to You for the work of Christ.*

Does Jesus Christ have first priority in your life, beloved, above all other relationships? If the answer is no, something is very wrong.

When we thoroughly understand that a covenant relationship supersedes all others, we can grasp the gravity of our Lord's call to those who would enter into covenant with Him. Luke 14:26 says: "If anyone comes to Me, and does not hate his own father and mother and wife and children and brothers and sisters, yes, and even his own life, he cannot be My disciple."

Examine your heart. If you've been giving Jesus second place to anyone or anything, confess it as sin right now, dear one. This should have been the agreement from the beginning. Jesus, your covenant partner, takes preeminence in all things, all relationships.

*I confess, dear Jesus, that I have allowed other commitments to take priority over my relationship with You. Please forgive me. It was ignorance and folly. Thank You for showing this to me and forgiving me. Show me how to nourish our relationship so that You are my all-consuming love.*

# AUGUST

---

# LEAD ME
# TO INTEGRITY

Can you say to others, "Follow me"? Or do you think to say such a thing would be absolutely presumptuous on your part? Perhaps your reply might be along these lines: "I wouldn't tell anyone to follow me. I would tell them to follow the Lord Jesus Christ."

You are right. They should follow Jesus Christ. But let me ask you another question: Are *you* following Jesus Christ? If your answer is yes, then why couldn't you say, "Follow me"? Sometimes people need role models they can see and hear. It was this way with the Thessalonians. They became imitators of Paul, Silvanus, and Timothy—and, consequently, of the Lord (1 Thessalonians 1:6).

Think about the words of the apostle Paul: "Be imitators of me, just as I also am of Christ" (1 Corinthians 11:1). "Join in following my example, and observe those who walk according to the pattern you have in us" (Philippians 3:17).

If you can't say, "Follow me," shape up your walk, beloved. We desperately need godly role models of Christ.

*Lord, help me to live with such integrity that I can urge others to follow my example. Let my life be a true reflection of Your Son, who entrusted Himself to You and did always those things that pleased You.*

Do you have integrity in all that you do, or do you fudge, as the expression goes, on the little things? Do you use postage stamps from the office supply cabinet for personal mail? Or "fib" about your child's true age so you can get a cheaper ticket? Or add just a little extra to your expense account in case you forgot something?

And what about your words? Do you stand by your commitments? Can people rely on your word to be trustworthy? Is your yes, yes and your no, no?

Your answer to these questions reveals a lot about your character. If you occasionally are guilty of fudging the truth—in word or in deed—you may justify your behavior by saying, "No one's perfect. Who could live by such high standards?"

Jesus did, beloved. He said, "I do nothing on My own initiative, but I speak these things as the Father taught Me.... I always do the things that are pleasing to Him" (John 8:28-29).

Since Jesus had integrity in all He did, can't you live the same way if He lives in you? Of course, dear one; it is simply a matter of obedience.

*Forgive me, Lord, for justifying my sin and measuring my behavior against the world's standards. By the power of the Holy Spirit who lives in me, I commit to living a life in keeping with Your holy standards of integrity.*

Have you been caught doing something wrong? It's embarrassing and painful, isn't it? The question is, why are you in pain—because you got caught or because you hurt God?

Think about that in light of 2 Corinthians 7:9-10: "I now rejoice, not that you were made sorrowful, but that you were made sorrowful to the point of repentance; for you were made sorrowful according to the will of God, so that you might not suffer loss in anything through us. For the sorrow that is according to the will of God produces a repentance without regret, leading to salvation, but the sorrow of the world produces death."

There are two kinds of sorrow: a worldly sorrow that produces death and a godly sorrow that brings salvation. Be sure, beloved, that your sorrow is prompted by genuine repentance.

*In true repentance and with a broken heart, I bow before You and confess my sin. I have done what is evil in Your sight, Lord, and I am ashamed. I ask You to forgive me and cleanse me from my sin.*

What kind of an employee are you? Would you be pleased to have your boss know everything you do from the minute you get to work until you leave? In other words, are you the best employee you can be? How is your stewardship in regard to time, supplies, and talents? Do you steal time from your employer or do you rob other employees of their time by engaging them in talk that keeps them from their jobs?

If Jesus Christ were your employer, would you work harder? Be more conscientious?

Do you know what God says about our work ethic? "Whatever you do, do your work heartily, as for the Lord rather than for men, knowing that from the Lord you will receive the reward of the inheritance. It is the Lord Christ whom you serve" (Colossians 3:23-24).

May that knowledge guide our work today.

*Gracious heavenly Father, I don't want to do anything that would bring shame to Your name. As I move through the day, help me to remember that people are watching to see whether my relationship with You makes a genuine difference in my life. Help me to work, talk, and act in a way that brings honor and glory to You.*

Do you want to run away from your responsibilities? From all that people are demanding of you? Where will you run? What will you do when you get there? Will you come to regret running away?

Sometimes we take a course of action without stopping to think about the consequences. We don't look ahead to the sense of defeat, failure, and shame that will plague us. We forget that our escape route may lead only to greater trouble.

When the urge to run strikes your heart, remember that God has promised never to desert you or forsake you. Meditate on the encouraging words of Isaiah 46:4: "Even to your old age I will be the same, and even to your graying years I will bear you! I have done it, and I will carry you; and I will bear you and I will deliver you."

The only place you need to run is into the all-sufficient arms of your Savior. They're open wide—as wide as Calvary.

*When the pressures of life seem overwhelming, I want to cling to the promises in Your Word. I will not fear, for You are with me. I will not anxiously look about, for You are my God. You will strengthen me, You will help me, and You will uphold me with Your righteous right hand. I believe this, and I choose to rest in You.*

Do you have doubts about something you are doing? Are you wondering if God approves of what you are doing? It seems a little "iffy," and you get a nagging feeling inside that your actions really aren't pleasing in His sight. Yet you have Christian friends who do the same thing, and it doesn't seem to bother them. As a matter of fact, they are telling you to get over your guilt trip, relax, and just do it.

What are you going to do?

You had better listen to God and not to your friends. God says, "The faith which you have, have as your own conviction before God. Happy is he who does not condemn himself in what he approves.... Whatever is not from faith is sin" (Romans 14:22-23).

Oh, dear child of God, are you going to base your decision on your friends' encouragement—or on the holy Word of God?

*Dear Lord, I want my actions to be pleasing in Your sight, no matter what anyone else thinks of me. I accept the fact that only I can take responsibility for my decisions. I believe that the hesitation I feel is a prompting of the Holy Spirit, and I am determined to turn from my sin and seek Your will.*

Are you a hypocrite? Maybe you're into pornography, or maybe you're mistreating your husband or wife. You're a lousy spouse and parent, but you're seen as a leader in your church—a Sunday school teacher, a deacon, or an elder.

Jesus warned His disciples: "Beware of the leaven of the Pharisees, which is hypocrisy. But there is nothing covered up that will not be revealed, and hidden that will not be known" (Luke 12:1-2).

The Pharisees pretended to be righteous, but inwardly they were not. Jesus compared their actions to cleaning the outside of a cup and a dish, while leaving the inside dirty. On the surface they appeared righteous, but inside they were "full of hypocrisy and lawlessness" (Matthew 23:28). So He said, "How will you escape the sentence of hell?" (verse 33).

You can pretend to be righteous, but nothing is hidden from God. Your mask will eventually be pulled off, and your sin will be revealed. The justice of God, the righteousness of God—the very character of God—requires it.

*Lord God, You know me better than I know myself. You probe my actions and examine my heart's attitude toward You. Please reveal to me any hypocrisy, any conflict between the truths I claim to believe and the actions that characterize my life, and then give me the strength to change accordingly.*

If you want to be blessed by God, to have peace in your heart, then you must live God's way, beloved. You cannot sin and expect to be blessed by God.

So how can you keep from sinning?

- Realize you're never above temptation. Your flesh is what entices you, and you'll live with your flesh until the day you die.
- Flee from lust. Get out of there fast, and stay far away (2 Timothy 2:22).
- Be careful about who you choose to spend your time with. "Bad company corrupts good morals" (1 Corinthians 15:33). "Pursue righteousness, faith, love and peace, with those who call on the Lord from a pure heart" (2 Timothy 2:22).
- Acknowledge that in your flesh there dwells no good thing, and "keep watching and praying that you may not enter into temptation," remembering that "the spirit is willing, but the flesh is weak" (Matthew 26:41).
- Keep eternity before your eyes. "Set your mind on the things above" (Colossians 3:2).

Do these things and you'll be blessed—mightily.

*I acknowledge my weakness, Lord, and I choose to rest in the strength of Your Holy Spirit. Help me to focus on eternity, resisting the enticing distractions of material and temporal things. I want to live Your way.*

Dear one, is your life sending mixed signals? Can people tell that you belong to Christ? Are you seeking to be holy by living a life of obedience to God?

Oh, beloved, if not, why not?

Let me show you 1 Peter 2:9: "But you are a chosen race, a royal priesthood, a holy nation, a people for God's own possession, so that you may proclaim the excellencies of Him who has called you out of darkness into His marvelous light."

Proclaim the excellencies of Him! Does your life do that?

Precious one, God is looking for men, women, and young people—someone just like you—who will tremble at His Word. He's looking for those who will seek to be holy as He is holy! Are you willing, beloved?

*Almighty God, You have called me to live in the world but come out of its mores, morals, and philosophies and be separate. In faith I willingly surrender my life to You, believing that through the Holy Spirit in me, I have the ability to live in obedience and holiness. O Father, I long to be a living testimony to Your excellencies.*

Adultery is an offense that causes much distress, and it has become appallingly common—even among those who call themselves Christians.

Physical adultery causes many a head to wag within the church—as well it should. But do we respond as strongly to *spiritual* adultery?

James 4:4 warns, "You adulteresses, do you not know that friendship with the world is hostility toward God? Therefore whoever wishes to be a friend of the world makes himself an enemy of God." Such spiritual behavior causes our covenant partner, God Himself, to weep. His "pure virgin" has been deceived, beguiled, led astray from pure devotion to Christ (2 Corinthians 11:2).

What about you, precious child of God, are you guilty of adultery—physical or spiritual? Confess it. And as Jesus said in John 8:11, "Sin no more"!

*Heavenly Father, I confess that my heart has been drawn away from pure devotion to You. I've tolerated sin in my life, looking to people for affirmation rather than measuring my actions against the unchanging standards of Your holy Word. Please forgive me and restore my relationship with You.*

Are you letting down your guard? Looking at things you shouldn't be looking at—on television, the Internet, or maybe from the video store? Buying sleazy magazines at the newsstand and then trashing them before you get home?

Many people justify such behavior by saying they're just curious. Be warned, my friend. It's a deadly, addictive curiosity that will destroy you. It awakens illegitimate desires. Introduces you to thoughts you've never entertained before. And while such material may be bringing you temporal pleasure right now, it will take you captive until you become its miserable slave, shackled by invisible chains that leave your soul raw and bleeding.

Listen to God's Word: "Beloved, I urge you…to abstain from fleshly lusts which wage war against the soul" (1 Peter 2:11). Don't get pulled into Satan's trap!

*Lord, thank You for the warnings offered in Your Word. I want to walk in obedience to Your instruction to examine everything carefully, hold fast to that which is good, and abstain from every form of evil. Open my eyes to anything that could lead me away from You.*

Beloved, how sensitive are you to sin?

We enjoy hearing about God's love, but we tend to skip over the fact that God is righteous and holy, a God of wrath.

His heart is grieved when we tolerate sin in our midst, closing our eyes to it in our own lives and in our own churches. God will not let our rebellion go unanswered; His character will not allow it.

Our holy, immutable God tells us in His Word that, "if we judged ourselves rightly, we would not be judged. But when we are judged, we are disciplined by the Lord so that we will not be condemned along with the world" (1 Corinthians 11:31-32).

Oh beloved, don't take this lightly. Watch what enters your mind. Watch your desires. Bring every emotion to Him, and if it's not in accord with His Word, reject it. Keep your heart pure! Determine what is sin! Have nothing to do with it!

*Lord God, break my heart with the things that break Your heart. Purify me, and eliminate any shred of rebellion or sin in my life. I want to walk in integrity, blameless before You.*

Are you being challenged because of your commitment to the Lord? Perhaps you're coping with the animosity of a loved one, the loss of position or reputation, or the loss of a dream.

Take some time today to read Daniel chapter 6. In this passage, jealous men sought Daniel's demise, but Daniel came out the victor. And the men who had maliciously accused him were themselves devoured by lions.

Do victories like that just happen? No! They are won just as Daniel's battle was won—on our knees, in our closets, clinging to all that we know of our God.

When your faith is challenged, when you feel threatened, remember that by faith Daniel shut the mouths of lions—and you can too.

"Therefore, my beloved brethren, be steadfast, immovable, always abounding in the work of the Lord, knowing that your toil is not in vain in the Lord" (1 Corinthians 15:58).

*Lord, You know my heart, and You know that I want only to please You. Give me the strength to stand firm in the face of unjust criticism, the pressure of my peers, or the loss of my position and my dreams. Give me the courage to be faithful and to trust You for the outcome.*

I wonder how many of us fully realize what it means to enter into the New Covenant—to become a covenant partner with the Lord Jesus Christ?

Oh, beloved, how I long to share with you what God has taught me about covenant. It's one of the most precious truths I've ever learned.

In John 6:35 Jesus refers to Himself as "the bread of life." Later He says, "He who eats My flesh and drinks My blood abides in Me, and I in Him" (verse 56). He was referring to the covenant meal, in which the two parties each committed themselves to serving the other for life. The disciples understood what Jesus was saying, and some walked away, unwilling to make such a sacrifice. They knew that covenant is a serious commitment—a commitment unto death—and Jesus' popularity was waning. They weren't willing to risk their lives for Him.

Have you given serious thought to your covenant relationship to the Lord Jesus Christ? Are you willing to serve Him, even when He's unpopular?

*Thank You for this reminder of the seriousness of my commitment to You. I have given my life to You as a living sacrifice, and I can't take it back—nor would I want to. The joy of my heart is to serve You faithfully, no matter what.*

Beloved, are you cheating God? Claiming to believe one thing yet doing another?

Years ago I met a remarkable Muslim woman. As we talked, she kept shaking her head and saying, "You know, if you really believe what you're saying, Kay, you couldn't do anything else but live the way you're teaching."

How right she is! Beloved, to truly believe on Jesus is to acknowledge that Jesus is God, my Savior, my Master, the Promised One, and to live in obedience to what I profess. We cannot swindle God by professing allegiance to Him and then living a life that's a sham!

In Malachi 1:14 God says, "I am a great King...and My name is feared among the nations."

How about you, beloved? Does your life give the reverence due His name?

*Dear God, in this moment I ask You to examine my heart and reveal any way in which my actions are inconsistent with my faith. I want my life to boldly declare my love for You and my commitment to You. I don't want to live any other way!*

My friend, what's keeping you from total commitment to Christ? Is it your career? Your ministry? What's hindering you?

When Paul wrote his letter to the Galatians, he was responding to a dangerous situation within the church. Some men had come in and preached another gospel, and the Galatians were in danger of believing it. Their faith had been sidetracked.

I hope you realize that some people today are teaching the wrong gospel. Sometimes it's referred to as "easy believism"—all you have to do is claim salvation; then you can continue on just as you were. But salvation isn't a matter of winning a door prize. Salvation is a call to walk, as Romans 6:4 says, "in newness of life."

Beloved, simply beginning the Christian life is not enough. It's a race to the finish—in God's lane, God's way! And if you're the real thing, you will finish, enduring to the end (Hebrews 3:6,14). If Paul sent a letter to you today, would he write, "You were running well; what hindered you from obeying the truth?"

*I confess that my faith has been sidetracked by the cares of this world, by my desire to achieve success. But today, fixing my eyes on Jesus, I choose to lay aside every encumbrance and the sin that so easily entangles me. In the strength of the Holy Spirit, I will run with endurance, following the path of righteousness.*

Beloved, we desperately need people who have determined in their hearts they will stand for what is right. We need men, women, teens and, yes, even children of character and conviction!

Dear one, you may be a quiet, reserved, behind-the-scenes kind of person, but you can be a brave and noble person. You can live boldly according to your convictions and the need of the hour.

The prophet Deborah was like that. The people were holed up behind the city gates without shields or spears to defend themselves. And Deborah decided, "That's enough." She arose, "a mother in Israel" (Judges 5:7), and God used her to lead her people to victory (chapters 4–5).

Oh, beloved, it's time for us to awake and arise, to be people of conviction, people who will stand for God in an evil and perverse generation!

*Lord, give me the courage to live boldly, to stand firm in my convictions, and to remain faithful to You in the midst of the evil of this world. I make myself available to You. Use me to lead others to the victory that is theirs in You.*

Dear one, do you live the way you believe? Do God's precepts permeate your marriage? Your business? Your daily life?

Oh, beloved, my life's passion is to help as many as I can to study God's Word *inductively*—to examine the Bible in depth and discern His truths for themselves—so that they will have God's plumb line to check out all they hear and are taught, rather than relying on interpretations by others. The world is looking for people who really believe and live what they say. And that's exactly the problem with much of the professing church, isn't it? We honor Him with our lips, but our hearts are far from Him.

Our marriages, our families, our churches, our society, our morals are eroding. Our nation needs the pure, unadulterated Word of God.

Didn't our Lord say to His Father, "Sanctify them in the truth; Your word is truth" (John 17:17)? We can't live what we don't know.

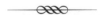

*Dear God, I so want to know, understand, and take Your Word to heart that it saturates my thoughts, my words, my entire life.*

Has anyone ever challenged the genuineness of your Christianity because your lifestyle isn't godly? How did you react? You ought to thank that person for loving God and you enough to risk your relationship. They're concerned for your soul because they know that real Christians don't live in habitual sin.

True Christians walk in obedience to God's commandments. That's not to say they don't disobey from time to time (1 John 2:1-2), but it's not the habit of their lives. To not obey His commandments is to be lawless, and "sin is lawlessness" (1 John 3:4).

"You know that He appeared in order to take away sins.... No one who abides in Him sins [habitually]; no one who sins has seen Him or knows Him.... The one who practices sin is of the devil.... The Son of God appeared for this purpose, to destroy the works of the devil. No one who is born of God practices sin, because His seed abides in him; and he cannot sin, because he is born of God" (1 John 3:5-6,8-9).

How does your life stack up against that?

*Lord, speak to my heart right now as I wait in silence. Reveal to me the truth about my condition. Show me whether my life is truly surrendered to You, whether I really have the anointing of the Holy Spirit abiding in me.*

Are you in a situation where you want to take the wrong way out? You're weary of the battle, exhausted from trying to do what is right. Or maybe you feel that, no matter how obedient you are, it won't change things anyway.

Have things gotten so bad that you simply want to check out, give up in despair, let your emotions and thoughts run amuck?

Whatever happens, don't do it, beloved. You have God's promise to walk with you no matter what, to help you overcome the temptation. If you give in, you'll have no excuse.

Remember Jude 24 says that God "is able to keep you from stumbling, and to make you stand in the presence of His glory blameless with great joy."

God can keep you from stumbling. Don't let go of His hand, beloved.

*You have promised, Father, that the testing of my faith will produce endurance. Your Word also says that You know how to rescue the godly from temptation. Rescue me, Lord. I need Your help and Your wisdom to keep from stumbling.*

Would you like to be unshackled—set free from ordering your life according to the dictates and philosophies of the world?

When I talk about being unshackled, I mean you would become confident in what you believe about life and how it is to be ordered and lived out. You would be so secure that you could walk with shoulders back and head held high on a path you know to be right—and do it graciously, with class! Wouldn't it be wonderful to have that kind of confidence?

You can! It comes by knowing and living according to God's precepts. The psalmist said, "And I will walk at liberty, for I seek Your precepts.... From Your precepts I get understanding; therefore I hate every false way" (Psalm 119:45,104).

Study God's Word inductively. The method will be an answer to your prayers, and the fruit will bring untold assurance to your life.

*Thank You for the confidence I have through Your Word, a confidence that enables me to draw near to You with a sincere heart, in full assurance of faith. I joyfully claim the promises of Your Word, confident in Your unwavering faithfulness.*

Are you dealing with a habit, a sin, or an addiction you can't seem to shake and therefore living in torment? You're ashamed. You hate it—and you're beginning to hate yourself for your weakness. Oh, beloved, this torture doesn't have to continue.

According to God's Word, if you're a true child of God you don't have to live that way. Romans 6 says your old self was crucified with Christ that your body of sin might be rendered inoperative. You no longer have to be a slave of sin; you've been set free. Therefore don't let sin rule in your physical body; don't give in to its cravings (verses 6-7,12).

The next time the craving, the desire comes simply say aloud, " I'm no longer a slave to my body. By God's power I will not do that." Walk away, liberated one. You don't have to yield. As you resist the devil and his temptations over and over again, you'll find that your body's power is rendered inoperative.

Start now, one desire at a time. Join others who've found freedom.

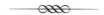

*My heart is filled with thanks for the Holy Spirit dwelling within me, who has set me free from the law of sin and death. I rejoice that by my identification in Jesus' death, burial, and resurrection, sin is no longer master over me. I have been freed from slavery to corruption.*

What kind of company do you keep, beloved? Friends have a tremendous influence on our lives. Who you spend time with may determine where you will end up or what you will be like. This is why God tells us, "Do not be deceived: 'Bad company corrupts good morals'" (1 Corinthians 15:33).

What we all need is godly friends, true friends. Ecclesiastes tells us, "Two are better than one because they have a good return for their labor. For if either of them falls, the one will lift up his companion. But woe to the one who falls when there is not another to lift him up" (4:9-10).

Now that you know what God says about friends, why don't you ask Him to give you a friend like this—and make up your mind to be this kind of a friend yourself.

*Dear heavenly Father, I pray that You will surround me with people who will encourage me to live according to Your Word, people who will hold me accountable to maintain integrity in every area of my life. And give me the wisdom and courage to be this kind of friend to others.*

Have you blown it? Made a mistake? Failed? Sinned? Are you reaping the consequences of your lack of integrity? You walked the wrong way because your thinking was skewed. Now you find yourself in trouble—with no apparent relief—because, as the Bible says, "She did not consider her future. Therefore she has fallen astonishingly" (Lamentations 1:9).

So what do you do? How can you make things right?

Remember the Word of God: "For if He causes grief, then He will have compassion according to His abundant lovingkindness. For He does not afflict willingly or grieve the sons of men" (Lamentations 3:32-33).

The trouble you're experiencing is a consequence of your sin, but God stands waiting to forgive you, if only you will turn to Him.

*God, I confess that I've been living in a way that's not pleasing to You, a way that deserves Your just judgment. Father, I'm sorry—truly sorry. Not just because I got caught and because others know about it, but I am sorry because this is displeasing to You.*

*I agree with You, Lord. I embrace what You say about my actions, and I want to think and act the way You want me to. I now commit myself to obedience, and I trust You to give me the power to live accordingly.*

Are you having a problem with your eyes? Are they drawn to the sensual, the forbidden, maybe even the perverted. You used to stand at the magazine racks and just casually look. Now you pick up the magazine and thumb through the pages. Or maybe you've started watching certain programs on television. It began with curiosity, but now you're hooked and you know it.

What does the Word of God have to say about this? "Everyone who looks at a woman with lust for her has already committed adultery with her in his heart. If your right eye makes you stumble, tear it out and throw it from you.... If your right hand makes you stumble, cut it off and throw it from you; for it is better for you to lose one of the parts of your body, than for your whole body to go into hell" (Matthew 5:28-30).

Break the habit, my friend, whatever it takes. It's leading you down a dangerous path—a path of destruction.

*Lord, this moment I reject the deception of Satan and embrace Your truth. With the psalmist I declare, "I will walk within my house in the integrity of my heart. I will set no worthless thing before my eyes" (Psalm 101:2-3).*

Are you suffering right now because you haven't compromised? You've determined to resist the pressure and stay true to God, but He hasn't vindicated you as of yet. You've stood for what is right, and as a result, you're distressed.

How does God respond to the questions in your heart, dear modern-day Joseph?

"If you should suffer for the sake of righteousness, you are blessed. And do not fear their intimidation, and do not be troubled, but sanctify Christ as Lord in your hearts, always being ready to make a defense to everyone who asks you to give an account for the hope that is in you, yet with gentleness and reverence; and keep a good conscience so that…those who revile your good behavior in Christ will be put to shame. For it is better, if God should will it so, that you suffer for doing what is right rather than for doing what is wrong" (1 Peter 3:14-17).

You are in the center of His will. Stand firm, beloved. Read Joseph's story in Genesis 37–50 and be comforted.

*O Lord my God, in You I have taken refuge. Save me from all those who pursue me. Vindicate me, O Lord, according to my righteousness and my integrity. Thank You for hearing when I call out to You.*

How pure is your life, my friend? Are your thoughts untainted by the world's philosophy, morals, and priorities? Are you satisfied with the way you are living, or do you wish you could be more pure, more holy? Are you running around to meetings, trying to force a revival in your heart? Are you channel-surfing, searching for some Christian program to help fill the spiritual gap in your life?

God's Word has the answer: "How can a young man [any person] keep his way pure? By keeping it according to Your word. With all my heart I have sought You; do not let me wander from Your commandments. Your word I have treasured in my heart, that I may not sin against You" (Psalm 119:9-11).

Quit running to meetings. Stop channel-surfing. All of those efforts will lead only to superficial solutions. Instead, sit down, open your Bible, and let God cleanse you with the washing of His Word and strengthen you in His precepts.

*Lord, Your Word spells out exactly what You expect of me: to do justice, to love kindness, and to walk humbly with You. Instead of pursuing superficial goals, I commit myself to spending time with You, meditating on the transforming truths in Your Word.*

Are you facing a difficult situation, feeling pressured to go against the clear teaching of God's Word?

Don't make the mistake of thinking you have no choice. When you cast yourself on Him and do all you can by responding obediently to God's leading yet nothing changes, God is still on His throne—and He is adequate.

His character has not changed. His name remains the same, and so do the promises of His Word. Our responsibility is to cling, to believe. He is Jehovah-jireh, the Lord who will provide all our needs.

According to Jeremiah 13:11, if you cling to the Lord, He'll make you a person of renown, honor, and glory. As you make your decision, remember that God, and God alone, is sufficient. He is able to carry you through the deepest waters.

*Lord, I cling to Your promise of strength in the midst of my trials. With the psalmist I pray that You will uphold me in my integrity and set me in Your presence forever (Psalm 41:12).*

When did you last pause to examine your life, asking yourself, "How does my life express the worthiness of the One who conquered sin and death by redeeming me with His own blood?"

Do your words and actions boldly proclaim the sovereignty and majesty of God? Or are you reluctant to make Him part of your everyday conversation, worried that people will think you're one of those religious nuts?

Over and over throughout the pages of Scripture, we're exhorted to be strong and courageous. And we can be because of Whose we are.

Dear one, remember that Jesus is worthy to receive power and riches and wisdom and might and honor and glory and blessing. Give it to Him now. He is worthy!

*"Behold, God is my salvation, I will trust and not be afraid; for the LORD GOD is my strength and song, and He has become my salvation" (Isaiah 12:2).*

Is life hard, beloved? God didn't promise it would be easy. We live in a world laden with sin. As a nation, our cup of iniquity runs over.

So what are you going to do? You must tell God you will not look at the temporal but the eternal, that you will not listen to the voice of ungodly men nor adopt their cynicism. Nor will you seek out their solutions for coping with life. Rather, beloved, you need to remember His words in Isaiah 25:6,8-9:

"The LORD of hosts will prepare a lavish banquet for all peoples.… He will swallow up death for all time, and the Lord GOD will wipe tears away from all faces, and He will remove the reproach of His people from all the earth.… And it will be said in that day, 'Behold, this is our God for whom we have waited that He might save us. This is the LORD for whom we have waited; let us rejoice and be glad in His salvation.'"

Today may be difficult, but your promised reward is coming—if you'll only endure.

*Thank You for the wonderful hope of a future reward, if only I will wait on You. Help me to keep Your promises at the forefront of my mind, so that I can focus on the eternal, ignoring the cynicism of the ungodly and pursuing Your solutions for my life.*

Oh, beloved, there is nothing—absolutely nothing—more satisfying than knowing you have favor with God.

Why? Because, dear one, you've been called for this purpose. If you can only see your suffering as having a purpose, it's much easier to take, isn't it? You're not a doormat to be trampled; you're a platform to be used to give everyone around you an up-close glimpse of God at work.

First Peter 2:19 says, "For this finds favor, if for the sake of conscience toward God a person bears up under sorrows when suffering unjustly." When Jesus suffered unjustly, He did not act or react independently of God. He did what pleased the Father.

When we are suffering unjustly, we must run to God and say, "O Father, what would You have me do? I will to do Your will!" Only in obedience will we find His favor—and in His favor is fullness of joy. Look at Jesus' example in 1 Peter 2:21-24.

*Father, what is Your will for me today? Whatever You ask, I am willing to do. I reaffirm my commitment to reject the world, take up my cross, and follow You. Lead me in Your truth, and teach me.*

# SEPTEMBER

---

# SEARCH MY
# ATTITUDE

Are you frustrated, my friend, because you have just been done in? Maybe you are even frustrated with God because He didn't seem to come to your defense. Evil triumphed, the wicked prevailed, and you—God's child—were deemed the loser.

Does God have anything to say to you about this? I think so. Read His words in Psalm 37:7-13:

"Rest in the LORD and wait patiently for Him; do not fret because of him who prospers in his way, because of the man who carries out wicked schemes. Cease from anger and forsake wrath; do not fret; it leads only to evildoing.… The wicked plots against the righteous and gnashes at him with his teeth. The Lord laughs at him, for He sees his day is coming."

Remember, God writes the end of the story—and He is the ultimate victor!

*Thank You for this reminder to rest in You, Lord. I will not fret about my circumstances or seek revenge. Instead, I will trust in Your sovereign will and wait patiently to see what You will do.*

Are you angry? Seething inside? You want to bang, to slam, to pound something, anything. In fact, you're so angry you're afraid you might hurt someone. Perhaps you already have. You've lashed out with angry, hurtful words—or maybe you have even fought back physically. Although you feel bad about your behavior, you've rationalized it. It was their fault. They shouldn't have aggravated you. They shouldn't have said what they said or have done what they did.

My friend, striking out at others—blaming them for your anger and your outburst—is not the solution. Your behavior is simply the manifestation of a problem—a problem between you and God. You're clinging to bitterness, and it's destroying your relationships.

Bring your attitude into submission with the Word of God: "Let all bitterness and wrath and anger and clamor and slander be put away from you, along with all malice. Be kind to one another, tender-hearted, forgiving each other, just as God in Christ also has forgiven you" (Ephesians 4:31-32).

*Forgive me, Lord, for failing to fully trust You in this situation. The Bible says that the anger of man does not achieve the righteousness of God. With this in mind, I turn to Your Holy Spirit to help me be quick to hear, slow to speak, and slow to anger.*

Are you a know-it-all when it comes to spiritual things? When someone tries to talk with you about God or about your relationship to the Lord Jesus Christ, do you brush aside his or her comments by saying, "Yeah, yeah, I know about all that stuff"?

If so, your response doesn't sound like the response of a genuine, honest-to-goodness Christian. It sounds more like the response of someone who has had a taste of religion or is involved in a church but who doesn't like these zealous people bugging them about Christ.

If this is so, it seems to me you are in grave trouble, my friend—possibly eternal trouble—and you don't know it.

If you were to stand before Jesus Christ, face to face, I think He would probably say to you, "Unless you are converted and become like children, you will not enter the kingdom of heaven" (Matthew 18:3).

It's time to humble yourself, beloved.

*Dear God, I come to You in humility and ask You to show me the true condition of my heart. I don't want to risk spending eternity in hell simply because I was too arrogant to listen to the truth.*

Are you feeling overwhelmed because of all the people depending on you? Are you worn out from taking care of others? Would you like to walk away from all your responsibilities? Do you long to be footloose and fancy free, focusing on yourself for a change? Are you eager to get a life of your own?

Our world would encourage you to break free. You have to look out for number one, they say.

You can listen to the world, join the multitudes, and do your thing, but I guarantee that later on in life you will be sorry.

Instead of giving into the pressures around you, look to the Word of God for guidance: "Do nothing from selfishness or empty conceit, but with humility of mind regard one another as more important than yourselves; do not merely look out for your own personal interests, but also for the interests of others. Have this attitude in yourselves which was also in Christ Jesus, who, although He existed in the form of God, did not regard equality with God a thing to be grasped, but emptied Himself, taking the form of a bond-servant, and being made in the likeness of men" (Philippians 2:3-7).

*Heavenly Father, I feel overwhelmed by the pressures of my life. I cannot possibly continue in my own strength, so I turn to You and ask You to renew my energy and refresh my attitude. Help me to press on.*

Do you walk in faith? Are you giving thanks in everything? The two go together because faith means taking God at His Word and doing what He tell us, and He tells us "In everything give thanks; for this is God's will for you in Christ Jesus" (1 Thessalonians 5:18).

Usually God doesn't let us know immediately why we should give thanks, but He asks us to walk in faith and to thank Him in faith. It's your choice: You can become stressed about your circumstances, or you can give thanks and rest in His sovereignty.

Because God is never out of control, because He rules *over all*—the small and the big things, the tragedies and the triumphs—and because He loves us with an everlasting love, we can give thanks in everything.

" 'For I know the plans that I have for you,' declares the LORD, 'plans for welfare and not for calamity to give you a future and a hope' " (Jeremiah 29:11).

These words were spoken first to Israel, but they are for all of God's children. Therefore, in all things—in everything—we can "give thanks."

*Thank You, Lord, for the assurance of Your awesome sovereignty. Thank You that everything that happens to me is part of Your will, and thank You that every aspect of Your will is based on Your love for me.*

God says, "In everything give thanks" (1 Thessalonians 5:18). Sometimes that's difficult to do, isn't it? Especially when things go wrong.

Although we may know this Scripture backward and forward, when we cannot see any earthly reason for what has happened, it's hard to believe we should give thanks. Our perspective is limited to the present time, the present situation, the present inconvenience, the present pain, the present trial.

Our present perspective ties our tongues, so that instead of using them to say, "Thank You, Lord, although I do not understand," they wag back and forth in murmuring, filling the air with discontent. Our nerves become taut with stress. The whole atmosphere becomes so charged with electricity that it could explode at any time.

It's difficult to give thanks. And yet, difficult or not, when you and I refuse to give thanks in faith, we are walking in unbelief. And unbelief is sin!

*Lord, I cannot see Your plan for my life at this moment. I do not understand exactly what You are working to accomplish through my difficult situation. But in faith I choose to believe that You will cause all things to work together for good.*

Are you a grouch? Is your conversation filled with demeaning comments and put-downs? Are you angry, bitter, unforgiving? Do others see you as consistently unhappy, a seething grump? You're dissatisfied with life, with others, and—if you are honest—probably with yourself. Yet do you excuse your behavior, saying that's just your personality and there's no point in trying to change? You've always been that way—and you're getting worse with each passing year.

Do you believe you have just cause to be this way? Oh no, my friend. There is no just cause. You don't have to go through life with a bad attitude; you can get saved. God will take you as you are, but He won't leave you that way. Jesus Christ will transform you into a loving—and loved—person.

Consider what God says: "Everyone who loves is born of God and knows God. The one who does not love does not know God, for God is love" (1 John 4:7-8).

*God, I'm sick of who I am, of what I do to others. My bitterness and anger are eating my insides, but I don't know how to get rid of them. I'm willing to let go, to forgive. Birth me into Your family by the power of Your Spirit. I want to receive the Forgiver—and forgive. Hear my desperate cry, God, and transform me into a loving, caring person.*

Dear friend, don't despair if this is your day of adversity! Continue in hope, even when your heart is crying out, "How long, O Lord, holy and true, will You refrain from judging and avenging our blood on those who dwell on the earth?" (Revelation 6:10).

Don't lose hope when it seems that the wicked go free and Satan moves forward unchecked. The Scripture says in Romans 5:3-5: "But we also exult in our tribulations, knowing that tribulation brings about perseverance; and perseverance, proven character; and proven character, hope; and hope does not disappoint, because the love of God has been poured out within our hearts through the Holy Spirit who was given to us."

Though others may be turning to their own ways and their own solutions, live as the redeemed should live. Remember, your redemption and your Redeemer draw nigh!

*Thank You, Lord, for this reminder that You are my hope and my confidence. Although things look bleak right now, I trust in You and in the promise of Your Word that this momentary affliction is producing an eternal weight of glory far beyond all comparison.*

Beloved, are you seeing things God's way?

If you're discontented and unhappy, maybe it's because you're not seeing things from God's perspective. How much is your attitude influenced by the movies and television programs you watch or by the books and magazines you read?

Our flesh says, "Things will make me happy. And besides, having things in abundance proves I'm fulfilled, successful, even blessed."

However, God's Word says, "Beware, and be on your guard against every form of greed; for not even when one has an abundance does his life consist of his possessions" (Luke 12:15).

If your thoughts and attitude are to match God's perspective, then you must be "transformed by the renewing of your mind" (Romans 12:2). My dear friend, get into the Word of God, and meditate upon it day in and day out. It's the light for your path!

*I confess, dear Father, that I have allowed an attitude of dissatisfaction to creep into my life. I ask for Your forgiveness, and I surrender my heart to You. I want to be able to echo the apostle Paul in saying, "I have learned to be content in whatever circumstances I am" (Philippians 4:11).*

Do you really trust God—in *all* things?

God holds your life and well-being in His hands. Oh, I'm sure you believe that most of the time, but...

Are there any "buts" in your thinking, beloved? If so, you need to be convinced in your heart that God alone is sufficient. Our help comes from the One who made the heavens and the earth, the One who loves us with an everlasting love.

"Blessed is the man who trusts in the LORD and whose trust is the LORD. For he will be like a tree planted by the water, that extends its roots by a stream and will not fear when the heat comes; but its leaves will be green, and it will not be anxious in a year of drought nor cease to yield fruit" (Jeremiah 17:7-8).

Trust in the Lord, beloved. He never changes. His name remains the same, and so do the promises of His Word.

Your responsibility is to believe!

*Your Word declares that You love me with an everlasting love. By faith I claim that promise, and I determine to stand firm in my faith, trusting my life to You no matter what happens.*

What is your greatest goal for your life? What brightens your outlook and makes you feel successful?

When our expectations are rooted in anything other than pleasing God, we'll know only distress, defeat, disappointment, and failure. But when our hope is rooted in Him, our attitude won't be affected by our circumstances.

Writing from prison, the apostle Paul said, "For to me, to live is Christ and to die is gain" (Philippians 1:21). It didn't matter to Paul that he was unjustly confined for three years. It only mattered that the work of his Lord continued. In fact, in the midst of his imprisonment, Paul's one hope and earnest expectation was that he would be ashamed in nothing, but that with all boldness, Christ would be exalted in his body (verse 20).

May you and I make knowing God and His Word our priority and passion so that in the day of testing we'll be able to rest in faith. And in doing so, we'll please Him, which above all is our calling!

*Lord, my heart's greatest desire is to know You and Your Word. I place my hope and trust in You so that I will be prepared to stand firm in the day of testing.*

Are you coping with financial problems right now? Are you unsure how to make ends meet? Is the family panicked? Or have you kept the truth from them? Are you struggling with worry, beloved, wondering whether God has abandoned you?

The apostle Paul faced similar trials. Spend some time today thinking about what he learned from his experience: "I have learned to be content in whatever circumstances I am. I know how to get along with humble means, and I also know how to live in prosperity; in any and every circumstance I have learned the secret of being filled and going hungry, both of having abundance and suffering need. I can do all things through Him who strengthens me" (Philippians 4:11-13).

Paul made it through Christ's strength. You can too, if you'll just lean on Him in faith.

*When I find myself worrying about money, struggling to achieve a sense of security, I cling to Your promise to supply all my needs. Give me an attitude of contentment, no matter my circumstances, and remind me that I can endure anything when I'm living in the strength of the Holy Spirit.*

First Peter 5:8 warns, "Your adversary, the devil, prowls around like a roaring lion, seeking someone to devour." What an evil picture this verse paints for each of us. Our adversary prowling and seeking to devour us, just waiting for us to let down our guard.

Did you know that one of Satan's favorite attack plans involves the five "deadly *D*s": disappointment, discouragement, dejection, despair, and demoralization?

If disappointment has ever caused you to go into an emotional tailspin, if you've ever felt you might drown in discouragement, then, my friend, you've undoubtedly engaged in warfare with the evil one.

Oh, beloved, seek God in every situation. Trust in Him to overcome your adversary! Declare with the psalmist, "But as for me, I trust in You, O LORD, I say, 'You are my God.' My times are in Your hand" (31:14-15).

*In obedience to Your Word and in the strength of Your might, I am determined to stand firm against the schemes of the devil. When disappointment comes my way, I will place my trust in You and determine to seek Your will.*

Do you have a ho-hum Christianity? You go through the motions, do the church scene—show-up, see friends, shake hands, and when they ask, tell everyone you're doing fine. Maybe you even go to Sunday school, and sometimes you read through the lesson.

Yet you live Monday through Friday basically the same way every one else does. You work hard, you're friendly to your neighbors, and you treat your family well. In the evenings you crash in front of the TV or crawl into bed.

That's all there is to your busy life. Any thoughts of spiritual things are limited to going to church and trying to be a nice person.

Maybe you misunderstood Jesus' call: "If anyone wishes to come after Me, he must deny himself, and take up his cross and follow Me" (Mark 8:34). Responding to this call isn't a once-for-all action; it means taking up your cross and following Him habitually, for the rest of your life. The cross is never ho-hum, my friend. You had better check out your commitment to Christ.

*I confess, dear God, that I do not have a passion to pursue spiritual things. I've lost sight of the seriousness of my commitment to You, allowing my schedule to be driven by worldly values rather than by Your priorities. Today I determine to make a change, to listen for Your voice and wholeheartedly obey its call.*

Fear never comes from God! Let me repeat that: Fear never comes from God!

John 14:27 is a not only a reminder, it's a promise: "Peace I leave with you; My peace I give to you.... Do not let your heart be troubled, nor let it be fearful."

So how does fear creep into our hearts and minds? Fear comes when we believe the father of lies, who constantly sows the seeds of doubt. Doubt breeds insecurity; insecurity breeds fear.

If you're ever going to find relief from fear's immobilizing power, you must first understand that God loves you unconditionally and sacrificially. He loved you before you ever loved Him. Romans 5:8 says, "But God demonstrates His own love toward us, in that while we were yet sinners, Christ died for us."

Beloved, God loves you more than you can possibly imagine. Let His love cast out all fear from your heart.

*Thank You, dear Lord, for this reminder of Your precious love, a love that never fails. By faith I believe that You love me even more than I can imagine, and I reject fear's power over me.*

What's overwhelming you today? Is it discouragement or rejection? Do you feel as if you've completely failed?

I know exactly what you're feeling. I've been there!

Beloved, run to your God, your Rock. Cry out to Him. If you feel He's forgotten you, then ask Him if He has. If you feel as if your enemies—physical, emotional, or spiritual—have overwhelmed you, ask Him why. Pour out your soul to your God. Hope in Him, and know you will again praise Him for the help of His presence. He has not abandoned you!

Second Corinthians 4:7-8 says, "But we have this treasure in earthen vessels, so that the surpassing greatness of the power will be of God and not from ourselves; we are afflicted in every way, but not crushed; perplexed, but not despairing."

There it is. His Word. Will you believe it?

*"Incline Your ear, O LORD, and answer me; for I am afflicted and needy. Preserve my soul.... Be gracious to me, O LORD, for to You I cry all day long.... In the day of my trouble I shall call upon You, for You will answer me.... For You are great and do wondrous deeds; You alone are God" (Psalm 86:1-3,7,10).*

The worries of this world are sometimes overwhelming, aren't they? Keeping up at work, holding our families together, coping with illness and all life's other crises. The demands of life are wearing! How are we to manage?

Satan's goal is to weaken you, to dishearten you, to make you lose courage. The cure for discouragement is encouragement. Encourage your heart by looking at your God and His promises.

Beloved, let me encourage you today. Habakkuk 3:19 (NIV) says, "The Sovereign LORD is my strength; he makes my feet like the feet of a deer, he enables me to go on the heights." In other words, no matter what life brings, you have the promise of God's strength.

And so what is God's word to you today? It's to be strong and courageous. Wipe away your tears and your fears by rejoicing in the God of your salvation. Smile, for He is your strength and He will enable you to stand.

*Thank You, God, that my attitude is not determined by my circumstances but is based on who and what You are. Hallelujah! Praise to Jehovah!*

*As I rest in Your sovereignty and rejoice in Your promises, I find encouragement, hope, and strength to continue.*

"If I have to put up with this another day, I think I'll scream!"

Sound familiar? Self-pity, complaining, and screaming are not the solution. When tension builds and your heart's in a panic, listen for God's voice. He'll gently whisper assurance that you're experiencing only those trials and temptations to which we're all continually subjected—with His knowledge and permission!

When testing or temptation threatens your peace, God has a promise for you in the midst of it all, and His Word is true! It's in 1 Corinthians 10:13: "No temptation [trial or testing] has overtaken you but such as is common to man; and God is faithful, who will not allow you to be tempted beyond what you are able, but with the temptation will provide the way of escape also, so that you will be able to endure it."

You *can* endure. Act, walk, and speak in the light of this promise!

*Before I go out to face the cares of the day, I take this opportunity to wait quietly before You, God, and listen for Your voice. Speak reassurance and peace to my heart, and prepare me with Your Word to endure the temptations ahead.*

What is your attitude about giving? When you drop your tithe in the offering plate, is it with hesitancy, possibly with a quiet sigh of regret? Do you think about all the ways you could use that money for yourself? Or do you justify giving less than your full tithe because you simply can't afford it?

Beloved, the way we handle our money reveals a lot about our relationship with God. When the Lord said to the Israelites, "Return to Me and I will return to you," they asked, "How shall we return?"

God's reply was quite interesting: "Will a man rob God? Yet you are robbing Me! But you say, 'How have we robbed You?' In tithes and offerings. You are cursed with a curse, for you are robbing Me, the whole nation of you!" (Malachi 3:7-9).

God has promised to supply all our needs, so what could we possibly gain from withholding our money from Him?

If your heart is totally surrendered to God, everything you have will be held out to Him in an open hand.

*Heavenly Father, I want to honor You with every aspect of my life, including my money and my material possessions. I acknowledge that everything I have comes from Your gracious hand, and I willingly offer it up for Your use.*

Beloved, you need to know about Satan's schemes! Do you remember in Genesis 3:1 when he approached Eve in the Garden of Eden? His first words planted seeds of doubt, "Indeed, has God said…?"

If you and I are to live by faith, then we must understand Satan's approach. His tactic is to make you doubt the power of God's words. If Satan can bring disappointment, discouragement, and despair, he can demoralize us totally. And since faith comes by hearing and hearing by the Word of God, isn't it only logical for Satan to try to convince us to abandon the Word?

Dear one, 2 Corinthians 2:11 warns us not to be ignorant of Satan's schemes. Remember, with the shield of faith "you will be able to extinguish all the flaming arrows of the evil one" (Ephesians 6:16).

*Thank You for the precious gift of Your Word, in which I can find truth and wisdom to resist Satan's attacks of deception. Like the psalmist, I want to meditate on its precepts and hide it in my heart so that I will not be led into doubt and sin (Psalm 119:9-16).*

How is your attitude today, my friend? Is this a time of disappointment? Discouragement?

Beloved, discouragement and disappointment are like twins! When you open the door to disappointment, you'll find discouragement coming in right behind.

Remember when the Israelites were about to go into the land God that had promised them? They sent spies ahead to check it out, and these agents came back with news of giants and fortified cities. The Israelites were afraid and discouraged, as if their God had become too small to handle human giants. Some forty years later, as they prepared to enter the same land, God said not once but three times, "Be strong and courageous! Do not tremble or be dismayed, for the LORD your God is with you wherever you go" (Joshua 1:9).

God's word is the same to you today, dear one. Encourage your heart. Look to your God and His promises.

*I love the portrait in Psalm 91:4 of Your protective presence. In the midst of my disappointment and discouragement, I picture myself huddled under Your sheltering wings and find new courage and strength. You are my God, and You are with me! What a wonderful promise!*

Beloved, you may feel abandoned today. You may think that if God were with you, you wouldn't be facing these problems or enduring this pain. But let me ask you a question: Will you walk in faith or live by feeling?

When we're discouraged and feeling abandoned, the enemy whispers lies into our ears. He wants us to believe that God is impotent—or worse, that He doesn't care about us. He knows that if he can cause us to lose heart, we are more likely to give in to temptation.

In Hebrews 13:5 God says, "I will never desert you, nor will I ever forsake you." In the Greek there are five negatives in that verse. Add two to the first "never," and read, "I will never, never, never desert you." Then add one more to "nor" and read it "nor never will I ever forsake you."

When you feel abandoned, answer Satan's lies in faith with verse six: "The Lord is my helper, I will not be afraid. What will man do to me?"

*You are my helper, Lord God. I refuse to allow my feelings to undermine my faith. Instead, I cling to the promise that You will never, never, never desert me, and I wait to see how You will bring good from my disappointment.*

Beloved, are you experiencing joy even in circumstances you don't like?

James 1:2 tells us to "consider it all joy...when you encounter various trials." *Consider it all joy?* How can you count it all joy when you're overwhelmed with pain, when difficulty seems to be your constant companion?

The disappointing situation is a test, precious child of God. It hasn't come because God wants to hurt you or make you miserable. It is permitted because He wants you to be perfect and complete in every aspect, lacking nothing. Hebrews 12:6-7 tells us, "Those whom the Lord loves He disciplines, and He scourges every son whom He receives. It is for discipline that you endure; God deals with you as with sons; for what son is there whom his father does not discipline?"

God will use the disappointments in your life to teach and train you, to make you more like Jesus Christ, to do something awesome in you!

Count it all joy, beloved. He's grooming you for eternity!

*I do not like my circumstances, Lord, but I choose to believe You are using my disappointments to mold me into something beautiful. I find joy in the knowledge that You are transforming me into the image of Your Son, and I long for the day when I truly am perfect and complete in every aspect.*

God loves you unconditionally, beloved. The question is, do you love Him unconditionally? Before you answer that, consider this: Do you doubt the reality of His love? If so, could it be because you're not really loving Him as you should?

When things weren't going their way, the people of Israel doubted God's love. They said, "How have You loved us?" (Malachi 1:2). They never once stopped to consider that maybe there was something wrong in their lives. They didn't realize that God might be permitting difficulties or disappointments to refine them as silver so that they might, as Malachi 3:3 says, "present to the LORD offerings in righteousness."

They were blind to God's purpose in their suffering. And that's often true of us today. We're only happy with God when things are going our way. But when God makes righteous demands of us, we pout and respond with insolence, "How have You loved me?"

God's love is unconditional; how can we ask for more?

*Please forgive me, heavenly Father, for sticking out my lower lip and doubting Your love for me, for focusing on my present circumstances rather than on Your eternal, unconditional commitment to me. Open my downcast eyes to Your purposes, and work in my heart to establish and perfect me in Your love.*

Think about it, beloved: What difference would it make to you if the doors of your church were barred shut? Would it simply give you two more hours a week to do your own thing without a guilty conscience, or would you, like multitudes in other countries where the gospel is banned, meet secretly at the risk of your freedom?

As I see our lack of zeal, our lack of discipline, I wonder how many go to church because it's part of their routine rather than because of a settled determination to worship God and to grow in the knowledge of Him?

My dear friend, if you're finding it tiresome to serve the Lord, I'd like you to prayerfully read Isaiah 1:10-14 in your Bible. It's hypocrisy to go through the motions of worship when you're not motivated by love's obedience. God calls such meaningless gestures "worthless offerings."

In contrast, read in Psalm 51:17 what God really wants from you: "The sacrifices of God are a broken spirit; a broken and a contrite heart, O God, You will not despise." God desires your pure offering, a heart that is totally committed to Him.

*Examine my attitude, God, and revive within my heart a zeal for You. Replace my apathy with a passion to grow in the knowledge of You and a yearning to spend time in Your Word, worshiping You in fellowship with others. I offer my heart, soul, mind, and strength in full surrender to You.*

What is your attitude toward people in need? Although you know they work (and work hard) do you secretly—or vocally—believe that they deserve to be where they are, that it is their lot in life? Or do you rejoice in the opportunity to share the blessings of God? Do you look for ways to help quietly?

In Luke 6:38 Jesus encourages us to be generous to those around us: "Give, and it will be given to you. They will pour into your lap a good measure—pressed down, shaken together, and running over. For by your standard of measure it will be measured to you in return."

Financial woes can happen to anyone—even to you. Consider Proverbs 19:17: "One who is gracious to a poor man lends to the LORD, and He will repay him for his good deed." I encourage you to memorize this verse, beloved. Let its truth sink into your heart so that the next time you hear of a need, you will find joy in giving what you can.

*Thank You for this reminder of the privilege I have in sharing my blessings with those around me. Your Word clearly tells me to give myself to the hungry and to satisfy the desire of the afflicted. Open my eyes and my heart to opportunities to love others in Your name.*

Beloved, is this one of those days when you're ready to give up? You just can't find the strength to continue. There's so much pressure, so many responsibilities that you wonder how you'll ever get it all done?

Rejoice in Isaiah 40:28, which says, "Do you not know? Have you not heard? The Everlasting God, the LORD, the Creator of the ends of the earth does not become weary or tired." What great news! "He gives strength to the weary, and to him who lacks might He increases power. Though youths grow weary and tired, and vigorous young men stumble badly, yet those who wait for the LORD will gain new strength" (verses 29-31).

Oh, my dear friend, through Jesus Christ God has become your strength. He has already compensated for your weakness. He is your loving covenant partner, gladly sharing with you all that is His. He has all the strength you need to make it through today.

*I need Your strength more than ever, Lord. Both my body and my spirit are worn out, and there is so much to do. Through Your Holy Spirit, help me to think clearly, respond compassionately, and endure faithfully through the pressures that come my way. I rely wholly on Your strength.*

You know the feeling: Your heart races, your chest tightens, and panic paralyzes your mind. How do you conquer the paralyzing fear that seems to strike you at your most vulnerable point?

Second Timothy 1:7 says: "For God has not given us a spirit of timidity, but of power and love and discipline." When fear strikes and you find yourself lacking in power and thinking irrationally, look at the cross of Christ. What does it tell you? It says your sovereign Father God loves you with a perfect love.

Remember this: Fear is to Satan what faith is to God. Satan operates on the basis of fear. He's working to immobilize you, to make you ineffective in serving God. He'll parade before you the fear of death, the fear of failure, of criticism, of rejection.

Beloved, God never operates on the basis of anything but faith. While fear immobilizes, faith energizes. Claim this truth, beloved: "There is no fear in love; but perfect love"—God's love—"casts out fear" (1 John 4:18)!

*I know and believe that You love me and that You are sovereign. Nothing can happen without Your permission. I will put my trust in You, pressing forward with complete confidence in Your ability to use this situation for my good and Your glory.*

Think about the people you admire most. What are their characteristics, their strengths? Do you find that you have the greatest respect for those people who have suffered the most and yet endured with grace?

My heart is stirred and often my eyes fill with tears when I hear those who in faith's courage say with Job, "The LORD gave and the LORD has taken away. Blessed be the name of the LORD" (1:21).

A perfect example is one woman who wrote to me saying her husband was an invalid, bound to a wheelchair and suffering from lupus and rheumatoid arthritis. They received no outside financial assistance, so she worked both night and day. "I sometimes wonder where the next meal will come from," she wrote, "but my God supplies."

Oh, beloved, memorize Hebrews 12:1. Make it the objective of your heart and life to "run with endurance the race that is set before us." You can do it with God's help.

*I fix my eyes on You, dear Jesus, the author and perfecter of my faith. I lay aside every encumbrance—my worries, my fears, my fleshly desires—and the sin that so easily entangles me. Relying on Your help, I am determined to run the race of faith with endurance and grace.*

Do you need reviving, my friend? Has your relationship with the Lord grown a little dull and routine? Has the blazing fire become a bed of tepid coals? Maybe you have become so busy you haven't had time for God and His Word.

Do you miss the joy you once felt? Are you feeling kind of guilty? Maybe even depressed, angry, jealous, or frustrated when you spend time with others who are bubbling over with love for the Lord. Do you long to join in when others share all that God is doing in their lives?

So why don't you make a change? It's time to dive back into God's Word and to spend time in prayer, listening to Him and becoming reacquainted with His heart. What a change it will bring in your attitude, not just toward God but toward everything and everyone in your life. You'll have His perspective once more—and that makes all the difference!

*"Turn away my eyes from looking at vanity, and revive me in Your ways. Establish Your word to Your servant as that which produces reverence for You.... Behold, I long for Your precepts; revive me through Your righteousness" (Psalm 119:37-40).*

---

# LEAD ME TO RIGHTEOUSNESS

Do you feel as if you can never measure up to what others expect of you? Are you worn out from trying? Or maybe you're worn out from beating yourself up about your failures and shortcomings. If so, I imagine you probably are also disappointed in your loved ones because they aren't measuring up either—at least not by your standards.

God says in His Word, "When they measure themselves by themselves and compare themselves with themselves, they are without understanding" (2 Corinthians 10:12). Beloved, God sets the criteria, not man nor the culture of the times. Romans 14:4 says, "To his own master he stands or falls."

God created you, put your genes together, saved you, gifted you with His choice of spiritual gifts, and foreordained the good works He wants you to walk in. Now be what God would have you be. His is the only standard you need to meet.

*Thank You for the reminder that I do not have to measure up to anyone's standards but Yours. My service is rendered unto You, not to men, and my reward will come from You. Help me to remember this same truth when I am tempted to criticize the actions of those around me.*

Are there specific criteria for the choices you make? Do you pretty much set your own rules? Do you have your own private standards of right and wrong? Or do you believe that right and wrong are relative, that there are no moral absolutes and people should simply live according to the dictates of their own hearts—as long as they don't hurt anyone, especially you?

What about the Bible? Does your lifestyle line up with God's word? Or are you uncertain what the Bible says about the various issues of life? Oh, my friend, you had better find out.

Proverbs 14:12 says, "There is a way which seems right to a man, but its end is the way of death."

That's not the way you want to choose, is it? *The way of death?* If not, you need to learn to look at life from God's perspective—and you will find that in the Bible.

*O Lord, lead me in Your righteousness; make Your way straight before me. Let my heart respond to the voice of Your Holy Spirit when He says, "This is the way, walk in it" (Isaiah 30:21).*

Have you found yourself looking at another person's mate and wondering what it would be like if that person were your spouse? You've found yourself wanting to hang around that person, to talk with him or her, to laugh and joke around together. Maybe you even joke about what it would be like if the two of you were married. Your behavior may look innocent, but in your heart you feel enticed.

What does God's Word say about this? "If my heart has been enticed by a woman, or I have lurked at my neighbor's doorway, may my wife grind for another, and let others kneel down over her. For that would be a lustful crime; moreover, it would be an iniquity punishable by judges. For it would be fire that consumes…and would uproot all my increase" (Job 31:9-12).

It's clear what you need to do: Repent and immediately get out of this situation before it goes any further.

*Forgive me, Lord, for entertaining sinful thoughts. Remind me that I can't get away with it; such thoughts lead only to danger and heartache. Purify my mind and give me the strength to flee temptation. I am determined that Your righteousness, not my own lust, will rule in my body.*

Do you feel absolutely overcome by the wicked, as if they are going to suck you into their evil schemes? You feel impotent to help yourself, but there is no one to rescue you. What are you going to do?

Maybe there's no one you can see, my friend, but there is One—and ultimately deliverance comes only from Him. Consider what God says: "The wicked have drawn the sword and bent their bow to cast down the afflicted and the needy, to slay those who are upright in conduct.… But the salvation of the righteous is from the LORD; He is their strength in time of trouble. The LORD helps them and delivers them; He delivers them from the wicked and saves them, because they take refuge in Him" (Psalm 37:14, 39-40).

Don't yield, beloved. Maintain your righteousness, and cry out to God. He's neither deaf nor impotent. He will deliver you.

*Heavenly Father, I am facing so much pressure to give in to wickedness. Sometimes it seems as if I'm the only one trying to live by Your standards. Help me to keep a holy fear of You, one that will spread to others. Thank You for upholding me and giving me the strength to live in a way that is sensible, righteous, and godly in this present age.*

Are you frustrated with God because He isn't answering your prayers? You ask and ask, but nothing happens. Hasn't God promised to respond to our prayers?

Let's see what God's Word has to say on this topic. Let me give you two things to check out. First, consider 1 Peter 3:12, which says, "The eyes of the Lord are toward the righteous, and His ears attend to their prayer, but the face of the Lord is against those who do evil." Therefore you need to make sure you are doing what God says is right. You cannot live in willful disobedience and expect God to answer your prayers.

Second, ponder 1 John 5:14, which says, "This is the confidence which we have before Him, that, if we ask anything according to His will, He hears us." Are you sure that what you ask for is really according to the will of God? John 15:7 will help you here.

Now then, if your life and request are in line with God's Word on this topic, keep praying and waiting on God.

*I pause right now, heavenly Father, to weigh the motives of my heart. Please bring to light anything hidden in the dark recesses of my heart that would prevent my prayers from being aligned with Your perfect will. And if it's simply a matter of persistence and patience in prayer, I'll be faithful to keep praying. I trust Your heart, Father.*

Is life hard, my friend, and full of trouble? Are you weary in well doing? A little faint? Wondering if it really pays to serve the Lord?

After taking a good look around, you realize you are a rarity anyway. Very few are committed to God and the cause of His kingdom. You're beginning to feel like Elijah, who experienced a great victory and then, discouraged by the power and threats of the wicked, fled in panic. When God asked what he was doing in a cave at Horeb, the despondent Elijah responded, "I alone am left" to serve the Lord (1 Kings 19:14).

But God reminded him that He had seven thousand others who had not bowed the knee to Baal. Then He sent Elijah forth on other tasks.

God offers similar encouragement to you today: Don't faint; don't quit; don't hide. You're desperately needed. Remember, "the lovingkindness of the LORD is from everlasting to everlasting on those who fear Him, and His righteousness to children's children, to those who keep His covenant and remember His precepts to do them" (Psalm 103:17-18).

*Lord, You know my frame; You are mindful that I am but dust. In my own strength I am nothing. But I choose to trust in Your strength to help me endure. Renew my zeal and passion as I rest in You.*

Genuine Christianity is a show-and-tell relationship with God. What do you have to show for your Christianity, beloved? So many profess to know God, but when you observe their lives, their Christianity doesn't show. And when you discuss the Bible, they have little to tell. They may know isolated verses and be able to tell you in broad terms what they believe about God and Christianity, but they cannot support their beliefs from the Bible. They're working from the knowledge they gained from others.

Occupying the pew of a church, the chair of a Sunday school class, or the seat on a board of deacons does not mean you are a child of God. Read Titus 1:16: "They profess to know God, but by their deeds they deny Him, being detestable and disobedient and worthless for any good deed."

These people were wrong in their deeds and their doctrine. What about your Christianity, my friend? Do you have something to show and tell?

*Lord, I want to measure my actions against the solid truths of Your Word, against the standards of what You deem righteous. Don't let me be deceived or deceive others by a profession or form of godliness that, in reality, does not produce what You would say are good deeds.*

Do you ever wonder how you are going to make it? Are you overwhelmed by the seeming futility of your efforts to do the right thing? Are you ever tempted to envy the world? To look at the temporal instead of the eternal?

What keeps you from slipping? From giving up? From walking out? From blowing it and dishonoring God?

The secret is found "in the sanctuary," a term used in the Old Testament for communing with God. When you spend time with Him, abiding in Him and learning His ways, you'll learn what the psalmist meant when he wrote, "Thus I have seen You in the sanctuary, to see Your power and Your glory. Because Your lovingkindness is better than life, my lips will praise You" (Psalm 63:2-3).

When you consistently spend time in God's sanctuary, you get God's perspective. He teaches you His way and leads you on a level path (Psalm 27). You won't feel alone, and you'll realize that His power offers all you need to endure.

*Lord, my heart is deeply troubled as I look at my circumstances. But when I come into Your sanctuary I realize that all this is nothing in the face of Your power and Your glory. Then I receive courage to cling to Your mighty hand as You uphold me to the end.*

What an awesome thing it is to serve God, to bear His name! It is not a privilege to be taken lightly.

God is a God of love and mercy, so when we fail Him we can find comfort in knowing that His lovingkindnesses never cease and His compassions never fail; they are new every morning (Lamentations 3:22-23). Yet because God is also holy—just and righteous in all His ways—we must remember that His judgment begins within His own household, with His own children (1 Peter 4:17).

"Be sure your sin will find you out," God warned the children of Israel in Numbers 32:23. He was speaking not to the heathen, the unbelieving, but to His own people. He wanted those who had promised to follow and obey Him to realize there would be consequences for disobedience.

Because of our identification with Christ, God cannot overlook sin in our lives. Rest assured, He will see that our sin will find us out. Let us remember the gravity of our commitment to follow Him.

*Thank You for this reminder of my responsibility to honor Your name in everything I do and say. Because I bear the name of Christ, I know I am not free to live for myself and my commitment to follow You is to supersede everything else.*

Do you know how to examine your heart for evidence of genuine salvation?

When you repent (have a change of mind) and believe on the Lord Jesus Christ, receiving Him as your God and Savior, you don't see anything spectacular or mysterious taking place at that moment. Yet in an instant you are a brand-new creature in Christ Jesus, indwelt by the Spirit of God, born again. And your life begins to bear fruit.

The Scriptures teach that the Holy Spirit bears witness that you belong to God. You begin walking in the light, following in the footsteps of Jesus. You may sin but you won't live in darkness, in habitual sin. You'll never permanently stray from God; rather you'll persevere in the faith.

Your attitudes and actions will reflect a change. You'll love others, and you'll walk in righteousness, overcoming the world. You will also have an inward hunger for God's Word and His righteousness.

"These things I have written to you who believe in the name of the Son of God, so that you may know that you have eternal life" (1 John 5:13).

*O Father, how wonderful it is to have confidence in my relationship with You! Thank You for laying out the evidence of true salvation in Your New Testament, so we can know that we know that we belong to You.*

Are you eager to go on, to become more like Christ? To be used of God? How wonderful! How absolutely wonderful! What an affirmation of Whose you are!

Once the Holy Spirit moves on a person's heart—bringing conviction of sin and prompting true repentance—there's a longing to be finished with sin and its awful harvest. Then when in salvation the Holy Spirit takes up His residence within a child of God, He causes him to set his mind on the things of the Spirit (Romans 8:1-8).

It is the Spirit who enables us to understand the things of God. This is one of the ways to know that you are truly born again: You have a hunger and a thirst for righteousness that drive you to the Word of God. And when you get there, you find that you can understand it! The veil comes off when Christ comes in! And it happens because of the indwelling Spirit.

Jesus said, "Blessed are those who hunger and thirst for righteousness, for they shall be satisfied" (Matthew 5:6). What a promise!

*Your Word says that eyes have not seen and ears have not heard the things You have prepared for those who love You. But You have revealed them through the Spirit to those who live in the Spirit. Thank You for the gift of the Holy Spirit, who enables me to have the mind of Christ and to know the things that are freely given to us by God.*

Are you tempted to return to something that once had a strong grip on you? You long for just one more drink... taste...look...touch....

Don't. The moment of pleasure is not worth the price.

God says it will bring forth sin, and sin will bring forth death (James 1:15). Sin destroys everything in its path, everything it touches. Sin is a child of desire. Therefore recognize your desires for what they are. If you rationalize them and accommodate them, beloved, you'll eventually find yourself in sin. And sin always results in death. You may not see how right away, but death will come—perhaps killing the trust in a relationship, destroying an opportunity to serve God, smothering a dream, or crushing your desire for righteousness.

Proverbs 11:19 tells us, "He who is steadfast in righteousness will attain to life, and he who pursues evil will bring about his own death."

Remember, beloved, the high cost of giving in to your flesh—and choose instead to "walk by the Spirit" (Galatians 5:16).

*Thank You, Father, for the fruit of the Spirit, which includes self-control. Now give me strength, dear God, to be steadfast in righteousness. When temptation hits, I want to walk in the power of the Spirit, refusing to damage my relationship with You for the passing pleasures of sin.*

Precious one, although society's values have changed, God's ideas about morality stay the same. Amidst the confusion, chaos, and conflict that come when a nation loses its respect and fear of God, the very foundations of our society are crumbling. It's the fruit of our ways: "The wrath of God is [being] revealed from heaven against all ungodliness and unrighteousness of men who suppress the truth in unrighteousness" (Romans 1:18).

If you're going to survive the holy judgment of God, which is here in part and is to come in greater measure, then you need to know that God and His Word never change! His truth endures from generation to generation.

When you're confused by the shifting values of our society, spend time in the Word of God. When all else is uncertain, "the firm foundation of God stands, having this seal, 'The Lord knows those who are His,' and 'Everyone who names the name of the Lord is to abstain from wickedness'" (2 Timothy 2:19).

*Lord, You say, "Let no one deceive you with empty words, for because of these things the wrath of God comes upon the sons of disobedience. Therefore do not be partakers with them; for you were formerly darkness, but now you are Light in the Lord; walk as children of Light" (Ephesians 5:6-8). May I stay far away from "the unfruitful deeds of darkness" and reprove them rather than condone them (verse 11).*

Are you engaged in warfare with the enemy of your soul, beloved? Do you find yourself losing the battle?

Oh, dear child of God, you don't have to lose the war! You can be set free from your enemy's prison. First John 4:4 reminds us that "greater is He who is in you than he who is in the world." Remember, beloved believer, the outcome of the war is already determined. Jesus is victor, and we are more than conquerors when we align ourselves with Him.

The promises of God are the concentration and mass of force that you need against the enemy. Make it your passion to prove these promises true. Spend time in prayer and studying God's Word. When you do, you'll find yourself winning every battle. God would never send you into a battle you can't win!

*Heavenly Father, I claim the promises to the churches in Revelation, which detail the blessings and rewards You will give to those who overcome. I cannot do it in my own strength, but I have faith that, with You as my protector, I can overwhelmingly conquer any weapon of Satan and emerge the victor in every spiritual battle. This is my birthright, and I won't despise it!*

How much do you hate evil, beloved? Do you tolerate evil, even call it good, just to avoid offending those around you? Are you afraid of being labeled a "radical"?

We live in a time where gray is the color of choice when it comes to moral issues. Some people even think there's a little bit of good in everyone, and they urge us to look for that good, to tolerate "evil" if we dare judge it to be so. "After all, God does!" they say!

Oh, does He?

It's a lie, beloved! God never compromises with evil; He only exposes evil for what it is and then judges it. Take a look at Malachi 2:17: "You have wearied the LORD with your words...in that you say, 'Everyone who does evil is good in the sight of the LORD.'"

Dear one, your only allegiance ought to be the love of God that mourns over sin and seeks to rescue all from the certain flames of judgment.

*God, I am determined to heed the warnings of Your Word, which says that those things that are highly esteemed among men are detestable in Your sight. I rely on Your Holy Spirit to give me discernment and to prevent me from tolerating sin in any form.*

Are you investing in things that build up, nurture, and edify? Or have you become caught up in things that will snare you, entrap you, shame you—eventually destroy you?

Our holy God commands and warns, "You shall be holy, for I am holy" (1 Peter 1:16). Now reason with me: If God says we are to be holy, then holiness is possible! He would never ask more of us than He equips us to do.

*Holy* means "to be sanctified, set apart unto God." Because God has set us aside for Himself, our lives—all that we are and do—are to be set aside for Him. You are not Your own; you are His. Even your very breath is given by Him. You cannot do as you please with your body, my friend, and expect God to stand idly by (1 Corinthians 6:19-20; Galatians 5:16-17).

If we sow to the flesh, we will reap corruption. Our sins will find us out (Numbers 32:23)! But if we sow to the Spirit, we will reap eternal dividends (Galatians 6:8).

*Lord, when I entered into covenant with You, I made a commitment to follow You in every aspect of my life. Cleanse my heart, dear Father, from any hint of compromise with the ways of the world. As I've told You before, I want to be a vessel for honor, sanctified and useful to You, prepared for every good work.*

"Judge not, that ye be not judged" (Matthew 7:1, KJV). It's the one verse the world knows and will readily quote to you whenever you point out that something is wrong or when you have the audacity to call something sin. "Who are you to judge!" they say.

Beloved, don't let them throw that at you. You need to understand the context of that verse. It is not forbidding us to call evil, evil. Rather it is saying that before you correct another about their misbehavior, their sin—trying to get that speck out of their eye—you first need to get the log out of your own eye. Note, the Bible says "first." It does not say, "Don't help others see and deal with their sin."

This verse, so often taken out of context, simply tells you to make sure you've dealt with your sin first, and then you can help the one in need.

Get rid of sin, my friend. Don't excuse or condone it in your own life or in that of others. You're supposed to be holy.

*Lord, You have called me to be holy as You are holy. Give me the courage to deal with sin in my own life and to admonish others to deal with their sin. I will not make excuses but will do what is necessary— reprove, rebuke, and exhort with great patience and instruction—to help others be sound in their faith.*

"Worthy is the Lamb!" Is your life demonstrating that the Lord is worthy of all power?

Someday we'll hear proclaimed with a loud voice that Jesus Christ alone is worthy. He is the overcomer! The One who redeemed us with His blood so that we might reign with Him on the earth.

Revelation gives us a dramatic glimpse into the future, a scene almost beyond our human comprehension: Around the throne of God there will be gathered multitudes upon multitudes, thousands upon thousands of living creatures, angels, and the elders, all saying with a loud voice, "Worthy is the Lamb that was slain to receive power and riches and wisdom and might and honor and glory and blessing" (5:12).

Why does God give us this preview of things to come? I believe one reason is so you and I will recognize and live in the expression of this truth now—so we'll live today in a way that testifies He is worthy!

How does your life—right now, beloved—demonstrate His worthiness?

*O Lord, it is my plea that You will be glorified in my life today. May everything in my body, this temple purchased by You, convey Your worthiness as I give You preeminence in my life in every way.*

Is it oh-so-tempting for you to be trying always to please someone else?

I've been there, beloved! One of my weaknesses is seeking to please other people.

It's so easy to be caught up in trying to fulfill the expectations of others. As we seek to serve them, we have to be careful that our lives are not lived at man's direction instead of God's. Try as we may, we'll never satisfy everyone in our human audience. Someone will always want something more from us, but we have physical limitations, and we can't expect to meet every request or need.

That's why it is critical to stay in close and constant communication with God. We need to make certain that when we serve others or seek to please them, it's what God would have us do. Can you see how important it is to listen to God, to consult Him for His leadership? So spend time in the Word, seeking God's direction. Remember that Psalm 37:23 (KJV) says, "The steps of a good man [or woman] are ordered by the LORD." Set aside time to be still so that you can hear His voice telling you, "This is the way, walk in it" (Isaiah 30:21).

*Lord, my heart is to act on what I just read. I trust You to order my steps, and I thank You for saying, "Man's steps are ordained by the LORD, how then can man understand his way?" (Proverbs 20:24). I may not always understand—but I'll trust.*

Have you wondered why we fail so often when that's never our conscious intent? Sometimes it's because we're attempting something we're not capable of completing. Sometimes we think we're smarter than God, so we get ourselves into trouble. And often we act before we think through the consequences.

Failure happens to all of us. We're born into a state of failure. Romans 3:23 tells us, "All have sinned and fall short of the glory of God."

But I have good news! God knows your "frame." He knows you're not perfect yet. But failure doesn't have to be the end of the story, not with God. Jude 24 describes God as the one "who is able to keep you from stumbling." Jesus is the One who rescues us from eternal death and destruction, brings us into eternal life, and protects us so that, with great joy, He can present us to God "blameless."

Believe it, beloved! You won't stumble so far that you can never recover—not if you're God's child and you hang on to Him in faith.

*O Father, just when I'm beginning to think I've learned my lesson, I find myself headed for the ground once more in defeat. Thank You for Your unconditional love, Your unfailing mercies, and Your faithfulness in forgiving my sins when I come to You in true repentance and for assuring me that You're still there, my help in time of need.*

Beloved, do you realize that it is God's intention that you succeed rather than fail! Did you grasp that with your heart and mind? Let me say it again: It is God's intention that you succeed rather than fail!

"And what will that success mean?" you ask. It means you'll become a woman, a man, a teenager "for renown, for praise and for glory" to God, because you're clinging to Him as you should (Jeremiah 13:11). So lift up your hands that hang down in defeat, set your feet on straight paths, as Hebrews 12:12-13 says. Throw yourself on God—and know that there's a future for you.

Memorize Philippians 3:13-14, or write it on a card and keep it in front of you: "Forgetting what lies behind and reaching forward to what lies ahead, I press on toward the goal for the prize of the upward call of God in Christ Jesus."

*By an act of my will, I choose to forget all my past failures and sins, even as You have, Father. I will concentrate instead on the path ahead. I believe that You will complete the work You have started in me, and relying on the Holy Spirit to guide me in truth, I press forward on the journey of faith.*

Do you feel utterly outnumbered? Outgunned?

Where will you turn, beloved? Where will you find the strength to stand fast and keep fighting the good fight?

Find your deliverance in God, your "Jehovah-nissi"— "the LORD My Banner" (Exodus 17:15-16)!

As children of God, the Lord Himself is our banner, a rallying point in a time of war. He's our confidence, the source of strength. You're not alone in this conflict; it's also His battle. Remember the encouraging words of Ephesians 6:10: "Be strong in the Lord and in the strength of His might."

Oh, beloved, if you don't learn anything else, learn this: Apart from Him you can do nothing. Only by abiding under the power, the standard, the banner, the ensign of your Jehovah-nissi can you win out over your flesh. Victory is assured under the bright banner of His name.

*Lord, I know that I can do nothing apart from You. In faith I ask that You would strengthen me through the power of Your Holy Spirit working within me. I believe that You are able to do far more than I have asked, and I trust You to work Your will in my life.*

Beloved, if you don't learn anything else from today, cling tightly to this truth: God is working in you.

The New Testament is passionate about saying that Christ is being formed in us, that we're to become more Christlike, to be conformed to Christ's image. Dear one, if you're being conformed to His image, then God is achieving His goal and you can rest, knowing all is well! "For I am confident of this very thing, that He who began a good work in you will perfect it until the day of Christ Jesus" (Philippians 1:6).

God is taking each of us through afflictions, difficulties, oppression, and humbling—all of them working together for our good and His glory. Beloved, accept every disappointing circumstance, knowing He is in control and He is transforming you into a perfect reflection of His Son.

*You are God. You're in control. You wound, You heal, You do according to Your will. I join the psalmist in proclaiming, "Bless the LORD, O my soul, and all that is within me, bless His holy name. Bless the LORD, O my soul, and forget none of His benefits" (Psalm 103:1-2).*

Has anyone ever said to you, "I saw an outfit the other day that looked just like you"? Clothes are often an expression of who we are.

In the Old Testament, when Jonathan made a covenant with David, Jonathan stripped himself of the robe that was on him and gave it to David. When two men entered into a covenant, the first thing they did was to exchange robes. The exchanging of robes symbolized the "putting on of one another."

This, beloved, is what the New Covenant is all about—our taking on Christ's likeness. Those who would enter into covenant with God must know that they are to bear the image of the heavenly. First Peter 1:16 tells us we are to be holy even as He is holy.

What about you, beloved? Have you put on Christ's robe? Are you clothed in His righteousness?

*In entering into covenant with You, I have laid aside my old self with all its evil practices. I have put on a new self—the Lord Jesus Christ—and I am being renewed by the Holy Spirit. Thank You for the wonderful knowledge that You now see the righteousness of Your Son in me, and I can be holy as He is holy.*

How does one live the Christian life? How do you serve God faithfully?

These are two important questions with a profoundly simple answer: by the Spirit! By the Holy Spirit of God.

Ezekiel 36:26-27 sums it up: "Moreover, I will give you a new heart and put a new spirit within you; and I will remove the heart of stone from your flesh and give you a heart of flesh. I will put My Spirit within you and cause you to walk in My statutes."

Under the New Covenant, when we accept the salvation offered through Christ Jesus, we're given the Holy Spirit of promise. John 14:17 says, "He abides with you and will be in you." And when the Spirit comes to live in you, He'll cause you to walk in keeping with God's statutes. "When He, the Spirit of truth, comes, He will guide you into all the truth" (John 16:13).

Oh, beloved, Jesus has left us, but He has not left us without a Comforter, without a Guide, without an Enabler. Live His life in the strength of His Holy Spirit! Serve Him in His power.

*Thank You, Lord, that I do not have to live a life of righteousness in my own strength. Instead, through the enabling power of the Holy Spirit, I can walk in Your statutes and serve You faithfully. I claim that power for today and praise You for making it available to all who call on Your name.*

It's difficult to go against the political, moral, and philosophical currents of the times, to walk against the wind of the culture. Yet when you live among people who have rejected God and chosen moral and spiritual anarchy, what can you do? You must be on the Lord's side, even though it will be costly. We can't "sleep with the enemy."

Jehoshaphat, king of Judah, had to be reproved for not resisting the pull of the world. Second Chronicles 19:2 says, "Should you help the wicked and love those who hate the LORD and so bring wrath on yourself from the LORD?"

The world hates righteousness because its standards are opposed to God; those who want to live their own way feel distinctly uncomfortable when confronted with His absolute moral standards. And those of us who want to live God's way should be distinctly uncomfortable when we confront the immorality of this world.

Beloved, when we enter into covenant with Jesus Christ, it's a mutual agreement—a commitment of both parties to defend the other against the assault of enemies. Will you stand strong for God today?

*Jesus, I belong to You as a bride belongs to her bridegroom. My love is fully committed to You, and I will not allow myself to be seduced by the things of this world. I am willing to defend You at all costs—and to live only for You as long as You give me life.*

Are you burdened to pray for someone right now? A son, a daughter, or a grandchild? Perhaps a wayward husband or wife? Or maybe you've given up, believing that person is beyond hope and help.

Beloved, God tells us in James 5:16: "The effective prayer of a righteous man can accomplish much." And in Luke 18:1, Jesus says that at all times men "ought to pray and not...lose heart."

Is there someone for whom you've prayed in the past but for whom you no longer pray because of discouragement? Oh, you must cling to that promise. Don't faint! It is the effective prayer of a righteous man that can accomplish much.

But remember, dear friend, there is a condition to this promise. It's the righteous man God hears. And the righteous are those who're walking "rightly," in accordance with the truths of God's Word and in accordance with God's will.

Walk in obedience and continue praying. Don't lose heart—the answer could be just around prayer's corner.

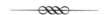

*"Hear my prayer, O LORD! And let my cry for help come to You. Do not hide Your face from me in the day of my distress; incline Your ear to me" (Psalm 102:1-2). If there is any sin that would hinder my prayers, reveal it. Look down from heaven, and be gracious to me.*

Do you really understand the value of your life, beloved? Do you realize the place you have, the purpose, the influence you have in the way you live? In the relationships you develop? Do you understand the value and impact of your words?

Your life has purpose, dear one. And if you don't think so, it's because you've believed the whispers of the evil one. Don't believe him; he's the father of lies. He's deceiving you with thoughts that, according to 1 Corinthians 2:16, are not according to "the mind of Christ," which was given to you as a child of God.

You've been loved by God, redeemed and created in Christ Jesus unto His good works. Someday you'll stand amazed at how He has used you even when you weren't aware of it.

Make the decision to be available to Him each day, to be used as He pleases, and watch what He does.

*Forgive me, Lord, for thinking You'll use everyone else before You'll use me. Forgive me for not seeing my importance to You and to the work You are doing, for not understanding that my life has a specific purpose. Please remind me to offer myself to Your service each day—and then to trust You to lead me step by step, one step at a time.*

Beloved, would it surprise you to know that love isn't always expressed with words of praise, kindness, comfort, or appreciation? Often love goes hand in hand with discipline!

God, speaking through the writer of Hebrews, said, "My son, do not regard lightly the discipline of the Lord, nor faint when you are reproved by Him; for those whom the Lord loves He disciplines, and He scourges every son whom He receives" (12:5-6).

Does that sound harsh? In our permissive age, it probably does. But listen: "He disciplines us for our good, so that we may share His holiness. All discipline for the moment seems not to be joyful, but sorrowful; yet to those who have been trained by it, afterwards it yields the peaceful fruit of righteousness" (verses 10-11).

Your righteousness is God's goal, beloved, so endure. It's all proof that you have a heavenly Father who loves you dearly and desires your highest good.

*Open my ears, Lord God, to listen as a disciple to Your words of rebuke. I believe with my heart that Your discipline comes from a heart of love, and I want to be wise enough to respond in obedience. I want to be a child who brings You great joy.*

Do you wonder why the world is experiencing such disasters? For all our brilliance, all our savvy, all our accomplishments, we're impotent in the face of these catastrophes. We can't stop the tornadoes, flooding, hurricanes, drought, earthquakes—or even war despite all our attempts to negotiate peace.

Do you realize, beloved, there is far more to come? This is but the beginning of sorrows. Read the book of Revelation. From chapter 5 on, it outlines the future. Those on the earth will not escape God's righteous indignation for all humanity's willful sin and rebellion against Him.

"Come, my people, enter into your rooms and close your doors behind you; hide for a little while until indignation runs its course. For behold, the LORD is about to come out from His place to punish the inhabitants of the earth for their iniquity; and the earth will reveal her bloodshed and will no longer cover her slain" (Isaiah 26:20-21).

Now is the time for us to seek God's face and to urge others to do the same. Only in repentance and righteousness will we escape His judgment and enjoy His grace.

*Father, you tell us in Isaiah 26:9 that "when the earth experiences Your judgments the inhabitants of the world learn righteousness." May I remember this and share it with others so that, by believing in Your Son, they might flee from the wrath that is to come.*

Believe it or not, beloved, much of the suffering you'll endure will come simply because we're living in a world that cannot understand our righteous lifestyle. The question is, how do we respond in such a way as to let Jesus Christ be manifested in our lives?

As Christians we're going to suffer rejection, abuse, contempt, defamation, and any number of cruel treatments man can impose on his fellow man. So, beloved, if at times you feel as if your heart will literally break, don't despair. Expressing your emotions doesn't show spiritual weakness. If Jesus cried, shedding tears, shall we not also cry?

When you suffer unjustly for your faith, remember the words of the apostle Paul who said, "I count all things to be loss in view of the surpassing value of knowing Christ Jesus my Lord,...that I may know Him and the power of His resurrection and the fellowship of His sufferings" (Philippians 3:8,10).

Remember, it's not the pain of suffering that reflects your Christlikeness; it's how you handle that pain!

*Dear heavenly Father, I want my life to be a true reflection of the righteousness of Christ. Though I may suffer for my faith, I embrace each trial because it deepens my knowledge of Him and brings me closer to You.*

# SEARCH MY THOUGHTS

Do you feel uneasy? Troubled? What's on your mind, my friend? I am sure it's not something pleasant, or you wouldn't feel as you do.

Did you know that what you think about, what you dwell on, is like setting the thermostat for peace or torment? Read with me Philippians 4:8-9: "Finally, brethren, whatever is true, whatever is honorable, whatever is right, whatever is pure, whatever is lovely, whatever is of good repute, if there is any excellence and if anything worthy of praise, dwell on these things...and the God of peace will be with you."

According to this, your level of peace is determined by two things. *First,* what you think. So frisk your thoughts at the door of your mind to make sure they meet the qualifications set in Philippians. *Second,* peace is affected by the way you are living. Is there anything you need to change in respect to your thoughts or your lifestyle to regain the peace of God? Do it, beloved. There's nothing like peace of mind.

*Heavenly Father, I need Your peace. When destructive thoughts come to mind, remind me that I don't have to think on them. I can refuse them—push them away—and focus on Your sovereignty.*

*I am determined to invest myself in those activities that draw me closer to You. And whenever the troubling thoughts come, by Your Spirit I will refuse them as many times as necessary. I will not give in!*

The way you think just may be killing you spiritually!

Beloved, if you're feeling discontented or unhappy, the root of the problem may be your inability to see things from God's perspective. Perhaps you've spent so much time concentrating on the world's perspective that your spiritual vision has become blurred. What we see, what we read, and the activities we engage in can have a destructive influence on our lives.

Our thinking says, "My mate isn't meeting my needs. I can seek love and a better relationship elsewhere." God's Word says, "Marriage is to be held in honor among all, and the marriage bed is to be undefiled; for fornicators and adulterers God will judge" (Hebrews 13:4).

Our thinking says, "Because God loves me, He won't allow me to suffer." God's Word says, "But in all these things [these sufferings] we overwhelmingly conquer through Him who loved us" (Romans 8:37).

Beloved, view the study of God's Word as food for your thoughts—more precious than food for your body. It is!

*Show me how to focus my thinking, Father. Cleanse my mind. Expose every thought that is based on the world's values rather than on Your standards. Sharpen my spiritual vision so that I can counter Satan's lies with the truth of Your Word.*

Are you thinking about having an affair? There's someone you're attracted to physically, drawn to emotionally. You're certain you won't be rejected because the interest is mutual.

You've thought about being with this person so much that he or she consumes your thoughts and has become the focus of your dreams. You have it planned, you know how it can happen. You're on the verge of taking the first step, and then, well, you'll see where it goes from there.

You're not alone, my friend. Many people have had to deal with the same thoughts and desires, but not all of us have succumbed. God has promised that no temptation will come your way that you will not be able to resist—all you have to do is claim the strength of the Holy Spirit.

The Word of God is quite clear on this subject: "Marriage is to be held in honor among all, and the marriage bed is to be undefiled; for fornicators and adulterers God will judge" (Hebrews 13:4).

Now, are you going to listen to God? Or will you walk after the desire of your flesh, grieve God, and eventually reap the consequences?

*Forgive me, Lord, for toying with temptation. I have entertained thoughts that are in direct contradiction to the righteous life You have called me to live. Help me see how destructive they are. Give me a holy fear of You before it's too late!*

Does what you feed your mind on really matter? Can't you watch, hear, read, and think what you want—as long as you don't actually participate in the evil acts? Surely intelligent people like us are too strong to be influenced by the movies, television programs, or advertisements we see or by the books or magazines we read.

"Do you not know that your body is a temple of the Holy Spirit who is in you…and that you are not your own? For you have been bought with a price: therefore glorify God in your body" (1 Corinthians 6:19-20). There is no justification for a Christian to fill his or her mind with the words, images, and sounds of people who are committing sin.

In Matthew 22:37 Jesus tells us that the greatest commandment is to "love the Lord your God with all your heart, and with all your soul, and with all your mind." You, as a child of God, have the mind of Christ and are to love Him with all your mind. Can you truly say your activities are in keeping with that command?

*No matter how powerful the temptation, I determine right here and now that I will set no worthless thing before my eyes. I will take refuge in You, God. Shield me from Satan's missiles as I walk in integrity.*

Are you struggling bitterly because you have failed so greatly, so horrendously, so obviously? Do you feel humiliated, devastated, ruthlessly shattered?

If so, what are you going to do? First, beloved, you must humble yourself before God. God resists the proud, but He draws near to the humble (1 Peter 5:5). Second, you must be willing to make right, as best you can, what you have done wrong or to restore the relationship with whomever you have wronged. Ask forgiveness, apologize, confess your transgression, not only to God but also to anyone you have transgressed against.

Then you must be sober-minded—you must bring every thought into captivity. No more dwelling on the past. You have just done what you could, what you should. Now remember and respect the fact that God is a redeemer. For thus says the Lord: "In repentance [returning] and rest you will be saved, in quietness and trust is your strength" (Isaiah 30:15).

Think on these things, dear one—and do them.

*Lord, I humbly confess that I have failed miserably. When I should have waited on You, I took things into my own hands—and now I'm paying the consequences. Please forgive me and restore what I have ruined. Then let me move forward in the confidence that You are my redeemer and You can use even my mistakes for Your ultimate glory.*

Do you realize, dear friend, that how you think really determines how you behave?

Consider your thought patterns. How do you think they affect you? Proverbs 4:26 (KJV) says, "Ponder the path of thy feet."

Be honest, how often do you "ponder" anything? We so seldom stop and do this; we just react! When things weren't going well, the Lord said to His people, "Consider your ways" (Haggai 1:5). Jesus called upon His followers to think!

Satan knows that if he can capture your mind, he can capture your body! Be careful, my friend, about what you let into your mind.

Either you will learn to take your thoughts captive or the deceiver will take you captive with your thoughts!

Romans 12:2 tells us to "be transformed by the renewing of your mind." Your mind is all-important. What is yours dwelling on?

*Lord God, I want to worship You fully—with all my heart, soul, strength, and mind. I determine to guard my thoughts, discarding anything that might give Satan an opening to attack. I choose to take my thoughts captive so I won't become a slave to them.*

Have you ever been doing just great, feeling secure and serene, and then someone says something or you see something or you remember something from the past—and suddenly your peace is gone?

You go from feeling fantastic to feeling like a failure. You wonder why you've done what you have done, or why you haven't done more, or why you haven't done things differently. As you begin to think about it all, a cloud of depression blocks out the warmth and contentment you felt just moments ago.

Where do these thoughts come from? So often we forget that we are in warfare, spiritual battle, and that Satan's target is our mind.

So take up "the shield of faith with which you will be able to extinguish all the flaming arrows of the evil one. And take the helmet of salvation, and the sword of the Spirit, which is the word of God" (Ephesians 6:16-17).

*Help me, Lord, to be aware continually that Satan is waging a battle for my mind. Only by the power of Your Holy Spirit can I stand firm, having done everything I can to protect my thoughts against Satan's attacks.*

Beloved, think with me a moment: What do you suppose our enemy, the devil, wants most?

He wants our minds, our thoughts! Satan chooses the mind for his battleground because he understands so well the principle laid out in Proverbs 23:7: As a man or woman "thinks within himself, so he is."

Isn't this the purpose of brainwashing as a form of combat? If you brainwash a prisoner, you can do with him as you please, and Satan knows this. What kind of thoughts does he attack our minds with? Paul described them in 2 Corinthians 10:5 as "speculations and every lofty thing raised up against the knowledge of God."

Beloved, spend some time today meditating on Philippians 4:8. Let it sink into your mind and direct your thoughts today. "Whatever is true, whatever is honorable, whatever is right, whatever is pure, whatever is lovely, whatever is of good repute, if there is any excellence and if anything worthy of praise, dwell on these things."

*Lord, help me to protect my mind from the onslaught of Satan's deception. Through the presence of the Holy Spirit, help me dwell only on those thoughts that are pleasing to You.*

Beloved, we cannot prevent the enemy from directing his fiery arrows of deceit toward our minds. But we can keep him from achieving a victory. Here's the secret: Never allow a penetration. Got that? You must never allow Satan to get his foot in the door. If you do, he'll have the leverage to push his way far deeper into your life.

Ephesians 4:27 says, "Do not give the devil an opportunity"—a place of occupation. First Peter 5:8-9 commands us to "be on the alert. Your adversary, the devil, prowls around like a roaring lion, seeking someone to devour. But resist him, firm in your faith."

Dear one, God has given each of us a full suit of spiritual armor and the two-edged sword of the Word of God. We are fully equipped for battle, if only we will gear up.

Take a few minutes today and read Ephesians 6. You'll discover that you have all the armor you need to keep the devil from making a penetration, and the Bible is the one and only weapon you need to bring him down. Go for it!

*Thank You, Lord, that You have not left me unprotected against the enemy. Through Your Word and Your Holy Spirit, You have provided everything I need to stand firm against the schemes of the devil.*

How are you doing, my friend? Honestly? How are you doing on the inside?

Are you hurting or feeling like a failure? Exhausted, tired of what seems like a rat race through the same old maze of life? Are you fighting a battle with disappointment, depression, or discouragement? Feeling unloved or unlovable?

Does the future scare you? Are you wondering about your job? Your health? Your children? How you are going to care for your parents? How you are going to provide for your family?

Are you worrying? Anxious because you may lose your job or because you can't find work? Concerned about the kids and what they are being exposed to? Are you worried about whether you're giving them the training they need to succeed as adults?

Whatever your situation, wherever you are, the answer is always the same: God knows your plight, your state of mind. He knows exactly where you are and what you are going through. The Bible says, "Cast all your anxiety on him because he cares for you" (1 Peter 5:7, NIV). Give it all to Him, beloved. It's too much to carry.

*O God, You have searched every corner of my heart. You are intimately acquainted with my anxious thoughts. Right now I purposefully surrender every one of my fears and worries to You, and I ask You to replace them with Your perfect peace.*

Are you sometimes troubled because you can't figure out what God is doing? Why He allows what He does? Why He doesn't intervene?

Remember, God is not man. Man is governed by his emotions, his desires, experiences, and limited knowledge—whereas God is infinite. He sees all, knows all, and is eternal. Whether it seems so or not, God *is* in control. The Bible tells us God creates good and He creates adversity (Isaiah 45:7). He can intervene—and many times He does—but only when it suits His eternal purpose (Proverbs 16:4). God's ways are not our ways, His thoughts are not ours.

If you are going to live in His peace, you need to embrace in faith the fact that "the LORD is in His holy temple" (Habakkuk 2:20). Embrace it and be silent before Him.

*Right now the road ahead seems to be dark and filled with danger, but, Lord God, I believe that You are doing something in my life—something I would not believe even if You told me. Until You reveal Your plan, I will wait quietly for You and rejoice in You, the God of my salvation.*

Have you ever looked at someone else and thought, "She has got it made! God has blessed her!"

She has what you want—great parents, wonderful heritage, a strong marriage, a spouse who loves Jesus, children who love the Lord. Maybe you envy her successful vocation, a rewarding ministry, or material blessings that have not kept them from loving Jesus.

Sometimes we look at the goodness of God in another person's life and wish we could experience the same. We find ourselves fighting feelings of envy or possibly even disappointment with God because we didn't get what we deem necessary for our happiness.

Until you make Christ your life, my friend, you'll never be satisfied or fulfilled. Remember Jesus' words to Peter when the fisherman wanted to know His plans for another disciple: "What is that to you? You follow Me!" (John 21:22).

*I confess, dear God, that I have looked upon those around me with envy, wishing to have their blessings for my own. But You have other plans for me, plans that may test my faith but that will ultimately make me perfect and complete. I rest in the knowledge of Your sovereignty.*

Anxiety, if left unchecked, can frazzle your nerves and eat away at your insides. When you find yourself worrying about your family, your finances, or your future, God says, "Be anxious for nothing." But you ask, "How?" Good question. Listen to His answer: "In everything by prayer and supplication with thanksgiving let your requests be made known to God" (Philippians 4:6).

It's a three-step process.

*First,* the moment anxious thoughts invade your mind, go to the Lord in prayer. Focus on God. Rehearse His character, His promises, and His works. Remember His names and His attributes and how they suit your situation. You will see the cause of your anxiety in a whole new light.

*Second,* pour out your supplications. The Greek word for supplication means "a wanting or a need." Get very specific in your petitions to your God, your Jehovah-jireh, the Lord who provides. Tell God exactly what you want or need.

*Third,* in faith give thanks. The act of thanksgiving is a demonstration of the fact that you are going to trust God.

Then lean back in His arms and watch the peace of God garrison your heart.

*Thank You, Lord, for telling me exactly what to do when I'm anxious. Now remind me every time anxiety intrudes on my thoughts. I need the peace that comes from trusting You.*

When was the last time you measured your thinking against the plumb line of God's Word? You want to make sure, beloved, that you haven't wandered off-center.

Our thinking says: "If my kids are going to make it in this world, they've got to be educated by the world." God's Word says: "I will destroy the wisdom of the wise, and the cleverness of the clever I will set aside.... Has not God made foolish the wisdom of the world?" (1 Corinthians 1:19-20).

Our thinking says: "Now that I'm a child of God, I'm safe. I can live any way I want because I have 'fire insurance.'" God's Word says: "You will know them by their fruits.... Every tree that does not bear good fruit is cut down and thrown into the fire" (Matthew 7:16,19).

Beloved, if your thinking is going to be changed, you must be transformed by the renewing of your mind. Get into the Word of God, and think about it all day long!

*Examine my thoughts and motives, Lord. I want them to be grounded in Your truths. As I spend time in Your Word, grant me discernment so that I may see where my thoughts are based in the deception of this world.*

Do you find your eyes searching the congregation just for the sight of him or her? Do you find yourself going out of your way in the hope that your paths will cross?

When you stand before the mirror, do you wonder what he would think? If she would like the way you look or find you attractive? Are you careful to look your best whenever there's a possibility you might encounter him or her?

And are you torn by a gnawing guilt because you know this attraction could lead to adultery in your heart, your mind—if not your body? Your attraction is illicit because one or neither of you is free to marry.

What does God say? "You shall not covet your neighbor's wife"— or husband (Exodus 20:17). Beloved, you must take "every thought captive to the obedience of Christ" (2 Corinthians 10:5). Repent of your fantasizing—before it's too late.

*I realize, dear God, that I put myself at great risk when I think that I am immune to temptation, when I tell myself that no harm could possibly come from a hidden fantasy. Thank You for the reminder that I am powerless when I disregard the prompting of the Holy Spirit. Forgive me for playing with temptation instead of fleeing from it.*

Dear one, what's driving you crazy? Is something from your past tormenting you, continually haunting you?

I constantly have to remind myself that whatever happened, happened. Once it's done, there's no changing it. No matter how hard you and I try, we can't remake our pasts. But with God we can handle the past.

Oh, beloved, do you realize how much depends on your perspective? Wouldn't it make a difference if we could see that each one of our hurts represents an opportunity to take God at His Word, if we could be thankful that each remembrance gives us a choice to turn to God? Jesus said in Matthew 21:21, "If you have faith and do not doubt…even if you say to this mountain, 'Be taken up and cast into the sea,' it will happen."

So, my friend, it boils down to this: Are we going to believe God, put away the thoughts, and press forward? Or will we live in bondage to the past?

*Sometimes my still moments and my nights are haunted by disquieting thoughts and regrets. Thank You for the reassurance that because You are God, the past is past—and there's a hope and a future. I can cope with the consequences of my past failures and move forward as I appropriate Your strength.*

Are you struggling with your self-image? Maybe you bitterly resent the genes your parents passed down to you. Maybe you agonize over the way you look, about some perceived flaw in your complexion or appearance.

The heart's cry of every human being is, "Why am I here?" We want to find the deeper meaning for our existence. We want to know there's a reason we were born and a reason we are as we are.

Oh, beloved, Colossians 1:16 tells us that "all things have been created through Him and for Him." Why were we created precisely the way we are? For Him!

Precious one, if you're not happy with yourself, with your appearance, or with your limitations, remember: God doesn't require you to understand; He simply asks you to trust in the name of your Lord.

*Heavenly Father, when my mind is filled with questions and I begin to doubt my own worth, remind me that Jesus came so that I might have abundant life. What greater proof could there be of my value in Your eyes? Thank You for treasuring me.*

Do you feel overcome by fear, sadness, or a sense of utter hopelessness? Does life seem overwhelming because of the constant nagging presence of your emotional pain? If so, and especially if these feelings are new, beloved, you could be suffering from a physical problem. Find a doctor who will check you out carefully and thoroughly.

Regardless of the cause of your emotional distress, you must cling in faith to what God says. You cannot allow your feelings to control your thoughts and your actions. Feelings are subjective; God's Word never changes.

Remember, the Bible says, "Faith is the substance of things hoped for, the evidence of things not seen" (Hebrews 11:1, KJV). So make yourself believe God. Don't let your thoughts wander. God promises He will keep you in perfect peace if your mind is stayed on Him, because you trust in Him (Isaiah 26:3).

*When waves of emotions leave me reeling in their wake, I make a covenant to cling to the solid foundation of Your Word, Father. In faith I claim Your promise to give perfect peace to those who trust in You. You are my everlasting Rock.*

Beloved, what are you doing right now? What are your thoughts? Are they wandering ahead to the responsibilities facing you—or are you focusing on the reason you opened this book?

Have you ever stopped to think that God has given you today, this minute? And every day and every minute is to be redeemed. "Be careful how you walk," Paul said in Ephesians 5:15-16, "not as unwise men but as wise, making the most of your time." In the Greek this phrase about making the most of your time literally means "redeeming the time"—buying it back.

Dear one, you're not your own. You've been bought with a price. You live only because God has given you life, and your moments and hours and days are to be lived for Him—above all else, above everyone else.

To live in light of this will prioritize where and how you spend all you are and all you have!

*O my God, in the strength of Your Holy Spirit, I surrender my thoughts to You. I refuse to waste my time on aimless thinking, but I commit my heart, soul, and mind to honoring You with every fiber of my being.*

Beloved, the fear of man sometimes causes us to forget God. Who is man in comparison to God? Think about that carefully, dear one.

When fear hits, remember you've been given a sound mind. You don't have to be thrown into a tizzy. Bring your thoughts, every one of them, captive to His obedience. Remember, His Word is truth. Psalm 56:3-4 serves as a great reminder: "When I am afraid, I will put my trust in You. In God, whose word I praise, in God I have put my trust; I shall not be afraid."

God has given you power, love, and a sound mind (2 Timothy 1:7, KJV). They are yours for the believing. Here's another psalm for you: "I will cry to God Most High, to God who accomplishes all things for me" (57:2).

That's right, precious friend. Cry to Him and know that His love will provide all you need!

*Father, when my anxious thoughts multiply within me, Your consolations delight my soul. Your loving-kindness, O Lord, will hold me up. You are my stronghold and the rock of my refuge.*

Are you thinking, "Why does life have to be so hard? I can't believe God wants me to be so miserable. Surely He doesn't want me to be unhappy. This is it. I give up on my marriage (my job, my family). I'm getting out—*my* way. No more waiting on God!"

Life is hard, and the world's way out is often very appealing. We're tempted on every hand. People—even many who profess to know Christ—have abandoned their commitments, leaving in their wake a trail of destruction that affects the church, our nation, our homes, and our individual lives.

God didn't promise it would be easy, but He did promise: "No temptation has overtaken you but such as is common to man; and God is faithful, who will not allow you to be tempted beyond what you are able, but with the temptation will provide the way of escape also, so that you will be able to endure it" (1 Corinthians 10:13).

Handle life's problems God's way, beloved, so you don't have to live with regrets.

*God, I don't believe that You want me to be miserable, but according to Your Word, trials are a necessary part of Your plan for me. Instead of focusing on the difficulty of my problems, I choose to rejoice in Your promise that in all things I can overwhelmingly conquer through the power of Your Son.*

Beloved, have you ever suffered through the "what-ifs"? Those times when you question yourself, the situation, and just about everything that comes in your life? "What if I should have responded differently? What if I didn't make the right choice?"

One Sunday our youngest son, David, came to say goodbye before returning to college. I had been taking a nap, so I prayed for him and then rolled over to catch another forty winks. Suddenly the "what-ifs" attacked. What if David had to face some trial at school? Had I been the mother I should have been? Had I adequately prepared my son for life? My peace was gone. I allowed myself to anticipate calamity rather than entrust David's future to my sovereign God.

Oh, dear one, what will you do when the "what-ifs" attack?

Think again about the words of 2 Corinthians 10:5: "We are taking every thought captive to the obedience of Christ." *Every thought,* beloved! Especially the "what-ifs"!

*Lord, I refuse to let my attitude be controlled by regrets and worries that reflect a lack of trust in You. My goal is to take every thought captive and destroy any thought that contradicts my knowledge of You. Through the power of Your Holy Spirit, I pray that You will enable me to do this.*

Do you ever hear a voice inside telling you that you are worthless? Do you ever wonder if life has any purpose?

Do you know where such thoughts come from? On the authority of God's Word, I can tell you they do not come from God. You exist because God gave you life; therefore God cannot possibly view you as worthless.

Your worth and purpose in this life do not depend on who you are, on what you have done, or on what has been done to you. Your worth and purpose depend on God and God alone—His will, His calling, His choosing, His love.

So where are these thoughts coming from? John 8:44 tells us the devil "was a murderer from the beginning, and does not stand in the truth.... He is a liar and the father of lies."

Don't believe Satan's lies. You're not worthless! God redeemed you, paying the ultimate price—His son.

*Your Word says that You chose me before the foundation of the world, to be holy and blameless before You. In love You predestined me to be adopted as Your child through Jesus Christ to Himself. Thank You for the riches of Your grace, which You have lavished on me.*

Have you ever felt trapped in a situation that seems absolutely insane, unbelievable? You watch, helpless, as your plans, dreams, and hopes are shattered.

"This can't be happening," you think. You wonder how you'll survive. You panic. What should you do? You have to do something, but what?

Fear not, little lamb; your Shepherd is watching over you. Isaiah 46:8-10 provides this comforting promise: "Remember this, and be assured; recall it to mind...for I am God, and there is no other; I am God, and there is no one like Me.... My purpose will be established, and I will accomplish all My good pleasure."

Oh, beloved, whatever happens, you can know that His will shall be accomplished in your life because you are His.

So rest, little sheep. Your Shepherd is here, and He's in control.

*You are God. You are in control. Your purpose and pleasure will be accomplished. O Lord, let these powerful truths rule in my mind, overcoming every fear and disappointment.*

"If I'm a child of God, I'm not going to suffer disappointments, am I?" Even if you've never asked this question out loud, has it entered your mind? If so, what is the answer?

Isaiah 55:8-9 says, "'For My thoughts are not your thoughts, nor are your ways My ways,' declares the LORD. 'For as the heavens are higher than the earth, so are My ways higher than your ways and My thoughts than your thoughts.'"

When adversity comes into your life, you can rest in the fact that it first had to be filtered through His sovereign fingers of love!

"Kay, I can't understand what you're saying! It doesn't seem fair!" Is that what you're thinking, dear one?

Rest and rely on God's Word, beloved. Remember what we just read in Isaiah? God's ways are not your ways. He's just, merciful, holy, righteous—a God of love!

*Dear God, I take You at Your word and rest in Your character. I believe with the conviction of faith that whatever disappointments enter my life are Your appointments to make me perfect and complete.*

Beloved, be alert to the lies the enemy whispers in your ear: "You're no good. You'll never amount to anything. No one loves you."

When such insidious thoughts invade your mind, meditate on these words from Psalm 103:17-18. They're just for you today, precious one: "But the lovingkindness of the LORD is from everlasting to everlasting on those who fear Him, and His righteousness to children's children, to those who keep His covenant and remember His precepts to do them."

Beloved, if you are God's child, you are no longer a sinner. You are a saint—one set apart for God, sanctified. You have received forgiveness for all your sins, past, present, and future.

If you are God's child, you are no longer bound to your past or to what you were. You're a new creature in Jesus Christ. The old has passed away, new things have come (2 Corinthians 5:17). Rejoice, beloved!

*Thank You, Father! Thank You, Lord! Thank You for the wonderful assurance that I am a new creature in You. I am no longer bound by or defined by the past. My identity is wrapped up in You, and all of my sins are completely forgiven!*

Do you feel like throwing in the towel, walking away from your marriage? "Why live," you say, "in the midst of a continual cold war! I feel nothing. We simply exist. I've stayed for the sake of the children, but they're old enough to handle it now. If I am going to get out, I had better do it while I still have time."

I hear you. Others who have felt this way have come up with the same reasoning. However, my friend, there is an alternative—an alternative that could keep you from making a disaster of your life. Why not be Christlike?

God says, "I hate divorce" (Malachi 2:16). Jesus said, "Everyone who divorces his wife and marries another commits adultery" (Luke 16:18). Will you listen to God or to your flesh?

I encourage you, my friend, to do your part to end the cold war. Start loving with the gut-level, unconditional love God gives each of His children. Love is an act of the will. That's why God can command us to love. This is true Christianity. Take up your cross and live what you profess.

*Lord, forgive me for not doing what I'm supposed to do, for reasoning like the world and not allowing the Spirit to take full control, for not presenting my body as a living sacrifice. God, in the power of the Holy Spirit, I will obey Your command to love my spouse and I will remain committed to my marriage.*

Have you thought, "We're losing our society, and there's nothing I can do about it. We're caught in a whirlpool of iniquity. There is no escape; our situation is too desperate. All hope is gone! Things can only get worse."

It does seem as if a reversal of our nation's moral decline is impossible, doesn't it? And I am sure it would be if not for the certainty that we have access to God through prayer, fasting, and the determination to obey Him no matter the personal cost or shame.

The book of Jonah says that when the people of Nineveh were warned of impending destruction, the entire city, from the greatest person to the least, believed God, called a fast, and put on sackcloth. When God saw their heartfelt repentance—when He saw them turn from their wickedness—He relented. If fasting, prayer, and repentance saved Nineveh, it can save us. The question is, will we repent?

*Thank You for this reminder that all hope is not lost. Help me to shift my thinking from resignation to repentance. May Your Holy Spirit draw others to join me in fasting and praying for our nation to turn from its wickedness and surrender to You.*

Are you disturbed when you see everything that is going on around the world—turmoil in the nations, terrorist activity, bomb threats, wars, persecution of Christians in various countries?

Do you wonder where it is all going to end? Do you feel powerless to do anything?

There is something you can do. You can read God's Word and learn the prophecies about what is going to happen. God doesn't want you to live in fear; He provided an outline of His plan so you can be prepared for what will happen. You can also act on God's Word: "You who remind the LORD, take no rest for yourselves; and give Him no rest until He establishes and makes Jerusalem a praise in the earth" (Isaiah 62:6-7).

Pray for the peace of Jerusalem, dear friend. When Jerusalem is a praise in the earth, our Messiah, Jesus, will be here, straightening it all out!

*Lord, please hasten the day when You will extend peace to Jerusalem like a river, the day You will gather all nations to witness Your glory. I long for Your soon return and an end to Satan's reign on this earth.*

Beloved, no matter what you see, no matter what you think, no matter what you feel, stay in God's Word!

And pray! Keep the communication lines open. You must be consistent in prayer. It's your greatest ally when life's problems and discouragement hit you like a ton of bricks!

God reminds us in Ephesians 6:18: "With all prayer and petition pray at all times in the Spirit, and with this in view, be on the alert with all perseverance and petition for all the saints."

Bring everything to Him in prayer. Oh, the power of prayer! Talk to God, and let Him deal with what's causing you grief, what's making you crazy with worry, what's troubling your loved ones.

Beloved, when you consistently pray and stay in God's Word, you won't ever doubt His love or concern for you as His child—no matter what circumstances you find yourself in!

*How amazing it is that I can come to You in prayer! Thank You for being a God who wants to hear from Your children, who finds joy in answering our petitions. It's such a relief to share my thoughts with You, to bring my cares to You and let You handle them in Your own way.*

---

# LEAD ME TO
# REST IN YOU

Is your spirit troubled not only at the blindness of people today, but at all that is going on in our world? When my spirit is troubled, I think of the book of Habakkuk, an incredibly appropriate book for our times.

The prophet Habakkuk was frustrated. He saw the deep sin within his nation—violence, iniquity, destruction, strife, and contention. The law was ignored. Justice never upheld. The wicked surrounded the righteous.

What was Habakkuk's recourse? And what is ours in a society that looks much the same as his?

It is God.

We must lay our questions, frustrations, anxieties, and impotence at His feet and wait for His answer. God assured Habakkuk that the ungodly would not go unpunished forever (2:16). Judgment will come.

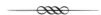

*Lord God, You are the everlasting Sovereign Ruler of all the universe, the Creator of heaven and earth, the One who sits on the throne. The wisdom and the cleverness of man have failed. Man's impotence is obvious; Your judgment is sure.*

*I rest in the firm belief that You are God— immutable, eternal. Everything is under Your control.*

Are you in a hard place? I do not know what your specific trial or frustration is. I don't know what troubles you. I don't know the anxieties of your battle. But God does—and you are precious to Him.

What you don't understand, what you feel unable to cope with can be overcome moment by moment if you will live by faith and walk in communion with Him. You needn't cry out, "Lord, where are You?" He's in His holy temple!

No matter how difficult your circumstances, you can rest in the sovereign power of God, knowing that He has promised never to desert you or forsake you. As you seek His face and place your trust in Him, you will find peace beyond all understanding. You'll be able to sing His praises along with Habakkuk:

*"Though the fig tree should not blossom and there be no fruit on the vines, though the yield of the olive should fail and the fields produce no food, though the flock should be cut off from the fold and there be no cattle in the stalls, yet I will exult in the LORD, I will rejoice in the God of my salvation. The Lord GOD is my strength, and He has made my feet like hinds' feet, and makes me walk on my high places" (Habakkuk 3:17-19).*

Are you undergoing a fiery trial? Do you feel as if your burden is more than you can handle? Don't despair; those are feelings, not facts.

So what are you to do? Consider these instructions from God's Word: "In this you greatly rejoice, even though now for a little while, if necessary, you have been distressed by various trials, so that the proof of your faith, being more precious than gold which is perishable, even though tested by fire, may be found to result in praise and glory and honor at the revelation of Jesus Christ" (1 Peter 1:6-7).

Like a metalsmith, God places His precious ore in a fire to consume the dross—to purify the metal, not to destroy it. And He never leaves the metal alone in the fire. He stays with it through each step of the refining process, until He can see His own image reflected in its surface.

Your trial is a test of your faith—a test that will produce endurance in your life. That endurance will make you perfect, mature, more Christlike. And as a result, dear one, you will be complete. The trial is permitted to make you what God wants you to be so that, characterwise, you lack nothing.

This, beloved, is why you can give thanks in every trial.

*Father, although it contradicts all the wisdom of men, I choose to rejoice in the midst of my trial. I believe in faith that You are testing me to produce endurance and maturity in my life. I will pass my test; I will trust You.*

When you find yourself in need, what is your first impulse, beloved? Is it to turn to man or to God?

Sometimes I think the material wealth of our nation has given us the illusion that we have no reason to call upon God. We seem to have everything we need, and we think all the answers are at our fingertips. Computers, libraries, universities, television, shopping malls, doctors, lawyers, psychologists are all easily accessible.

Is it any wonder that we seem to have forgotten the promise of Jeremiah 33:3: "Call to Me and I will answer you, and I will tell you great and mighty things, which you do not know"?

Oh, for the childlike faith that would flee to the throne of grace crying, "Abba, Abba, Father, I need you!" Oh, for the faith that would turn to God before it ever turned to man.

*Forgive me, Father, for trying to find solutions in my own strength and in the wisdom of men. I turn to You now with the confidence of a child, trusting You to meet my need beyond all that I ask or imagine.*

When was the last time you were still before your heavenly Father? The last time you read His Word, prayed, and just listened?

Beloved, time alone with God means being quiet, being still. And that's so hard to do, isn't it? I understand. Life gets full, and even when we mean well, we find ourselves giving less and less time to seeking God in prayer and studying His Word.

But there is a solution. Ask God to awaken you each morning. He will! Isaiah 50:4 says: "The Lord God has given Me the tongue of disciples, that I may know how to sustain the weary one with a word. He awakens Me morning by morning, He awakens My ear to listen as a disciple."

Your Father waits for you to join Him each day. He knows the change your time spent together will make, the strength and confidence it will impart, and the rest of faith it will bring.

*Lord, my body and soul are weary. I long to be refreshed by Your presence. Please awaken me each morning, early enough that I can spend time alone with You before I become caught up in the hectic pace of the day. I need the strength, the peace, the confidence that only You can give—and the refreshment it will bring.*

Do you wish, my friend, you were closer to God, more intimate with Him? Is your prayer life so weak that the only time it breathes is when you utter a quick, "Lord, I need help"? And does that prayer come only after you have tried everything you could think of and nothing worked?

You say you've tried to have a decent prayer life, but it just doesn't happen. It's frustrating, isn't it? It almost makes you think God plays favorites—and you've lost out. Have you ever thought of telling God, "I give up. I cannot make it happen? If I am going to have a decent prayer life, You are going to have to do it"?

That's a great idea—and very biblical. You're impotent; He's not. So get up every morning, pull out your Bible, and read for awhile. Then spend some time talking with God. Turn what you've read into prayer. The Bible is the best prayer book in the world.

*I am failing at prayer, Lord, and I ask You to take over. I don't know how to pray as I ought, but I know that You live inside me and this is your body. Now, Holy Spirit, I ask You to make intercession through me according to the will of God, just as Romans 8:26-27 says You will.*

Have you yearned for someone to take you by the hand and walk you safely through the traumas of life? Do you long to rest in someone's arms?

In each of us there is a longing for the spiritual. And we're never more aware of it than when we come up against something we cannot control. Dear one, there is One who is always available to listen, to guide, and to mark your life with the imprint of His own. God wants to speak to your heart right now through His Word and by His Spirit. Won't you spend time with Him, praying and reading His Word, letting Him speak to you?

Look at Psalm 27:8. It says, "When You said, 'Seek My face,' my heart said to You, 'Your face, O LORD, I shall seek.'"

Precious one, will you put your hand in His in childlike trust? He's reaching out to you today, eager to walk by your side through all of life's trials. He's reminding you that His everlasting arms are ready to sustain you.

*Dear heavenly Father, I need to feel Your loving presence here beside me, walking with me through this difficult day. Speak to my heart as I wait in silence, meditating on Your Word. Give me the peace only You can give.*

Oh, beloved, how often have you tried to live in your own strength? How many times have you approached God on the basis of your own merit rather than on His grace?

When we fail to appropriate His grace, there's nothing to cover our failure and save us from despair. We need our heavenly Father. We need His wisdom, direction, help, and support. You'll never outgrow Him.

"My grace is sufficient for you," He says in 2 Corinthians 12:9, "for power is perfected in weakness." And how does the surrendered follower respond to this promise? "Most gladly, therefore, I will rather boast about my weaknesses, so that the power of Christ may dwell in me."

We will always need His grace, beloved. It's not a well that will run dry; it's an ocean, the depths of which you can never plumb.

Oh, dear friend, trust His grace! It will never fail.

*Thank You for the promise that Your grace is always available to me; all I have to do is ask. Today I appropriate that grace so that in Your power, I can face the challenges ahead.*

If you're not in the midst of a trial, then you can be sure one is on its way. That's the way of life on this earth, so we need to acknowledge it and be prepared.

And how do you prepare? By realizing that God, and God alone, holds your life and well-being in His hands. He alone is sufficient! Our help comes from the One who made the heavens and the earth, the One who loves us with an everlasting love.

"Blessed is the man who trusts in the LORD and whose trust is the LORD. For he will be like a tree planted by the water, that extends its roots by a stream and will not fear when the heat comes; but its leaves will be green, and it will not be anxious in a year of drought nor cease to yield fruit" (Jeremiah 17:7-8).

Indeed, we—you and I—can have green leaves in times of drought. Even then we can bear fruit if we will place our trust in the Lord.

*Lord, I thank You that my fruitfulness, my survival in drought, does not depend on the weather but on where I'm rooted. O Lord, I purposely extend my roots to You, the eternal spring, the fountain of living waters. Thank You for the promise of green leaves even in times of drought.*

You can be certain that God will never allow anything to happen in your life that you cannot handle. Whatever the trial, testing, or temptation, He wouldn't permit it if you could not endure it in a way pleasing to God.

Keep in mind that temptation doesn't come from without but from within. The opportunity to sin is always present in a world invaded by Satan. However, it's not the world or the devil that causes you to be tempted—it's your own flesh! What a difference it makes to realize this. Suddenly you see your total accountability, something few want to acknowledge.

God says temptation comes when you are enticed by your own lust. *Entice* means "to catch in a snare or trap" or "to lure a fish from behind a rock." *Lust* refers to a strong desire of any kind.

It's our own lusts—our desires—that would trap us or lure us away from God, our Rock (Deuteronomy 32:4). Hide in the cleft of the Rock, beloved. He'll give you the strength to endure.

*Heavenly Father, I run to You for deliverance from temptation. You are my hiding place, and I ask You to keep me safe from trouble. Instruct me and teach me in the way that I should go.*

Beloved, you say you're secure in your salvation; you know without a doubt that you'll go to heaven when you die. But are you secure enough to really live? To experience true joy?

God has given us His incredible gift of grace, but at times we act as if it's our own skill that determines the quality of the Christian life. Nothing could be further from the truth!

In 2 Corinthians 12:9 the apostle Paul writes of God, "And He has said to me, 'My grace is sufficient for you, for power is perfected in weakness.' Most gladly, therefore, I will rather boast about my weaknesses, so that the power of Christ may dwell in me."

You may very well be secure enough in the grace of God to die, but what about the grace to live? To experience joy, satisfaction, peace, and fulfillment?

Remember, you'll never cease to need the Father's wisdom, direction, and support. You'll never outgrow Him. You'll always need His grace.

*Heavenly Father, Your grace is all I need to face life with joy and courage. Resting in the security of Your promise to be faithful, I press on toward the goal of being conformed to the image of Your Son.*

Why is it some people remain strong through their difficulties and others don't?

My friend, if you don't understand and embrace in faith what God says about you, you'll lack confidence in God, in His unconditional love, in His help, in His promises, and in His desire to use you.

When you're not living in faith, your attention turns to what's wrong in you and your circumstances—and it's the pits!

So what does God say about you? According to the apostle Paul, writing in Ephesians 1, you've been accepted in the Beloved just as you are, chosen "in Him before the foundation of the world" (verse 4). You've been adopted as God's dear child and are sealed by His Spirit, who guarantees you'll live with God forever.

Take a moment to thank God for the truth of this scripture! Then in faith tell Him you want to think and act accordingly. You'll find life taking on a whole new dimension.

*Dear heavenly Father, thank You for adopting me as Your own child. Thank You for Your Word that opens my eyes to the surpassing greatness of Your power in my life. When storms come, I will wrap myself in the truth of Your love, knowing that You have redeemed me for Your glory.*

Where do you turn when you can't run away any longer, when your strength is drained and your hope is gone?

Proverbs 18:10 says, "The name of the LORD is a strong tower; the righteous runs into it and is safe."

"But how," you ask, "could His name defend me?" In biblical times a name represented a person's character; God's name represents His attributes, His nature. It's a statement of who He is.

Dear friend, knowing your God means everything. *Everything.* It makes the difference between rest and constant turmoil. It makes the difference been victory and defeat. It makes the difference between life and death!

In times of trouble or need, we're to run to our God and put the full weight of our trust in Him. In Psalm 50:15 (KJV) God says to us, "Call upon me in the day of trouble: I will deliver thee, and thou shalt glorify me."

*Lord, I want to know You more intimately than ever before. As I study Your Word, open my eyes to who You are. Reveal to me Your holiness, Your love, Your justice—all of Your attributes—so that I can place the full weight of my trust in You.*

"Is there no balm in Gilead? Is there no physician there? Why then has not the health of the daughter of my people been restored?"

Beloved, those words are from Jeremiah 8:22. Gilead was a city in Israel known for its healing ointment. The soothing salve of Gilead brought both healing and beauty. But Jeremiah knew his nation needed more than a topical salve, more than a bandage. Judah's wounds went all the way to the soul.

There was only One who could heal, only One who could restore health and beauty to a sin-sick nation. God's people learned there is a Physician, One who could bring refreshment, One who could take the bitterness of life and make it sweet.

Do you know Him today, dear friend, as Jehovah-rapha—the Lord Who Heals?

*Your Word says that You heal the brokenhearted and bind up their wounds. You support the afflicted. Thank You for being my physician today, dear God. I need Your tender mercies and healing touch. Restore my soul to health and bring refreshment to my spirit.*

Are you feeling as if you've been tossed aside like some worthless rag? When you long for acceptance and love, do you feel only rejection and pain?

"Where is God?" you ask. "Does He know? Does He see? Does He care?"

Oh, beloved, He sees! It's His very name; He is El Roi, the God who sees. Remember Hagar? Lonely, exhausted, discarded. A servant girl treated as an object, a thing to fulfill someone's desire for a child, before being cruelly rejected. Did God see her in her distress?

Genesis 16:7 says, "Now the angel of the LORD found her by a spring of water in the wilderness." This was none other than the Lord Himself in the form of an angel.

He knew right where to find her.

He knew her name.

He knew her heartaches.

The omnipresent God is there, beloved. He sees. He's not caught off guard!

*How could I ever doubt You, Lord? I do believe that You see my pain and You care. No matter how isolated I feel, by faith I know that I am never out of the protection of Your loving hand, and I rest in that wonderful promise!*

Oh, beloved, have you experienced God as your strength? Your El Shaddai? Have you claimed for yourself the words of God Almighty, El Shaddai, in Isaiah 49:15-16: "Can a woman forget her nursing child and have no compassion on the son of her womb? Even these may forget, but I will not forget you. Behold, I have inscribed you on the palms of My hands."

As a young woman, I found out that God was my El Shaddai. As a single mom with two boys, I longed for a man stronger than I was, someone who would put his arms around me and hold me and protect me and keep me. I wanted a place of refuge, a place where I could run when I was hurting or afraid. God met every one of those needs in Himself.

Beloved, the Almighty has all the might you could ever require!

*Lord, You are the strength of my life. I place all my hopes in You, and I rest in Your everlasting arms of love. When others overlook me, I know that You will not forget. Thank You for being my refuge and for Your promise to meet all of my needs—spiritual, physical, and emotional.*

Do you feel silly asking God for something you think you can do for yourself? Dear one, God's provision for you is complete.

I don't want you to miss this precious truth. I want you to know all that it means to call upon your God, your Jehovah-jireh—your provider. He provides more than your salvation. He also takes care of your day-to-day needs. Nothing is so small or insignificant that it escapes His attention.

Matthew 6:7-8 says, "And when you are praying, do not use meaningless repetition…for your Father knows what you need before you ask Him."

Yes, He sees our needs and knows them. He specifically instructs us to pray, "Give us this day our daily bread." You can't get any more mundane than that!

Yes, His provision is complete! From miraculous redemption to the mundane needs of daily life, the Lord will provide!

*Almighty God, I confess that I have tried to look out for myself, to be independent and in control. But in doing so, I have missed out on the wonder of watching You meet my needs. Today I embrace You as Jehovah-jireh, my provider. You are sufficient for me, and I turn to You for my every need.*

Beloved, are you at the end of your strength? Does it seem as if the odds against you are overwhelming? Maybe you're facing trouble at work, a crisis in your marriage, problems with your children.

When there seemed to be no other recourse for deliverance, the children of Israel came to know God as Jehovah-sabaoth—the Lord of hosts. It's God's name for man's extremity. And it's not until we, as God's redeemed, find ourselves failing and powerless that we realize our need to run into the strong tower of His name.

This name of God is yours to claim in the time of conflict and warfare. And believe me, precious one, our warfare is going to get more blatant as the day draws near for our Lord's return.

Scripture says in Proverbs 18:10, "The name of the LORD is a strong tower; the righteous runs into it and is safe." What better place could you go?

*Why do I wait so long, Lord, to turn to You? Why do I try to succeed on my own? All I do is wear myself out, digging a deeper hole. I repent of my willfulness, dear God, and confess that I am powerless to help myself. I take refuge in the fortress of Your name.*

It's one thing to know God created the earth. But what then? Did He just walk away?

Of all the names of God, no other name means as much to me as El Elyon, "The Most High." It has sustained me through every trial of my life. It's a name that has enabled me to live with my past and empowers me to face whatever lies in my future.

"For I am God," Isaiah 46:9 says, "and there is no other; I am God, and there is no one like Me, declaring the end from the beginning."

Beloved, begin to grasp the depth of the name El Elyon, submit to that name, bow to the all-embracing sovereignty of God Most High, and you'll experience a deep and abiding peace in the very core of your being.

It will defy description!

*Lord, You are too marvelous for words. I bow before Your majesty. The heavens are Yours, the earth is Yours, the world and all it contains—including me. As I catch sight of all You are, I rest in the assurance of Your unchanging grace and Your all-encompassing sovereignty.*

Are you feeling the pressure of the holidays? I understand. If we're going to get the family together and have a pleasant celebration, the responsibility falls on us. And of course a multitude of mini-crises pop up to complicate our juggling act. "How," we wonder, "am I going to get it all done? And why am I even bothering? I just end up exhausted, disappointed with the whole holiday, and in debt for things we don't need."

We've allowed the superficial values of our culture to rob us of what Christmas is all about. This is the year to change. What can you do? Get alone with a pad and paper. Talk to God and ask Him to show you what to let go of, where to cut back, what to delegate to other family members. As you contemplate your priorities, consider Jeremiah 15:19: "And if you extract the precious from the worthless, You will become My spokesman."

Call a family meeting to reevaluate how you celebrate Christmas. Post your decisions on the refrigerator door, and listen for the message God gives you to share with others.

*I am worn out, dear Lord, from trying to juggle all of the tasks of the holidays. I confess that my family has become increasingly caught up in the commercial side of Christmas. Show me, please, what I need to change so that our family can experience the true joy of Christmas as You intended.*

Are you already taxed by the season? Going deeper into debt to buy everyone presents? Have you wondered what started all this gift giving at Christmas anyway?

It goes back, my friend, to the real meaning and purpose of Christmas. It's supposed to be the celebration of the birth of the Lord Jesus Christ. The celebration of the gift of God's Son so that you and I who are sinners, spiritually dead and separated from God, might have the gift of eternal life and change our destination from hell to heaven. Jesus was born for the express purpose of dying for our sins—paying for us the penalty, which is death (1 Corinthians 15:3).

Jesus paid the penalty in full. This is what we are supposed to celebrate at Easter: Jesus' death for our sins, His burial, and His resurrection three days later. It all started with the gift of a newborn baby, the Son of God incarnate. Why don't you return to the real meaning of Christmas? It will change your perspective—and your life.

*Thank You, Lord, for this reminder about why we observe the Christmas holiday. The marvelous gift of Your Son, Christ Jesus, sent to redeem all of humanity, makes all the difference in my life. Through Him I have been reunited with You. I want to spend this season rejoicing in that truth.*

Is this a disappointing season of the year for you? Would you perhaps describe it as "depressing"? You're not alone. Christmas is the hardest time of year for multitudes because loneliness is magnified to overwhelming proportions.

The images of Christmas portrayed on television and in magazines center around home, family, loving, caring, sharing, and beauty—but the season is not like that for most. Christmas instead serves as a reminder of broken homes, broken relationships, our overwhelming emptiness and poverty of the soul.

If you're feeling alone, precious one, let me tell you about someone who longs to keep company with you. He knows loneliness. The world has shut Him out, even though Christmas is supposed to be the celebration of His birth.

His name is Jesus Christ. He lived, died, and rose again so you might never be alone. The Bible says He stands at your door and knocks (Revelation 3:20). Won't you invite him in? Tell Him you want to know Him better. He's listening for your voice.

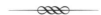

*Oh, Jesus, how comforting to know that I am not alone, that You are right here with me. Rather than wasting my time growing depressed about all that I do not have, I want to fill the next few days with learning about You. As I study Your life and words in the Bible, speak to my heart and give me a new vision of Your love.*

What a wonderful time of year this can be if you will take time to talk to God about Christmas! If you'll wait on Him to show you how He wants you to celebrate the birth of His Son. If you'll ask how He wants you to express His love to His children and to the world for which He died.

I know that if you will focus on others this Christmas season—on their spiritual, emotional and physical needs—you will feel a renewed sense of purpose, obedience, and joy. Christmas won't seem like such a whirlwind waste of time, energy, and money.

There is nothing like getting outside of ourselves and doing for others. When you do so, you take on the character of Jesus, whose birth we are celebrating. He's the Son of Man, who came not only to die for our sins but also to show us how to live.

"Have this attitude in yourselves which was also in Christ Jesus" (Philippians 2:5). What a Christmas you will have!

*Open my eyes, dear God, to see how I can show Your love to others. Give me a sense of purpose as I celebrate the birth of Your Son in a way that is pleasing to You. Through Your Holy Spirit reveal the needs You would have me meet in the name of Jesus.*

Are you dealing with failure, my friend? Do you feel like the greatest of failures? You thought you could be perfect—perhaps others expected it too—but such delusions no longer exist. The verdict is in: You are a failure.

And the worst of it is, you don't think there is any hope for recovery. The weight seems almost unbearable, robbing you of joy, of your zest for life. It inhibits your relationships, and it keeps you from trying to do anything for fear you will only fail again.

Oh, beloved, this is what Christmas is all about— recovery from the failure to be perfect. Every one of us has missed the mark. We've fallen short of God's standard of perfection. Christmas is the celebration of the gift of Jesus Christ, who forgives you for missing His standard of perfection. Christmas is also about celebrating the gift of Jesus, who lives inside you to help you become the man or woman of God you can be.

Will you accept that gift—and all that it means for you—today?

*Thank You, Lord, for the wonderful gift of new life through Your Son. Because of what He did on the cross, I don't need to wallow in my regrets; I can embrace the joy of the Holy Spirit living within me. What an incredible reason to celebrate!*

What is Christmas all about? It's about salvation. It's about God keeping His covenant promise and giving us His Son so that we could be His people. Before the world tarnished Christmas, it was the day we recounted God's incredible and incomprehensible love. It was the day we thanked Him for sending His Son to be made flesh so that He could die in our place for our sins and offer us absolute forgiveness and the sure promise of eternal life.

Spend some time today thinking about Luke 1:68-79: "Blessed be the Lord God of Israel, for He has visited us and accomplished redemption for His people, and has raised up a horn of salvation for us...salvation from our enemies, and from the hand of all who hate us;...to grant us that we, being rescued from the hand of our enemies, might serve Him without fear, in holiness and righteousness before Him all our days.... To give His people the knowledge of salvation by the forgiveness of their sins, because of the tender mercy of our God, with which the Sunrise from on high will visit us, to shine upon those who sit in darkness and the shadow of death, to guide our feet into the way of peace."

A blessed Christmas to you, my friend.

*More precious to me than any other gift is the joyous news of salvation through Your Son. Thank You, Lord God, for Your blessed gift of redemption. Out of gratitude for Your loving sacrifice, I commit myself to serving You in holiness and righteousness all the days of my life.*

Are you spiritually prepared to deal with the fears in your life? The days in which we live are so difficult, so full of uncertainty. How can you be equipped to handle every contingency?

In the Word when God says, "Do not fear," in the same breath He also tells us why: "I am the Lord." "I am with you." "I am your shield." And it's all possible because of Christmas—Christ dwelling with man.

Remember, God is never anything less than He has been in the past, and He's always in charge. He knows the cause of your fear, and He's right with you, offering Himself as your fortress and defender.

Beloved, when fear strikes, you can find refuge in God and His infallible Word. Read until His peace mounts a guard around your mind, heart, and soul.

Fear not, little sheep. Your Shepherd walks with you through every valley, every shadow.

*Your Word says that You have chosen me, Lord, and in faith I believe that to be true. I will not fear, for You are with me. I will not look anxiously about at my circumstances, for You are my God. I trust You to strengthen me, to help me, and to uphold me with Your righteous right hand.*

Have you ever loved someone who would only return your love on his or her terms? You knew the terms were unfair, but that person simply refused to listen to reason.

If you've ever experienced anything like this, you have had a glimpse of the pain God endured in His love for Israel. He loves His church, Christ's bride, in the same way.

Matthew 23:37-38 says: "Jerusalem, Jerusalem, who kills the prophets and stones those who are sent to her! How often I wanted to gather your children together, the way a hen gathers her chicks under her wings, and you were unwilling. Behold, your house is being left to you desolate!"

Too often we only want God's love on our terms. We want His protection, but we want to go our own way. And we can't have both. He loves you, precious one, but if you've wandered, He wants you to return. Are you ready to listen?

*Lord God, I confess that I have tried to set my own terms on our relationship. I have rebelled against Your standards and wandered from the path of righteousness. Forgive me, please. I return to rest under the shadow of Your wings.*

Beloved, is there a major failure in your life, a sin that haunts you and makes you feel as if you're cut off from God?

Whether your sin has been gross and blatant or delicate and disguised, there's only one way to receive God's forgiveness. It's through the blood of the Lord Jesus Christ, the One born to die so that you might live. Second Corinthians 5:21 tells us that Jesus, the sinless One, was made sin for you so that you might be made "the righteousness of God in Him." God's forgiveness is always an act of grace, His freely given favor.

To refuse to believe that you're forgiven is to turn your back on the love of God, the love expressed in the holiday you just celebrated. He loved you, dear one, so much so that He gave His only Son, so that if you believed on Him, you would not perish but have everlasting life.

Jesus paid for all your sins—past, present, and future. Are you certain you have accepted God's forgiveness?

*Yes, Lord, I embrace Your forgiveness. In faith I believe that You have removed my sin from me as far as the east is from the west. I reject the lies of Satan that would keep me in bondage to the past, and I thank You for the promise of redemption through Jesus' death on the cross.*

Do you feel loved today, my dear friend? I'm talking about love in its richest form, love that doesn't fail.

Beloved, because God loved you so very much, He entered into a covenant with you. Because God's love is unconditional and unqualified, He took on your humanity (Christmas) and He even paid in full the debt for your sin (Easter).

That's love. Unconditional, unqualified love—for you. In addition to being moved by the immensity of His love, do you recognize the practical implications? You have a covenant partner who can be touched with the feeling of your infirmities. Hebrews 4:15 contains the promise that He can sympathize with the weaknesses of your flesh, because He was "tempted in all things, as we are," yet He was without sin.

Precious one, your covenant partner is your High Priest. Run to Him for help in time of trouble, of need, of failure, of weakness, of temptation. Run! That's why He was born!

*Here am I again, Father, seeking Your help. I rejoice in Your unfailing love for me, a love that will not let me go but continually draws me back into Your presence. Thank You for Your Son, who understands my flesh, who loved me where I was but hasn't left me there. Thank You for Your love, which moves to make me more like Jesus.*

Is this one of those days when you'd give anything to find relief from the fear that marks your life?

Beloved, I have great news for you! God has given you power, love, and a sound mind. Consider the powerful words in Isaiah 51:12-13: "I…am He who comforts you. Who are you that you are afraid of man who dies and of the son of man who is made like grass, that you have forgotten the LORD your Maker, who stretched out the heavens and laid the foundations of the earth, that you fear continually all day long because of the fury of the oppressor?"

Fear of man causes us to forget God. And who is man in comparison with God? Is not the Sovereign God of Calvary in control? Of course! Dear one, cry to Him and know that love, through faith, provides all you need! Rest, beloved. Rest.

*I claim You as my defender, almighty God. In faith I believe that nothing can touch me apart from Your will. I renounce the fear that turns my heart from You, and I rest in the protection of Your loving embrace.*

If you're going to live a life of peace, beloved, a life of rest and contentment no matter what your circumstances, you must never forget that you're a sheep—and God has provided a shepherd.

God's shepherd is not a hireling, so He'll never run away. He's a shepherd who came that you might have life and have it abundantly (John 10:10). The Lord is your shepherd, and you'll never want. He offers you a life of rest in green pastures, protection from your enemies, and the promise that He'll walk with you through the valley of the shadow of death. Nothing—not any situation or any person—can snatch you out of His loving hands.

So hold tightly to His grip, dear one! Whatever He does—whatever He permits—is all in love. Rest little sheep, your Shepherd is there. He's in control! When life comes to an end, you'll discover goodness and mercy followed you all your days. And you'll dwell in the house of the Lord forever. What can you do but bleat submissively and contentedly as He takes you into His arms?

*Thank You, Jesus, for being my good shepherd. I believe Your promise that I am safe in the palm of Your hand, and I choose to rest there quietly, listening to the soothing sound of Your voice, as the storms of life rage all around me.*

Precept Ministries exists for the purpose of establishing people in God's Word, producing reverence for Him.

The ministry serves hundreds of thousands of men, women, and teenagers across North America and around the globe by offering multiple and varied opportunities for learning how to study the Bible inductively. More than nine thousand Precept Bible study classes are conducted annually throughout the country. In addition more than ten thousand people are equipped each year to study the Bible inductively through the ministry's Institute of Training. Precept Ministries offers training and Bible study classes in 42 languages and in 112 countries.

Kay Arthur's extensive daily and weekly radio programs, as well as her television outreach, give voice to Precept's heartbeat, proclaiming the Word of God around the world.

For information about Kay's teaching, radio and television ministry, the Institute of Training, Precept study materials, Precept classes in your area, or how to become a Precept leader, write or call:

Precept Ministries
P.O. Box 182218
Chattanooga, Tennessee 37422
Attention: Information Department
(423) 892-6814
Or visit the Precept Ministries website at:
http://www.precept.org